Praise for
Helping Teachers I

Helping Teachers Learn *is a remarkably ambitious and comprehensive work that describes how principals may effectively exercise leadership in support of teacher learning within schools. It is about learning-oriented leadership, filled to the brim with ideas of genuine value for every reader. Informed by deep understandings of adult learning and development, the book is an extraordinary treasure chest of real world examples, insights and uncommon sense.*

—Richard H. Ackerman
Author, *The Wounded Leader*
Co-Director, International Network of Principals' Centers
Harvard Graduate School of Education

Helping Teachers Learn *addresses an extremely important theme—the developmental aspects of teacher learning and how principals can support them. The framework is new and generative.*

—Andy Hargreaves
Author, *What's Worth Fighting For in Your School*
Thomas More Brennan Chair in Education,
Lynch School of Education, Boston College

Helping Teachers Learn *is a 2-for-1 bargain! First, it teaches an important lesson: the success of the school principal–known in the community as its chief child-educator–may depend more on the principal's abilities as its adult educator. Second, through her respectful and illuminating attention to 25 talented principals from a variety of circumstances, Drago-Severson has created an indispensable resource for anyone who wants to learn how to be a school's "principal adult educator."*

—Robert Kegan
Meehan Professor of Adult Learning and Professional Development
Harvard University Graduate School of Education

Teaching can be a very isolating profession. In the midst of the many constraints and pressures inherent in education today (limited resources, teacher turnover and shortages, debates on standards and accountability), there exist some distinctive messages of hope. **Helping Teachers Learn** *focuses on some of the best practices found in a broad spectrum of schools—public, independent and parochial. Through her research study of 25 school leaders, there emerge patterns and characteristics that can lead to what Drago-Severson describes as transformational learning: " . . . learning that helps adults better manage the complexities of work and life." The end result is models and possibilities that lift professional development out of the realm of "sit and git," or "one size fits all," and into an informed conversation of how adults in the profession learn best and grow. Teaching need not be so isolating. Drago-Severson's important research points the way to greater reflective practice, personal growth and professional satisfaction.*

—Joe Marchese
Dean of Faculty, Westtown School (PA)

Helping Teachers Learn *is full of so many wonderful examples, stories, real people and real events and REAL experiences. But above all, the idea of the school itself as an organization devoted to learning—for everyone—comes alive, in ways that the organizational theorists can't always capture. How are we going to educate a new cadre of teachers? By making schools places of learning for teachers in just the way we want them to be for kids. And who is the "teacher in charge" of that classroom of teachers? The principal's primary job is not to be the teacher of all the kids, but the teacher of teachers—and to teach in ways consistent with how he or she would want teachers to interact with kids. Drago-Severson's book is full of that tone of mutual respect which lies at the heart of a strong school—whether we are talking kids or teachers.*

—Deborah Meier
Author, *In Schools We Trust*
Co-Principal, Mission Hill School, Boston (MA)

More than students learn and grow in schools. Principals who think hard about their staffs' development and act upon it will improve both teacher confidence—and thus morale—and student learning. **Helping Teachers Learn** *will help those school leaders with this essential task.*

—Nancy Faust Sizer and Theodore R. Sizer
Harvard University

Helping
Teachers
Learn

*For the many teachers whose attentive and caring leadership transforms
and brings joy to lives—and especially for my parents,
Dr. Rosario P. and Mrs. Betty L. Brisgal Drago,
the Drago boys and girls of them,
and David, my love.*

Eleanor Drago-Severson

Helping Teachers Learn

Principal Leadership for Adult Growth and Development

Foreword by Susan Moore Johnson

CORWIN PRESS
A Sage Publications Company
Thousand Oaks, California

For information:

Corwin Press
A Sage Publications Company
2455 Teller Road
Thousand Oaks, California 91320
www.corwinpress.com

Sage Publications Ltd.
1 Oliver's Yard
55 City Road
London EC1Y 1SP
United Kingdom

Sage Publications India Pvt. Ltd.
B-42, Panchsheel Enclave
Post Box 4109
New Delhi 110 017 India

Printed in the United States of America

Library of Congress Cataloging-in-Publication Data

Drago-Severson, Eleanor.
Helping teachers learn: Principal leadership for adult growth and development / Eleanor Drago-Severson.
    p. cm.
Includes bibliographical references and index.
ISBN 0-7619-3966-0 (cloth)
ISBN 0-7619-3967-9 (pbk.)
  1. School principals—United States. 2. Educational leadership—United States. 3. Teachers—In-service training—United States. I. Title. LB2831.92.D72 2004
371.2'012'0973—dc22

                                2003027097

This book is printed on acid-free paper.

04 05 06 07 10 9 8 7 6 5 4 3 2 1

Acquisitions Editor:	Robert D. Clouse
Editorial Assistant:	Jingle Vea
Copy Editor:	Carla Freeman
Typesetter:	C&M Digitals (P) Ltd.
Indexer:	Kathy Paparchontis
Cover Designer:	Michael Dubowe
Graphic Designer:	Lisa Miller

Contents

". . . that is the way of the place: down our many twisting corridors, one encounters story after story, some heroic, some villainous, some true, some false, some tragic, and all of them combining to form the mystical, undefinable entity we call the school. Not exactly the building, not exactly the faculty or the students or the alumni—more than all those things but also less, a paradox, an order, a mystery, a monster, an utter joy."

—Stephen L. Carter, *The Emperor of Ocean Park* (2002)

Foreword

Research about education is replete with contradictory findings. Teachers unions, found to be agents of reform in one study, are judged to be obstructionists in another. Small class size, shown by one scholar to positively affect student performance, is judged by another to make little or no difference. Data about teacher training lead some analysts to predict that alternative routes to certification will improve the quality of the teaching force and others to warn of their dire consequences. One finding, however, has emerged reliably in study after study for the past 25 years: The principal is key to building a better school. A strong and supportive principal can enable a faculty to succeed in the most challenging conditions; a weak or authoritarian principal can undermine the work of even the most able and committed teachers.

Although it is possible to identify strong principals, it is not obvious what makes them so. And despite some reformers' claims of a leadership formula that works for all principals in all schools, none exists. Each person and each setting is different, and a principal who seeks to be an instructional leader must chart a course that is right for a particular school and faculty. Eleanor Drago-Severson never overlooks this complexity. She begins by celebrating the variety that exists among schools, principals, and teachers, and then she richly describes and astutely analyzes the ways in which exemplary principals understand and undertake their work as instructional leaders.

By studying various types of schools—public, Catholic, and independent—in an array of communities, Drago-Severson demonstrates that differences in resources, mission, and policy environments deeply affect what a principal in a particular school can and must do. The principal of a Catholic secondary school has different options and opportunities than the principal of a comprehensive public high school. But Drago-Severson does not stop at these institutional and social differences, for she further understands that the teachers in any school differ as well, bringing to their work different kinds of experience and different levels of personal development. Just as a successful teacher adapts instructional approaches to the developmental stages of individual students, a successful principal recognizes and responds to teachers as a diverse group of learners at different stages of readiness.

Regrettably, public education has long been organized to discount differences among teachers. The egg-crate structure of the school, in which each classroom is separate and each teacher autonomous, has led not only to isolation among teachers but also to practices that treat teachers as if they are all the same. Thus teachers routinely are expected to do the same job on the first and last days of their career. Drago-Severson reminds us, however, that teachers differ markedly from one another and that relying on a uniform strategy to improve their work is sheer folly.

Robert Kegan's theory of adult development stands at the center of this book, and Drago-Severson makes fine use of it in her explorations of principals' work with teachers. As many readers know all too well, staff development programs in most schools pay little or no attention to the learning needs and capacities of the individual teacher. They are, as Drago-Severson explains, designed to be "informational"—convey facts, build skills, and inculcate procedures—rather than "transformational"—to effect fundamental changes in how teachers conceive of their work and roles. Drago-Severson convincingly illustrates how individual teachers' capacities to be changed depend, in part, on their own stage of development—development that does not track neatly onto years of experience in the classroom.

A principal seeking to support and promote teachers' learning must recognize that within a school's faculty, there are certain to be teachers at various stages of adult development, which means that they will bring to their work different ideas about what they need and how they might improve. Some teachers will primarily seek explicit rules and surefire approaches ("instrumental knowers"); other teachers will try to understand what authorities want and work for their approval ("socializing knowers"); yet other teachers will take responsibility for their own work and seek opportunities to reflect on it ("self-authoring knowers"). Devising strategies for professional development that simultaneously accommodate the demands and needs of teachers at all developmental levels presents a significant leadership challenge. These 25 principals' descriptions and explanations, which Drago-Severson skillfully compares and contrasts, enable the reader to see how strategies can be tailored to particular settings and individuals. By focusing closely on the experience and reflections of Sarah Levine, one principal whose work Drago-Severson studied intensively, we can see how deliberate and sustained principals' efforts must be, as they simultaneously support and challenge their teachers as learners.

From these principals' accounts, Drago-Severson identifies four "pillars" of practice that support effective, differentiated approaches to adult learning and professional development in schools: establishing teams, providing leadership roles for teachers, promoting collegial inquiry, and relying on mentoring for the induction of new teachers and the further learning of experienced teachers. The approaches are notable because they not only accommodate teachers' needs for professional growth but also create opportunities for interaction among teachers at different developmental levels. Implicitly, these approaches acknowledge that all teachers are not the same; some are ready to take on special roles with their peers—as leaders of teams, facilitators of discussions, and mentors.

At the Project on the Next Generation of Teachers, my colleagues and I have found that the majority of new teachers today have no intention of remaining in the classroom for a lifetime. Some expect to teach for a few years before moving on to different lines of work. Others plan to remain in education (but not the classroom), taking on specialized roles as administrators, instructional coaches, curriculum coordinators, or staff developers. Unlike teachers from the generation of teachers about to retire, new teachers entering classrooms today expect to work in teams, to have access to leadership roles, to reflect with colleagues about their work, and to rely on expert teachers for guidance. They are eager to work in the very kinds of schools Drago-Severson depicts here. Unfortunately, however, few schools are organized to meet such expectations, and, as a result, many promising teachers will abandon teaching for other workplaces that are more responsive and encourage them to grow. If schools are to become new centers of learning that effectively support teachers at all levels of experience and development, it will be because principals take the lead in making them new centers for learning. As principals set out on this challenging path, this book will surely help them find their way.

Susan Moore Johnson
Pforzheimer Professor of Teaching and Learning,
Harvard Graduate School of Education

Preface

School principals are a critical component in the revitalization of our teachers and our schools. Developing a deeper understanding of practices that support teacher learning will promote more effective leadership.

Teacher shortages, teacher turnover, standards-based reform, accountability, and an increasingly diverse population are among the many issues facing principals in the 21st century. What's more, just as the work of school leaders is becoming increasingly complex and more demanding, the country faces an anticipated shortage of experienced principals (Kelley & Peterson, 2002; Stricherz, 2001). More and more principals are leaving their posts because of the inherent stress and extremely complicated nature of their work (Ackerman & Maslin-Ostrowski, 2002; Kelley & Peterson, 2002). Furthermore, training has been inadequate to help them manage that work (Klempen & Richetti, 2001). There is thus an imminent need for designing more effective supports for principals. One way to accomplish this is to share with principals how to better support their teachers, a principal's most valuable resource.

ABOUT PROFESSIONAL DEVELOPMENT

One important way to provide teacher support is through professional development. As Roland Barth (1990) said, "Probably nothing within a school has more impact on students in terms of skills development, self-confidence, or classroom behavior than the personal and professional growth of teachers" (p. 49). To be effective leaders, principals need to understand what makes for effective professional development. The research on which this book is based focuses on how principals effectively exercise leadership in support of teacher learning. The primary way in which teachers are supported in their personal and professional growth is through professional development programs. However, the lack of time to be devoted to these programs is a recurrent theme in practice (Cochran-Smith & Lytle, 2001; Darling-Hammond & Sykes, 1999; Little, 1990, 2001; Mann, 2000; Meier, 2002; Sizer, 1992).

In reviewing literature on professional development models currently practiced (Drago-Severson, 1994, 1996, 2001), six types of models emerged: training; observation/coaching/assessment; involvement-in-an-improvement process; inquiry, individually guided or self-directed; and mentoring. Sparks and Loucks-Horsley (1990) identified five distinct models in their review of staff development. My developmentally oriented review of this literature furthers their fine work by focusing on the demands embedded in these models and the different types of supports and challenges teachers need in order to engage effectively in professional development activities and grow from them.

The models described in Table P.1 are in a sequence that reflects an increasingly internal or self-developmental focus. Table P.1 summarizes their characteristics.

As shown in Table P.1, there is a lack of clarity and consensus as to *what* constitutes teacher development, *how* to support it, and *how* models are translated to practice (Darling-Hammond, 2003; Lieberman & Miller, 2001; Peterson & Deal, 1998). Currently practiced models of teacher growth operate on different assumptions and expectations about how teacher growth can be supported (Cochran-Smith & Lytle, 2001; Drago-Severson, 1994, 1996, 2001). Furthermore, much of what is expected of, or needed from, teachers in order for them to succeed in these professional development models demands more than an increase in their funds of knowledge or skills, or *informational learning*. Successful participation in some models may demand *transformational learning*. I define transformational learning as learning that helps adults better manage the complexities of work and life.

Educational researchers and practitioners emphasize the need to reassess what constitutes professional development (Darling-Hammond, 2003; Lieberman & Miller, 2001). Recently, researchers maintain that effective professional development for teachers must be (a) embedded in and derived from practice, (b) continuous and ongoing rather than one-shot experiences, (c) on-site and school based, (d) focused on promoting student achievement, (e) integrated with school reform processes, (f) centered around teacher collaboration, and (g) sensitive to teachers' learning needs (Hawley & Valli, 1999). Yet Cochran-Smith and Lytle (2001) question this consensus and emphasize that these new visions for professional development are implemented in significantly different ways.

Joellen Killion (2000) offers insights into teacher preferences for learning in her discussion about eight schools that were selected as "model professional development schools" (p. 3). Killion's research showed teacher preferences for informal, diverse, and continuous development practices, concentrating primarily on their preferences for spontaneous rather than planned opportunities. Informal learning for the teachers in her study meant that teachers were able to determine how they preferred to learn, based on their work contexts. Killion (2000) discusses informal learning as "teacher planning, grade-level or department meetings, conversations

Table P.1   Summary of Professional Development Models

Characteristics	Training	Observation/ Coaching/Assessment	Improvement Process	Inquiry, Collaborative Action Research	Self-Directed	Mentoring
Target of development?	Information, knowledge, and skills development	New teaching methods through skills development	Increased knowledge and skills needed to participate in decision making	Improved decision-making skills, collegiality, collaboration	Increased self-direction pursuing self-interests	Psychological development of self through context of relationship
Types of initiatives	Most inservice, Hunter model	Peer coaching, clinical supervision, teacher evaluation	Developing new curricula, research into better teaching, improvement processes	Collaborative action research, collaborative research, study groups, roundtables	Self-directed learning, journal writing, evaluation with teacher, setting goals	Supportive, longer-term relationship
Goals	Improved student achievement, improved teacher knowledge, and skills	Improved student achievement by improving teacher performance	Improved classroom instruction practices and improved curriculum	Improved teaching practices and improved student learning	Improved collegiality and opportunities for reflection	Psychological development of self
Mode of delivery	Mostly "single-shot" experiences	Several conferences and/or meetings	Longer term, may span several years	Variable, depends upon context & current problems	Variable, depends upon context and current problems	Usually longer term, may extend over several years
Underlying assumptions	Techniques and skills are worthy of replication	Colleague observations will enhance reflection and performance	Adults learn most effectively when faced with important and meaningful problems to solve	Self-managed and nonhierarchical; teachers have knowledge and expertise that can be brought to inquiry	Adults are capable of judging their own learning needs; adults learn best when they are agents of their own development	Development occurs in the context of a relationship; mentoring skills can be taught to adults

SOURCE: This table adapted from Drago-Severson (1994), *What Does Staff Development Develop? How the Staff Development Literature Conceives Adult Growth* (p. 57).

about students, reflection on students' or teachers' work, problem solving, assisting each other, classroom-based action, research, coaching and supporting one another, making school-based decisions, developing assessments, curriculum, and instructional resources" (p. 3).

Creating these types of learning opportunities, Killion (2000) discovered, ignites and sustains teachers' excitement for "learning, growing, and changing their classroom practices" (p. 3). Furthermore, she contends that these types of experiences can be created in schools regardless of financial resources, provided that other nonfinancial resources, such as human resources and time, are available. She found that teachers said the "alignment of school goals with student learning needs" (p. 3) was also key to their development preferences and that adequate resources in terms of time and funding, as well as a "strong principal," were also important.

Blase and Blase (2001), among others (Fullan, 2003; Hargreaves, 1994; Killion, 2000; Rallis & Goldring, 2000), emphasize the key ingredients for support of teacher learning. They also advocate for a collaborative approach to leadership for teacher learning. This is critical because collaborative approaches provide greater access to pertinent information and alternative points of view, assist reflective practice, help cultivate a culture that supports learning and growth, and facilitate change. The principal's role in such an approach is as a facilitator (rather than the authority) who provides resources for effective work, including creating opportunities for teachers to engage in dialogue and reflection. But how do principals create these new and desired opportunities for teacher learning and development? This book addresses this question and illuminates the ways in which the principals in this study implemented four pillar practices to support adult learning and growth and designed reflective contexts in which teachers had opportunities to work collaboratively in support of their own and other's learning. In summary, research on professional development indicates that teachers seek collaborative, ongoing, informal, and democratic forums to support their learning.

SCHOOL LEADERSHIP

Finding better ways to support those adults who teach and care for children should be a priority (Howe, 1993; Levine, 1989; Lieberman & Miller, 2001; Renyi, 1996). Current theories on school leadership and the principal's role in relation to adult learning suggest four possible ways in which principals can support adult development. Principals can (1) create a developmentally oriented school culture (Evans, 1996; Sarason, 1982, 1995); (2) build interpersonal relationships with teachers (Barth, 1990; Bolman & Deal, 1995); (3) emphasize teacher learning (Johnson, 1990, 1996; Johnson et al., 2001); and/or (4) focus on teachers' personal growth (Elmore, 2002; Fullan & Hargreaves, 1992; Sergiovanni, 1995). However, the question of how *specific* leadership practices support teacher growth within a school has not been explored (Danielson, 1996; Donaldson, 2001; Guskey, 1999; Levine, 1989; Lieberman & Miller, 2001). Thus work that explores connections between adult development and leadership holds great promise.

Despite some theoretical discussions about the need to support adult growth and development in schools (Kegan, 1994; Kegan & Lahey, 2001; Levine, 1989, 1993; Oja 1991), the leadership roles and practices of principals in relation to adult development in school settings remains virtually unstudied (Boscardin & Jacobson, 1999; Leithwood & Jantzi, 1998, 2002; Lieberman & Miller, 1999, 2001). Lieberman and Miller (2001) emphasize the need for developing a better understanding of *what* principals do to facilitate teacher development, as well as *how* they do it. Theories of adult development can be powerful tools for supporting the development of adults in schools (Brookfield, 1987; Cranton, 1996; Daloz, 1986, 1999; Glickman, 1990; Kegan, 1994; Levine, 1989; Mezirow, 1991, 2000; Oja, 1991).

The research on which this book is based employs such a constructive-developmental perspective to learn about how a group of principals effectively exercise their leadership in support of teacher learning within their schools. The need for practices and practical information—informed by theories of adult learning and development—about how to better support teacher learning is *real* and urgently needed. How do principals effectively support teacher learning? This book addresses this question. In presenting the principals' stories, I hope that I have painted a picture of what these practices are and why they work to effectively support adult learning, development, and growth.

ORGANIZATION OF THE BOOK

Each chapter in this book is organized around three core themes: (1) the principal as principal teacher developer; (2) principles of adult learning and constructive-developmental theory (i.e., illuminating underpinnings of reflective practice, teaming, leadership roles, and mentoring and discussing how constructive-developmental theory can be employed as a powerful tool to inform practice); and (3) the school as a context for teacher learning.

In this research, I examined how 25 school leaders from public, Catholic, and independent schools with varying levels of financial resources across the United States understand the effectiveness of their leadership practices on behalf of supporting teacher learning and growth. The study was built upon lessons from an earlier four-and-a-half-year ethnography, in which I examined how one principal exercised leadership on behalf of teacher development and how adults in her school experienced her practices. This new research describes how the larger sample of principals understand how their leadership practices work, and describes the challenges associated with implementing them in their particular school contexts. In addition, most chapters present a case from the earlier study to illustrate how particular initiatives work within one school and how teachers within that school make sense of these practices.

Chapter 1 introduces the need for a learning-oriented model of school leadership, exploring connections between adult learning, developmental theory, and leadership practices. I describe the setting for this research and its methodology. Next, I orient readers to the four pillar practices of my *learning-oriented* model of school leadership: teaming, providing leadership roles, engaging in collegial inquiry, and mentoring. The principals in this sample employ these mutually reinforcing, broad *forms of adult collaboration*, to different degrees, in support of adult learning and development.

Chapter 2 presents an overview of the principles of psychologist Robert Kegan's (1982, 1994, 2000) constructive-developmental theory of adult growth and development, since I draw primarily on it throughout this book to interpret the principals' practices that support transformational learning. I also employ this theory to call attention to the diverse ways in which teachers might experience the practices constituting my learning-oriented model of school leadership and to show that supports for teacher growth need to take different forms, depending on individual needs. This chapter provides an overview of three key ideas from Kegan's (1982, 1994, 2000) framework: (1) theoretical principles, (2) three essential "ways of knowing" that are most common to adulthood and why they matter when considering how to support adult learning in schools, and (3) the central aspects of a "holding environment" (Kegan 1982, 1994).

Chapter 3 describes how the principals have conceived and enacted their roles in shaping positive school climates that support teacher learning. While nearly all principals voiced the importance of building a positive school climate by appreciating teachers, they have different priorities and ways of working to create cultures supportive of teacher learning. I discuss the challenges they encounter and how they define their leadership approaches, and present contextualized examples of practices they use for shaping school climates that support teacher learning. I also introduce three grounding ideas for their leadership in support of teacher learning: (1) sharing leadership (e.g., engaging in dialogue and inquiry, seeking feedback, participating in decision making); (2) building community (e.g., involving teachers in policy development, encouraging relationship building among adults, developing a collaborative mission and value sharing); and (3) embracing and helping adults to manage change, and foster diversity (e.g., annual evaluation and goal setting, ideas for curricular and policy improvement, and implementing changes).

Chapter 4 discusses the financial resource challenges that these principals encounter (serving in schools with varying levels of financial resources) and how these challenges influence their leadership practices with regard to teacher learning. The principals named several important context-specific challenges, including school size, mission, student population, teaching staff, their own past experiences, and school location. But by far the most common challenges cited, across all school types and economic levels, were resources: *financial, human,* and *time.* This chapter provides examples of the creative strategies principals employed to garner needed resources and implement practices that effectively support that learning. In so doing, I highlight how the types of initiatives that the principals employ to support teacher learning are differently influenced by their schools' location on a continuum of financial resources.

Chapter 5 focuses on the use of "teaming" to promote personal and organizational learning through various forms of professional partnering and adult collaboration. I discuss principals' views of this practice and weave in the adult learning and developmental principles informing the practice that support teacher learning and growth. Through case examples (e.g., curriculum teams, literacy teams, technology teams, teachers teaching in teams, and diversity teams), I show how many of these principals organize their schools for teamwork and describe their thinking about how teaming opens communication, decreases isolation, encourages collaboration, creates interdependency, and builds relationships.

Chapter 6 discusses how these principals understand the practice of providing adults with leadership roles and how they can support transformational learning. Examples include principals' conceptions of how this practice invites teachers to share ownership of leadership, authority, and ideas in their roles as teacher leaders, curriculum developers, or school administrators as they work toward building community and promoting change.

Chapter 7 explores how most of these principals focus on inviting adults to engage in collegial inquiry within the school. According to the majority, setting up situations in which adults are regularly invited to reflect on and talk about aspects of their practice in the context of supportive relationships encourages self-analysis, which can improve individual and the school community's practice. In addition, collaborative goal setting, evaluation, and conflict resolution can facilitate both adult learning and the growth of the institution. I discuss how collegial inquiry connects to developmental principles and how it works in practice to support teacher learning and growth.

Chapter 8 describes how the principals, across school types and resource levels, see their mentoring programs as initiatives that support teacher learning and development. I discuss various programs, at different stages of development, and how program purposes vary from "mission spreading" to exchanging information to providing emotional support for new and experienced teachers and/or staff. I also show how the principals select mentors according to different criteria, including understanding of the mission, teaching experience, disciplinary focus, and/or other characteristics (nonacademic), and how these programs work in their schools. I emphasize why principals value this practice and how they think it supports teacher growth, and illuminate the adult learning and developmental principles informing this practice.

Through an in-depth case, Chapter 9 illustrates how one principal and her school approached their self-study evaluation as an opportunity for learning. By exploring the experiences of one principal, a few teachers, administrators, and staff, I highlight how teaming, providing leadership roles, collegial inquiry, and mentoring—the four pillars of my school leadership learning-oriented model—can work together to create a context supportive of teacher learning and development. This chapter illustrates how a school's self-evaluation process provided an opportunity for broadening perspectives, building community, and helping adults manage change and foster diversity. It was also an opportunity for adults to share leadership, power, and decision-making authority, demonstrating how principals can tailor forms of support and challenge to individual needs. The power of combining these practices to support teacher learning and development with the self-study evaluation process, common in schools across this sample, can serve as a context for growth.

Chapter 10 explores the range of ways the principals discussed the need for, and their efforts toward, self-renewal while balancing the demands of multiple responsibilities and the complex context-specific challenges of leadership (e.g., school size, student population, teaching staff, their own past experiences, and school location). In addition, I highlight a particularly powerful finding: the importance of reflective practice to principals in better supporting their *own* development, while they support the development of other adults in the school.

Chapter 11 discusses the implications and promise of the four practices discussed in this book for other school leaders. These developmental initiatives are the pillars of a learning-oriented school leadership model that can be adapted and used effectively by school leaders in different settings. In stressing the importance of considering each school's particular characteristics in supporting the learning and growth of all its members, the chapter highlights a qualitatively different way of thinking about professional development and leadership supportive of adults' transformational learning.

In summary, these principals, who serve in low-, medium-, and rich-resource schools, work creatively and differently to support teacher learning effectively—despite the constraints, challenges, and complex demands of leadership in the 21st century. By focusing on the practices they employ to support adult learning and growth within their schools, the challenges they encounter, and their creative solutions in the midst of resource limitations, this work can serve as a map for other school leaders. Moreover, given the demands of leading in a nation with an increasingly diverse population, researchers, policymakers, school reformers, and school principals themselves are searching for more effective ways to train and support school leaders. This book offers insight into another way to accomplish these important national goals. Helping principals to more effectively exercise leadership in support of teacher learning and development is an initiative I believe is directly tied to improving the quality of teaching and fostering children's growth and achievement.

Acknowledgments

What the eye sees better the heart feels more deeply. . . . For we are moved somewhere, and that somewhere is further into life, closer to those we live with. They come to matter more. Seeing better increases our vulnerability to being recruited to the welfare of another. It is our recruitability, as much as our knowledge of what to do once we are drawn, that makes us of value in our caring for another's development.

—R. Kegan, *The Evolving Self* (1982)

I have come to deeply appreciate the importance, power, and gift of wonderful and caring people in my life. The support I have enjoyed from generous and gracious people has made this work all the richer. I have been honored to work with and learn from them. I am delighted to acknowledge the inspiration given to this research and the faithful support given to me in preparing this book by many individuals and institutions. I am deeply grateful to them, and ask forgiveness from those I have failed to mention who also made a difference to this project and to the joy I found in their wonderful company.

The research upon which this book is based was made possible by a grant from the Spencer Foundation. I gratefully acknowledge and express my appreciation to the Spencer Foundation for their support. The data presented, the statements made, and the views expressed are solely my responsibility as author.

Deep gratitude and greatest appreciation go to the 25 remarkable, courageous, and inspiring school leaders who participated in this research. They generously shared their experiences and opened their hearts and minds so that all of us could learn from their good work, dedication, and passions. These busy professionals gave freely of their time, with commitment. Their warm welcome of me into their schools, their thinking, and their lives continues to inspire. I am grateful to each of them for the privilege to learn from the gifts of their insights into the triumphs, challenges, and joys of leadership in support of teacher learning—in the hope of improving schools for children, who deserve our very best. I thank all of you for your genuine interest in this work, and for your meaningful contributions to making it all it has become. I shall not forget your leadership.

During earlier ethnographic research that inspired this larger study, I had the privilege of learning from Dr. Sarah Levine. Sarah contributed her best thinking and energies to my study over countless hours. She welcomed me into her school and her practices, and she shared her thinking with courage and tenacity. I thank Sarah for believing in this work and in me, and for the gift of our enduring friendship.

The talent and gifts of many people enhanced this work. Their generosity of heart and mind—and their company on the learning journey—helped me make this work better in many ways. I hope that I have, during our work together and in these public expressions, offered a sense of my immeasurable appreciation for them.

Since first having the delightful gift of learning from Dr. Robert Kegan of Harvard's Graduate School of Education (HGSE) in 1988, I have come to know Bob Kegan as the very best kind of educator. His teachings have been and always will be an inspiration to me. Bob is a master teacher and wise mentor. He is also a wonderful person. This work and my own learning and development would not be as strong without the wisdom offered by Bob's exemplary thinking. His special brand of educational leadership supports learning and development.

Bob embodies his constructive-developmental theory that enlivens the pages of this book. I admire his devotion to helping others and his integrity. Bob has changed the directions and contributions of my life in ways I could never adequately acknowledge. My respect and regard for him and his work are surpassed only by my deep appreciation for all he has offered me and gives so freely to anyone working hard to make schools better by helping everyone grow. Thank you, Bob, for your company and support—each and every step along the way.

HGSE doctoral students Kristina C. Pinto and Deborah Helsing contributed to advancing this work through their assistance with initial data analysis. Their individual and collective knowledge strengthened the research. I thank them for their help in making this work rest on a solid foundation.

Many others must be acknowledged for their help with this work along the way. Anne Amatangelo Korte, Joelle Pelletier, and Christopher Soto transcribed interviews. Kristina C. Pinto and Christopher Soto conducted several literature reviews. Marcia Brownlee provided invaluable administrative support and encouragement. Heartfelt thanks to all!

My thanks in particular go to Kristina C. Pinto and Dr. Sue Stuebner Gaylor, who generously shared their fine thinking during extended conversations about how to best present some of the ideas found in this book. I also thank them for their careful reading and thoughtful comments on key chapters. For me, they embody the ideals of Big heart and Big mind. Always gracious, they cheered me on. India Koopman also offered editorial suggestions that accompanied me in important parts of this writing. I thank Kristina, Sue, and India for the gift of the thoughtful questions offered in the spirit of making this work most accessible.

Senior Acquisitions Editor Robb Clouse of Corwin Press, Inc., kept communications open during project conceptualization and responded excellently to my questions. He offered valuable suggestions that helped improve the transformation of this work from research into accessible ideas for educators everywhere. I thank Robb sincerely for noticing my work and for staying with the promise of it during development. I also express my appreciation to Carla Freeman for her caring expertise during the copyediting process and for her support of this work. In addition, Corwin Press and Ellie Drago-Severson would like to thank the following reviewers, whose thoughtful suggestions made this work better:

Andrew Hargreaves
Professor
The Thomas More
  Brennan Chair
Lynch School of Education
Boston College
Chestnut Hill, MA

Joyce Kaser
Senior Program Associate
WestEd
Albuquerque, NM

Robert D. Ramsey
Educational Consultant
Minneapolis, MN

Barbara L. Brock
Professor
Creighton University
Omaha, NE

Kenneth D. Peterson
Professor
Portland State University
Portland, OR

Sandra Lee Gupton
Professor
University of North Florida
Jacksonville, FL

Bill Sommers
NSDC Board Member
Principal
Eden Prairie Public Schools
Eden Prairie, MN

Sharon Powers
Principal
McAdams Early Learning School
New Carlisle, OH

Stephen D. Shepperd
Principal
Sunnyside Elementary School
Kellogg, ID

Douglas H. Pierson
Principal
Hamilton Elementary School
Narragansett, RI

Richard H. Ackerman
Associate Professor
College of Education and Human
  Development
Orono, ME

Robert Kegan
Meehan Professor of Adult Learning
  and Professional Development
Harvard Graduate School of
  Education
Cambridge, MA

Joe Marchese
Dean of Faculty
Westtwon School
Westtown, PA

Deborah Meier
Co-Principal
Mission Hill School
Boston, MA

Nancy Faust Sizer and Theodore
   R. Sizer
Professors
Harvard Graduate School of
   Education
Cambridge, CA

Jed F. Lippard
Director
Prospect Hill Academy Chapter
   School
Cambridge, MA

Susan Moore Johnson
Pforzheimer Professor of Teaching
   and Learning
Harvard Graduate School of
   Education
Cambridge, MA

Many others have supported this work in lasting ways. My K–12 students and their master teachers, such as Ted Hill, Barbara Myerson, and Gerry Murphy, helped my love for teaching to grow. Gratitude goes to them and also to Dr. Susan Moore Johnson, Dr. Howard Gardner, Dr. Eleanor Duckworth, Dr. Neville Marks, Peggy Kemp, Dr. Millie Pierce, and Linda DeLauri for their thoughtful support, wise counsel, and encouragement of me. Among the many graduate students who helped advance this work, I especially thank students in my Leadership for Transformational Learning Class at HGSE. Their questions and curiosity have made this work stronger.

My acknowledgments conclude with deepest gratitude for the love and support from those people most associated with shaping my life in my family. Dr. Rosario and Betty Drago are my parents and finest teachers. With wisdom, joy, and care, they modeled learning and leadership that transformed me. Holding me all along the way, they helped me learn to love and stand for something. I thank them for the impossible-to-measure gifts, encouragement, and love they have given to my life. By example, you taught me to love learning and hard work and contribution to the lives of others. Their belief in me, and support for all I choose to do, are but two of the precious life gifts they have given me. It is on their shoulders that I stand in order to see farther. I thank my parents for showing me how to appreciate the important roles that roots and wings play in building a happy and productive life.

I thank my siblings and their families for their constant encouragement and warm love. My five brothers and only sister, all but one older than I, walked some of my paths before I did. They taught me some things about leadership, love, and what can be found and what can be lost. I thank my siblings and their children for teaching me, showing me the way, being there for me, and cheering me on. You are my loves.

Anyone who has engaged in a labor of heart such as this knows that it requires sacrifice, patience, love, and support from many, especially one's lifelong partner. I now thank my husband and love, David Severson. Thank you for believing in me and for the sacrifices, compromises, and insights you make and give so freely. Thank you for your enduring support, precious care, and for sharing your own learning journeys with me. Thank you for being my cherished love, my touchstone—and for being in my life.

About the Author

 **Eleanor (Ellie) Drago-Severson** is a lecturer on education at the Harvard Graduate School of Education, where she teaches courses on school leadership and qualitative research methods. Prior to her research into adult learning and leadership, she was a teacher, administrator, and staff developer in K–12 schools in New York, Florida, and Massachusetts. Drago-Severson teaches, conducts research, and consults with teachers, principals, and other educational leaders on issues of school leadership, adult learning, and professional development. Her work is inspired by the idea that schools must be places where adults as well as children can grow. She grew up in the Bronx, New York, and lives in Cambridge, Massachusetts, with her husband.

CORWIN PRESS

The Corwin Press logo—a raven striding across an open book—represents the union of courage and learning. Corwin Press is committed to improving education for all learners by publishing books and other professional development resources for those serving the field of K-12 education. By providing practical, hands-on materials, Corwin Press continues to carry out the promise of its motto: **"Helping Educators Do Their Work Better."**

1

Developing a New Model of School Leadership for Teacher Learning

R ecently, I've noticed talk about "the heart of leadership" in the press, in professional conversations between school leaders, and amongst researchers. Leadership, like teaching, is about heart—dedication and profound caring. There's a special kind of satisfaction and joy in supporting another person's growth. You *see* and *feel* that your efforts to support another human being have made some difference in his or her sense of self and ability to make a difference for a student or a fellow teacher. As one principal in this study said, "You see it. And it makes all the difference. Not just for the teacher. But for teachers and for students' learning, even if it's one student at a time. It makes all the difference for all us here at the school."

My work in support of school leadership and teacher development on behalf of children has taught me the power of heart in the form of paid attention. I like to learn what people think and how they tend to make sense of their learning and growing experiences. Over a recent dinner with student educators new to the Harvard Graduate School of Education master's program, I asked about interests and reasons that led the already successful professionals to decide in favor of additional study.

Marie said she came to Harvard to learn more about school reform. "I want to focus on how to support low-income students of color in my hometown. I want to learn more about issues of race and ethnicity, and how theory can inform practice. I want to give back to my hometown, to help kids there, to give them a model for what they can do. I want to lead a program that I design for teachers and students of color to help them achieve and learn—and grow." Bob offered that he was keen on what he was learning in a class he was taking on promoting students' academic achievement. Rose stated, "I'm working on this exciting research project where we're focusing on how to support teachers' professional development through technology." Teal shared with noted enthusiasm, "I came here to take a year away from my school to reflect on my work and next steps. I'm interested in finding better ways to support adult learning, so that teachers can more effectively attend to children's learning and achievement in schools." At this point, Jody chimed in, "I'm really enjoying my classes, but I miss my students so much that I've decided to continue teaching part-time while I take my classes. It's a lot to juggle, but the kids give me energy. So that's what I've decided to do."

And then, after a pause, Elizabeth, who was seated at the far end of the table, shared, "I remember crying one year after an August staff meeting when I realized I would not have any free time with the other teachers who taught U.S. history. I was so mad at my principal for not recognizing how important it is to collaborate with peers and to make it a priority in scheduling." She continued, "I really cherish my time here at Harvard if only because it is a breather from the last six years of teaching. I've always had my summers free to detox and reflect, so I thought it was weird how much I felt 'free' when August and September rolled around and I wasn't writing lessons. It is so hard to reflect on your teaching when you are in the thick of it."

As postgraduation plans were discussed, I was reminded of many other conversations I've had with teachers and principals over my own years of teaching, researching, and consulting to schools. For example, Bob's comments rang true for me as they echoed what I have learned from many. "I love teaching and I love my kids," he said. "But the new state regulations for permanent certification demand that I earn a master's in my discipline. I just can't see taking another year off, or managing part-time study while teaching in order to pay for another master's degree. I plan to attend medical school after this year." Rose added, "Teaching is tough work. I love it, and I love my kids. But it has become increasingly frustrating for me, and sometimes I feel like all I'm doing is jumping through hoops, hoops, and more hoops with no time to reflect on my teaching. My days are so full, that I rarely get the chance to talk with my colleagues when we're in school. That's what I'm really enjoying about my time in this program. I finally have time to think and talk with others about teaching. It's so stimulating, and while I think it will make me a better teacher, I'm not sure that I'll go back to the classroom. I'd like to go for a doctorate and then become a principal."

Kristina, who had been listening carefully to the conversation, said, "My mother has been a second-grade teacher for 25 years, and she loves it. This year she's working toward national certification. It's an intense program, she says. It requires that she reflects on her practice, and she's finding it so satisfying. It's helping her stay fresh, and she feels it's making her a better teacher. That's why I'm here. To take some time to reflect."

These heartfelt stories and experiences of teachers, school leaders, and my own experiences resonate with stories from principals and teachers across the country. My students and many other school leaders I have met in workshops and conferences have helped me better understand their important work and their caring. The best educators love students. They care for them, and they care for their learning. They dedicate themselves—with BIG hearts and minds—to their vocation, and they also crave time to reflect on their teaching and leadership practices toward becoming ever better in service to students and each other.

Walking home from dinner that evening, I reflected on my own past experiences as teacher and administrator in middle and upper schools. What was it that made the difference for me in terms of working in a healthy school environment, one where I was able to support children's learning and achievement while also making time to reflect on my own practice so that I could be more effective? I have worked in schools where very few structures were in place for engaging conversations about teaching with my colleagues, where few faculty meetings were held for purposes other than administration or announcements. Outside speakers were occasionally invited to present their work, which was one form of important learning. The presentations offered good information and, often, new skills with promise to improve our teaching and leadership practices.

It has also been my privilege to teach in a school where many opportunities were made available for collaboration and reflection. I knew that I was growing in some important ways from participation in the conversations for learning. The faculty in this school was encouraged to visit each other's classes, so that we might learn from conversations about the work we were doing. Our principal also sat in on class meetings, and he joined in reflective discussions afterward. Teachers at the school were in mentoring relationships toward supporting and enhancing our teaching. We met often to discuss our practice—our craft—and to develop new ideas for improving student achievement and our school. Our principal, like those you will read about in this book, made support for adult learning a priority. He secured time for us to talk about our work, and he attended to adult learning with the same zeal he brought to student learning. He created structures for reflective practice among all adults in our school, structures that incorporated both challenges to and support for each other's thinking. I believe that all of us working at the school during those years experienced profound learning that changed our ways of thinking about education. Those teachers, and especially a principal who made support for adult learning a demonstrated personal priority, made all the difference.

When I arrived home after talking with my advisees, I decided to e-mail them to ask if I might share some of their heartfelt stories and passions in this book. Within minutes, they replied. Rose was the first to respond, "If it helps to get the word out about how important it is to support teacher growth, please use anything you'd like." Julia explained, "I realize I was quiet at dinner tonight. I was listening, and beginning to learn that I was not alone. I have lots to share. Here are a few examples, if you need more, please let me know!" Elizabeth included three more stories in her e-mail about her thirst for time to reflect with colleagues in her school and how she "depended on [her] principal to create those" opportunities. It reminded me of my own life in schools in various roles, including as a university professor. Their enthusiasm for sharing resonated with my own. Most important, their energy resounded with the enthusiasm of the principals in my study as they voiced stories of supporting teacher learning and development. Their words also resonated with the principals' stories of both triumph and struggle and made me think about what I have heard from other leaders in workshops and conferences.

Recently, while delivering a workshop on how to support adult learning and development in schools, I had the privilege of talking with school leaders from a large district about their goals for the coming school year. One principal, Brisgal, expressed ideas that sounded so very much like what others had said. She passionately voiced her determination to "make this school year different" from the past 20 she had experienced in education. As Brisgal discussed plans for the coming year, her sixth as principal, I asked about the hopes she held for her teachers. After a pause, Brisgal explained that she wanted to teach her 33 teachers to "be confident, be able to handle conflict situations, and to present their views and take stands for the things they believe in, even when others disagree with them." While inspired by Brisgal's enthusiasm to "teach" new behaviors to her teachers, I could not help but wonder *how* she might go about doing this. Such behaviors are not a kind of content that can be mastered. Rather, they are capacities that adults can develop if they are provided with appropriate supports and challenge in order to grow.

After the workshop, Brisgal told me that she now understood that these behaviors she sought for her teachers were not simply skills to be taught but were expressions of certain developmental abilities or capacities that adults could grow toward. "Something more than teacher training is needed to achieve my hopes," she offered; she would have to create a stronger environment within which teachers would be supported in their own growth and development. This was why Brisgal attended the workshop, and, essentially, this is why I have written this book: to share theories and practices of adult learning and development to help school leaders build school environments that are supportive of teacher learning.

This book illuminates the ways in which 25 principals make sense of the challenges they face as they work to support adult learning and development, the creative strategies they employ to overcome financial and human resource barriers, and the practices they courageously implement as they strive to support adult learning within their schools. Of course, they face significant obstacles in their efforts, such as the challenges of time and faculty resistance. While I will point these out, my primary focus in this book is to illuminate the practices that they employed to effectively support teacher development and growth. I focus on what works well in supporting teacher learning because my aim is to offer these practices to others who want to support students and teachers in their growth. Toward this end, I will present four specific leadership practices that are the core of what I call a new model of *learning-oriented leadership* and illuminate the principles of adult learning and adult development that inform these practices.

The study was inspired by the question: What would school leadership practices look like if they were designed to support adult development? In other words, how would a model used to support children's development appear if applied to adult learning? When thinking about how to best support children's development, we consider their developmental capacities, such as the capacity for concrete versus abstract thinking. We also keep in mind how they will experience our efforts to support learning, and how to offer developmentally appropriate supports and challenges. Just as children's development needs to be considered in this way, so too does adult development.

My work stems from three premises. First, principals have a key role in supporting teacher learning and a responsibility to develop a clear vision of how school contexts can better support this learning. While they certainly do not have the *only* role, they have an important one. Second, leadership supportive of teacher development makes schools better places of learning for children (Barth, 1990; Fullan, 2003; Howe, 1993; Kegan, 1994). And last, schools need to be places where *the adults as well as the children* are growing (Donaldson, 2001; Greene, 2001; Levine, 1989; Sizer, 1992).

THE STUDY

This work focuses on honoring the uniqueness of each participant's story while also identifying patterns of similarity and difference among the 25 school leaders' stories. It offers a new and meaningful perspective to the current conversation about how leadership practices can better support teacher learning within schools. I hope that it furthers the current conversation.

ORIGINS OF THIS WORK

My first experiences working in schools were as teacher, program director, coach, and staff developer in several different K–12 school contexts. Having had the privilege of serving in different educational settings in these capacities and as a consultant, I have observed what wonderful places schools can be, and also the complex problems that exist in schools. My need to understand how I could help in making schools better learning places has long inspired my work. For nearly two decades, I have been studying teacher development and leadership in support of adult learning within schools through research, the teaching of K–12 and graduate students, and practice. The research questions informing this study grew from my own commitment to improving schools through attention to school leadership that fosters adult development. I bring these experiences to my listening and attention to the principal's stories reported in this book.

This particular study of 25 principals is built on lessons from a prior four-year ethnographic study (Drago-Severson, 1996) that I conducted with one school leader, Dr. Sarah Levine, to learn about how Sarah practiced leadership in support of teacher development. This type of leadership process in schools had not been studied previously. I invited Sarah to participate in this study because she had an explicit intention to support adult learning in her school. Her experiences represented an "ideal type" (Freidson, 1975) or "critical case" (J.A. Maxwell, personal communication, October 1, 1992) that demonstrated what seemed to work in the practices of a principal who actively supported adult development. This case also allowed for understanding practices that need improvement or were difficult to implement, even under ideal conditions. That is, they were implemented by a principal who had a developmental stance toward adult growth and assumed a strong leadership approach within a school.

In moving from the study of this one in-depth case to the study of a larger group of principals, I was able to develop a richer and more complex picture of school leadership and the support of adult development in schools. (Sarah has also participated in this current research as principal at a different school.)

My purpose in this current study has been to understand what a range of principals, who work in a variety of school contexts with strikingly different levels of financial and human resources, do in support of teacher learning and to understand why they believe the practices are effective. Put simply, I wanted to understand how these principals make meaning of their work in support of teacher learning so that I would be able to share their good work and stories of triumph and challenge with others.

METHODS

Participant and Site Selection

Marshall and Rossman (1989) maintain that "The researcher's question is the primary guide to site selection" (p. 54). My research questions were site specific. The 25 participants for this research were purposefully selected for their school leadership responsibility in support of teacher learning (see also Drago-Severson, 2002; Drago-Severson & Pinto, in press). Furthermore, each had served as a school leader for at least three years. As Table 1.1 indicates, this sample is diverse with respect to number of years as school principal, number of years at their current schools, gender, race, ethnicity, and educational background.

I selected school leaders serving in public, private, and Catholic schools that differed with respect to several factors, including level of financial resources (high, medium, and low). Financial resource levels were determined by using school Web site information, budgets, publication materials, and public school system financial reports (e.g., Boston Public Schools Fiscal Year Budget, 1999, as cited in Boston Plan for Excellence and the Boston Public Schools, 1999). In some cases, when these measures were not available, the principals themselves identified what they perceived to be their schools' resource levels relative to other schools of the same type in similar locations (e.g., urban Catholic schools). When determining a school's financial resource level, I did not include funding that resulted from principals' creative strategies to secure additional grant funding or funding from other sources (e.g., gifts or development funds).

I also made selections based on type of school (elementary, middle, high school, and K–12), populations served with varying degrees of racial and ethnic diversity, and location (urban, suburban, and rural). Human resource levels (i.e., how many people—faculty, staff, and administrators—worked at each school) were learned through Web sites, school documents, and principal reports.

Thirteen of the 25 leaders were recommended by professional colleagues as being known for their support of teacher learning, employing practices that create opportunities for different modes of teacher reflection (see, for example, Harbison, with Kegan, 1999). I sought to include principals who wanted to create contexts and opportunities *within their schools* for teachers to reflect on their practices. My goal was to achieve a sample that was diverse with respect to the school characteristic criteria listed above. I selected principals who were identified by professional colleagues or myself as leaders who:[1]

1. Provide various forums for teachers to discuss new theories and reflect on practice through writing and discussion

2. Seek out additional resources to provide professional development opportunities (e.g., ensuring substitutes for teachers when they are

Table 1.1   Characteristics of the Sample[1]

Type of School	Grades	# of Years Experience	# of Students	# of Teachers	Name of School/Location	Student Diversity	Resource Level/Endowment or School Budget (in Hundred-Thousands)[2]
Public Schools							
Mr. Kim Marshall[3]	K–5	13	600	28(31)[4]	Mather School Dorchester, MA: Urban	High	Low/$2.6
Mr. Joe Shea	K–5	20	607	55	Trotter School Boston, MA: Urban	High	Low/$3.0
Dr. Mary Nash	K–8[5]	25	120	15(27)	Mary Lyons Alternative School Brighton, MA: Urban	High	Medium/$1.5[6]
Mr. Len Solo	K–8[7]	26	370	22(47)	Graham & Parks Alternative School Cambridge, MA: Urban	High	Medium/$3.2
Ms. Muriel Leonard	6–8	18	690	60	McCormick Middle School Dorchester, MA: Urban	High	Low/$3.7
Ms. Kathleen Perry	9–12 +GED[8]	31	3,167	165(180)	Lake Worth Community High School Lake Worth, FL: Urban	High	Medium to High/$37
Dr. Jim Cavanaugh	9–12 +GED	22	768	60	Watertown High School Watertown, MA: Urban	Medium-High	High/$24.5
Dr. Larry Myatt	9–12 +GED[9]	19	300	35	Fenway Pilot High School Boston, MA: Urban	High	Low to Medium/$1.9

Type of School	Grades	# of Years Experience	# of Students	# of Teachers	Name of School/Location	Student Diversity	Resource Level/Endowment or School Budget (in Hundred-Thousands)[2]
Catholic Schools							
Mrs. Deborah O'Neil	K–8	10	235	13	St. Peter's School Cambridge, MA: Urban	High	Low/$800K
Sr. Barbara Rogers	5–12 (all girls)	20	325	59	Newton Country Day School of the Sacred Heart Newton, MA: Suburban	Medium	High/$6
Mr. John Clarke	9–12	8	910	67	Cardinal Newman High School West Palm, FL: Urban	High	Medium/$5.1
Sr. Judith Brady	9–12 (all girls)	35	283	24	St. Barnabas High School Bronx, NY: Urban	High	Low/$1.2
Mr. Gary LeFave	9–12	29	535	36	Matignon High School Cambridge, MA: Urban	Medium	Low/$3.2
Sr. Joan Magnetti	Pk–12	24	626	58	Convent of the Sacred Heart Greenwich, CT: Suburban	Low	High/$5.2

(Continued)

Table 1.1 Continued

Independent Schools

Type of School	Grades	# of Years Experience	# of Students	# of Teachers	Name of School/Location	Student Diversity	Resource Level/Endowment or School Budget (in Hundred-Thousands)[2]
Mr. John (Jack) Thompson	K–9	40	352	45	Palm Beach Day School Palm Beach, FL: Suburban	Low	Medium to High/$3
Dr. Sarah Levine	Pre-K–6 7–12	30 30	200 840	26 ft/6pt 108	Belmont Day School Belmont, MA Suburban Polytechnic Pasadena, CA: Urban	Medium High	Medium High/$30
Dr. Dan White[10]	7–12	20	391	41	Seabury Hall Maui, HI: Rural	Medium	Low to Medium $700K
Ms. Barbara Chase	9–12	21	1,065	218	Philips Andover Academy Andover, MA: Rural	Medium-High	Very High/$535
Dr. Sue David[11]	9–12	< 10	Approx. 300	<75	Anonymous Suburban	Medium	High/< $60
Mr. Joe Marchese[12]	9–12	30	590	87	Westtown School Westtown, PA: Suburban	Medium	High/$60
Dr. Jim Scott	K–12	25	3,700	281 (334)	Punahoe School Honolulu, HI: Urban	High	High/$68
Mr. Scott Nelson	Pk–12	16	770	125	Rye Country Day School Rye, NY: Suburban	Medium	Medium-High/$13
Ms. Mary Newman	Pk–12	22	950	170	Buckingham, Browne, & Nichols Cambridge, MA: Urban	High	High/$30

Type of School	Grades	# of Years Experience	# of Students	# of Teachers	Name of School/Location	Student Diversity	Resource Level/Endowment or School Budget (in Hundred-Thousands)[2]
Mr. Jerry Zank	Pre-K-12	30	520	62	Canterbury School Fort Myers, FL: Urban	High	Low/$800K
Ms. Shirley Mae[13]	9–12	<25	N/A	N/A	CA: Urban	High	N/A

Notes:
1. I thank Kristina Pinto for sorting through some of the materials I gathered and helping to compile some of the information depicted in this chart. I also thank Sue Stuebner Gaylor for her help with adjusting the format of this chart. A similar version of this chart appears in Drago-Severson (2002).
2. As mentioned, 2000–2001 financial resource levels were determined either by using school Web site information or publication materials (i.e., district financial reports), or in a few cases, the principals themselves identified their schools' resource levels in comparison to other schools of the same type in similar locations (e.g., Florida Catholic schools). This determination, for any school type, *does not* include the principals' creative strategies to secure additional external grant funding or funding from other sources (e.g., federal, state, development fundraising, or gifts). For the independent schools in this sample, including Catholic independent schools, I have listed their 2000–2001 endowments. In the case of the Boston public schools, I have also listed their approximated school budgets for the "General Fund [which] refers to money that is allocated to the schools by the city budget" (Boston Public School Fiscal Year Report, 2001, p. 203). For Catholic parochial schools, I have listed their 2000–2001 operating budgets. Reported numbers are listed in millions, unless otherwise noted, and have been rounded to the nearest half million. In places where no amount appears, information was not available, or the participant preferred not to share it.
3. Principals whose names appear in *italicized* font have left their positions as school principals, for a variety of reasons.
4. Parenthetical numbers indicate the number of teachers *and* support staff (i.e., assistants and specialists).
5. This school is designated as an alternative school for children with special needs.
6. Dr. Nash has a great deal of autonomy over her school budget, because it is an alternative school and because it was one of the first schools of its kind in the city. She also spoke about the ways in which she was able to negotiate with the district to secure additional funding for a needed after-school program for her students, which added to the available financial resources.
7. Graham-Parks school is an alternative school based on John Dewey's philosophy of education and constructivist thinking. The classrooms are multigraded, self-contained, and open. Learning is considered to be a social activity that transpires through social interaction. Len Solo, this school's former principal, served as interim principal of a public high school in Cambridge, MA, in 2001–2002.
8. Lake Worth Community High School is a magnet school with ROTC programs, bilingual programs, and day and evening GED programs.
9. Fenway High School, founded in 1983, became an alternative pilot school in 1995. This status gives the school freedom from the Boston Public School System. In other words, it is allotted some funding from the Boston Public School System but does not have to conform to all of the same guidelines as the other Boston public schools.
10. Principals whose names appear in **bold** font serve in boarding schools.
11. This participant preferred to remain anonymous; I have assigned a pseudonym.
12. Westtown is a Quaker boarding school.
13. This participant preferred to remain anonymous; I have assigned a pseudonym.

working on collaborative projects, encouraging teachers to attend and present at professional conferences and share their learning with colleagues at school, encouraging teachers to work together to implement their ideas for practice)

3. Provide opportunities for shared leadership (e.g., through mechanisms such as cross-disciplinary, or cross-functional, teams as defined later in Chapter 5)

4. Hold teachers accountable for creating high expectations for children while they (the principals) provide feedback and encourage dialogue to achieve these goals

For the sake of diversity, I also included a second group of principals who were *not identified* as exemplary in terms of their support of teacher learning. In other words, the principals in this second group were not identified as leaders who incorporate teacher learning as part of their *explicit* beliefs or mission. I sought a balanced sample, and selection was guided by balancing the following criteria: personal or colleague referral, school's financial resource level, school type, school level, and location.

Above, I explained that I focus primarily on the principals' successful practices to provide readers with effective ideas for their own work. Another reason I emphasize these principals' successful practices, rather than shortcomings, is because 23 of the 25 participants elected to use their real names in this book. Also, in fairness to my entire sample, I do not name which principals belonged to the group of leaders who were recognized for excelling in their work and which principals did not. It is important that readers bear in mind that the unreferred participants were not necessarily *unsuccessful* in their leadership.

Research Questions: What Did I Want to Learn?

These research questions guided my exploration of leaders' efforts to support teacher learning:

1. How do school leaders, who serve in different school contexts with varying levels of financial resources, exercise their leadership to promote adults' transformational learning (i.e., learning that helps adults to better manage the complexities of work and life)? How do they understand and experience their role in support of teacher learning?

2. What are the actual practices they use to support teacher learning within their schools, and why do they think that the practices are effective?

3. How do these leaders support their own development and sustain themselves in their complex work?

4. What developmental principles, if any, inform the practices that support transformational learning?

Data Collection: How Did I Investigate the Research Questions?

To better understand the questions guiding this research, I conducted in-depth qualitative interviews and document analysis. A grounded theory (i.e., an understanding derived inductively from their stories) was developed about how these principals support teacher learning within their schools by triangulation of data (i.e., examining different sources of data for alternative perspectives). Various literature cited in this book also informed my analysis.

Interviews

With the sample of 25 principals selected, I conducted 75 hours of semistructured, in-depth, qualitative interviews (tape-recorded and transcribed). On average, these interviews lasted two to three hours, though some were longer and others shorter.

Most often, before beginning the interview or after completing it, I toured the school with each principal to get better acquainted with the school context. In-depth interviews allowed for exploration of principals' goals for supporting teacher learning and what they experienced as the challenges and benefits of supporting teacher learning within their schools. They also articulated the kinds of practices they employ on behalf of teacher learning, how and why they believed these initiatives were effective, and what other kinds of practices they would like to implement. Finally, I was also interested in learning how these school leaders supported their own development. To make sure the data I collected were comparable, I asked participants very similar questions about these overarching topics; however, additional questions specific to each participant and his or her school context were included. For example, if a person wanted to talk about a certain topic raised during the interview (e.g., a special project in support of teacher learning that he or she was contemplating and the challenges associated with it), I encouraged the person to elaborate. Also, I did my best to let the participants stay with questions that seemed important to them.

I gave each school principal the opportunity to review and comment on the interview transcript. They were also encouraged to elaborate on their comments and to omit any comments that they did not want to have published (e.g., identifying features of their school if they opted to remain anonymous). Twenty-two of 25 principals reviewed their interview transcripts, and 6 of these made minor syntax changes to the transcripts. Any additional comments that they offered at this time were incorporated into analysis.

Documents

Approximately 60 documents were analyzed, including written communications from principals, demographics, Web site information, school budgets, mission statements, speeches and letters (official correspondence written by the principals) to faculty members and parents, school self-study documents, published articles, and various other private writings by the principals. I also collected e-mails, letters, and memos the principals sent to me that contained their thinking about the research, as well as responses to additional questions I posed.

The documents were important because some were vehicles by which the principals shared their thinking with school boards, parents, faculty, and administrators. Many of the principals told me that they used these as tools for communicating their visions, policies, and priorities to various constituencies on whom they depended for achievement of objectives. Other documents produced by the principals that made public their thinking to educators, practitioners, and educational researchers were included. Weekly notices (written by some of the principals) and the self-study evaluation documents created by school community members helped me to better understand each school context and culture. These also helped me to better understand community members' activities and oftentimes parental involvement with and influence on the school and its practices and programs. Collectively, these documents served as important validity checks for the information gleaned in my interviews and provided alternative perspectives on data.

Data Analysis: Making Sense of the Learning

Data analysis strategies were developed to address each research question. Techniques included coding for important concepts and themes (from theory, and from the participants' own language—emic codes, Geertz, 1974), creating narrative summaries (Coffey & Atkinson, 1996; Maxwell, 1996), and crafting vignettes (Seidman, 1998). I built my understanding inductively from the participants' stories (i.e., a grounded theory approach) while informing analysis with the literature cited herein.

I undertook an early and a substantive phase of data analysis.[2] In the early phase, I wrote field notes immediately after each interview about the interview, my observations of the school context, and how the literature cited herein informed the principals' stories and vice versa. This initial analytic phase focused on creating a set of more than 60 codes that were employed to analyze data from all interviews, cross-checking codes from each interview, writing summary analytic memos (Maxwell & Miller,

1998), and identifying consistencies and discrepancies within and across participants' data.

In the substantive phase, I grouped interviews by school type and financial resource level to examine patterns across categories (e.g., principals' views about mentoring) within and across groups. I created detailed narratives and visual displays (Miles & Huberman, 1994) that were analyzed through a developmental lens.

Throughout analysis, I tracked the ways in which the literature on adult development and school leadership informed the data, through questions and the use of analytic memos (Maxwell, 1996). For example, how do the principals' reported practices serve as "holding environments" (Kegan, 1982, 1994) for growth? What developmental principles inform practices that these principals name as being supportive of teacher learning? How might teachers at different developmental levels, phases of their lives, and stages of their careers experience these practices? I used additional questions to explore themes in the literature of school leadership and organizational learning. For example, what features of these principals' reported practices appear to support reflection and the development of critical thinking (Brookfield, 1987; Schön, 1983; Senge et al., 1994)?

Last, I traced participants' descriptions of their roles and practices across groups to illuminate qualitative and developmental patterns. Profiles and narratives (Coffey & Atkinson, 1996) for each participant were created to explore patterns in 15 core categories and their subcategories (Strauss & Corbin, 1998) within and across school type, resource level, and the sample as a whole. Looking particularly for similarity and contrast, I analyzed the factors (e.g., level of financial and/or human resources) that coincided with critical themes and developed cases of participants, whose stories served as examples. Having identified practices that were transformational and those oriented to informational learning (e.g., skill acquisition), I examined how principals described both kinds of practices and how they said they worked within each school. The learning-oriented model of school leadership that I present in this book is informed by data from the study itself, as well as the literature cited herein.

In interpreting the data, there are several ways I attended to their validity. Multiple data sources (e.g., interviews, documents, correspondence of principals) allowed for multiple perspectives on data. Myself and at least one additional researcher employed various strategies during all analytic phases. For example, coding, data displays, emerging interpretations, and other aspects of analysis were discussed with other researchers in order to incorporate alternative interpretations.

In addition, I worked to incorporate the principals' feedback and interpretations of the data in several ways. As noted, all principals received copies of their interview transcripts to check for accuracy, add to them, and/or clarify their statements. Their feedback was incorporated into analysis. All principals received and were invited to comment on a dissemination packet and a detailed executive summary, which presented the overarching findings reported in this book. Each principal also received drafts of articles (Drago-Severson & Pinto, 2003, in press) that were written about this work (before publication in journals) and invited to comment on my interpretations of the data. These constituted opportunities to follow up on interviews and to further investigate their understanding of how they supported teacher learning. Their comments were incorporated into analysis.

Throughout analysis, I looked for and examined both confirming and disconfirming instances of themes (Miles & Huberman, 1994) to test both the power and scope of my developing understanding (Merriam, 1998). Finally, in this analysis, I have attended to various levels of data and multiple perspectives on their interpretation by attending to patterns that emerged from the individual narrative, from group level patterns (e.g., similar resource level and school types), case write-ups, and the sample as a whole (Glaser & Strauss, 1967). When data collection and analyses are continually integrated, analysis gains depth and focus (Strauss & Corbin, 1998). This study benefited from this type of intentional and continual synthesis of data.

Strengths and Limits of This Study

This study illuminates what these principals actually pointed to with examples in terms of the specific practices they used in their schools to support teacher learning in practice (i.e., reported or expressed practices). Because I had a sample size of 25, I was not able to conduct in-depth observations at every principal's school, which would have helped me to see their practices at work in their school contexts. However, all but one of the initial interviews were conducted on-site, which allowed me to become somewhat familiar with their school contexts. In this study, I invited principals to tell me, concretely, the specific practices they use in their schools to support teacher learning. These principals told me about what they do, and, for the most part, I was not able to see their practices at work. I have been mindful of differences between espoused theory (reported practice) and theory-in-use (what they actually do in practice) (Argyris & Schön, 1974) when analyzing interviews, by noting gaps and possible inconsistencies in the interview material itself.

Since all principals interviewed offered to continue conversations with me, I did meet with many of them a second time to check interpretations and share findings. These conversations provided important validity checks on their meaning making and my interpretations. This study examined principals' support of adult development through a particular theoretical lens. Although other theoretical perspectives could also yield findings about school leadership and supporting adult growth (i.e., gender analysis), they were beyond the scope of this particular study.

A NEW MODEL OF LEARNING-ORIENTED SCHOOL LEADERSHIP

This book offers a new model of learning-oriented school leadership that facilitates transformational learning. I define *transformational learning* as learning that helps adults better manage the complexities of work and life. In contrast to *informational learning*, which focuses on increasing the amount of knowledge and skills a person possesses and is often the goal of traditional inservice professional development programs, transformational learning constitutes a qualitative shift in *how* a person organizes, understands, and actively makes sense of his or her experience. When transformational learning occurs, a person develops increased capacities (i.e., cognitive, interpersonal, and intrapersonal) for better managing the complexities of daily life and work. This increase in capacities enables people to take broader perspectives on themselves and others—and on their work and life (Cranton, 1994; Mezirow, 1991, 2000). For this to occur, attention needs to be paid to shaping school contexts wherein adults have opportunities to examine their own assumptions (i.e., taken-for-granted beliefs that guide thought and action) and convictions in the learning process. In other words, we hold our assumptions as big Truths and rarely question them unless provided with opportunities to consider them.

Examining assumptions is essential for the development of lasting change and the successful implementation of new practices. While both informational and transformational learning opportunities are important, initiatives supportive of transformational learning can help us develop a heightened awareness of our assumptions so that we can examine their influence on performance. Doing so creates opportunities for development. My learning-oriented school leadership model presents the principal as professional developer and educator and employs adult developmental principles to inform leadership practices that support teacher learning.

The Four Pillars of the Model

The principals in this study employ four mutually reinforcing initiatives that support adult growth and development; they form the four pillars on which the weight of this new learning-oriented model rests. They are (1) teaming/partnering with colleagues within and outside of the school, (2) providing teachers with leadership roles, (3) engaging in collegial inquiry, and (4) mentoring.

Teaming

Working in teams enables teachers to question their own and other people's philosophies of teaching and learning, consider the meaning of the ways in which they implement the school's core values in the curriculum and school context, reflect on the meaning of their school's mission, and engage in collaborative decision making. Teaming is a practice that creates an opportunity for teachers to share their diverse perspectives and learn about one another's ideas. This practice creates a context wherein teachers can explore new and diverse perspectives and grow.

Providing Leadership Roles

By assuming leadership roles, teachers share power and decision-making authority. A leadership role is an opportunity to raise not only one's own consciousness but also a group's consciousness with regard to ideas. These roles are a way for principals to share their own leadership and to practice distributive leadership, since the roles enable the school to benefit from teachers' expertise and knowledge. I use the term "providing leadership roles" rather than the commonly used term "distributive leadership" because of the intention behind these roles, which is to not merely distribute leadership duties. In contrast to assigning tasks, "providing leadership roles" offers supports and challenges to the person who assumes such a role so that he or she can grow from them.

Engaging in Collegial Inquiry

"Collegial inquiry" is an example of a larger developmental concept known as "reflective practice," which can occur individually or in groups. In this book, I define collegial inquiry as a shared dialogue in a reflective context that involves reflecting on one's assumptions, convictions, and values as part of the learning process. Collegial inquiry is a practice that creates a context for teachers to reflect on their practices, proposals for change, and schoolwide issues (e.g., developing a school mission). It enables principals to provide teachers and staff, and themselves as well, with opportunities to develop more complex perspectives by listening to and learning from one another.

Mentoring

When adults engage in mentoring, it creates an opportunity for each person to broaden perspectives, examine assumptions, and share expertise. The practice of mentoring invites teachers to share leadership. Mentoring takes myriad forms, including pairing experienced teachers with new teachers, pairing teachers who have deep knowledge of school mission with other teachers, and pairing experienced teachers with graduate student interns from local universities. Mentoring enables adults to explore their own thinking and contradictions, enhancing self-development.

Underpinnings of the Model: Adult Learning and Development

Scholarship on adult development and learning, like the staff development literature, discusses how principals can benefit from reframing their practices in a developmental perspective (Brookfield, 1987, 1995; Kegan, 1994; Kegan & Lahey, 1984, 2001; Levine, 1989; Mezirow, 2000; Osterman & Kottkamp, 1993; York-Barr et al., 2001). Adult developmental theory can be a strong tool for understanding *how* adults develop during engagement in professional development programs (Drago-Severson, Helsing, Kegan, Broderick, Popp, & Portnow, 2001; Drago-Severson, Helsing, Kegan, Broderick, Portnow, & Popp, 2001; Kegan, 1994).

Developmentalists have criticized current approaches to supporting teacher development (Kegan et al., 2001; Kegan & Lahey, 2001), arguing that adults at various stages of ego and intellectual development respond differently in terms of their understanding of the options provided by these programs. In fact, Kegan (1994) contends that much of what is expected and needed from teachers for them to succeed and grow within widely used staff development models demands something more than an increase in their fund of knowledge or skills (i.e., informational learning). It may demand changes in the ways they know and understand their experiences (i.e., transformational learning). In other words, the expectations intrinsic to some of the models may in fact be beyond the developmental capacities of those using them. Knowledge about theories of adult development can be a robust tool for considering how to better support the development of adults in schools. Yet the role of principals in supporting teacher development is only beginning to be explored.

Since this book draws centrally on the work of Kegan (1982, 1994, 2000) to shed light on *how* the practices employed by the 25 principals in this study support teachers' transformational learning, I will discuss his framework in the next chapter. There is a hopefulness in this new model of learning-oriented school leadership. It offers a way to support adult learning within schools—so that teachers do not have to leave schools to grow and have time to reflect. The simplicity and power of the model is the power of paid attention for the development of not only a skill set, but the person.

CHAPTER SUMMARY

This chapter introduced the study on which this book is based and presented its methodology, including sample selection, data collection, and analysis. The study was guided by three principles. First, principals are key to supporting teacher learning and envisioning how schools can better support this learning. Second, leadership that promotes teacher development also fosters the learning of children. Finally, schools need to be contexts for both adult and youth development. Based on these premises, I investigated the following question: What would school leadership look like if designed to support adult development?

My findings inform a new learning-oriented model of school leadership, which is supported by four pillars: teaming, providing leadership roles, collegial inquiry, and mentoring. In practice, these tools contribute to the effectiveness of leadership in service of teachers' transformational learning and professional development. Through case examples, this book focuses primarily on successful leadership practices to assist school leaders in their efforts to better support teacher learning, growth, and development.

REFLECTIVE QUESTIONS

Please take a moment to reflect on these questions. They are intended to help you consider the ideas discussed in this chapter and can be used for internal reflection or to open up a group discussion.

1. What are two or three practices you engage in to support your own or other people's learning? How are they working?

2. In what ways does this chapter help you in thinking about the practices you named above? What, if anything, resonates with your own experiences?

3. If you were a participant in this research, how would you respond to the research questions presented in this chapter?

NOTES

1. Peggy Kemp, Director of School Partnerships at Harvard University and Dr. Millie Pierce, Director of Harvard University's Principal Center, assisted me in creating a list of principals who fit the selection criteria for supporting adult development in their school contexts.

2. I thank Deborah Helsing and Kristina Pinto for their contributions to different phases of data analysis. Collaborating with each of them at different points in the analysis was an invaluable resource that strengthened this work.

2

Constructive-
Developmental Theory
and Adult Development

Throughout this book, I draw primarily on principles of psychologist Robert Kegan's (1982, 1994, 2000) constructive-developmental theory to interpret the principals' practices that support transformational learning. I also employ this theory to call attention to the diverse ways in which teachers might experience the practices constituting my learning-oriented model of school leadership and to show that supports for teacher growth need to take different forms, depending on individual needs. This chapter provides an overview of the key ideas from Kegan's (1982, 1994, 2000) framework.

Constructive-developmental theory and theories of adult learning offer tools for understanding and reviewing leadership practices and models of teacher development that can inform practice. Certainly, there are other frameworks that could be employed to understand and illuminate different aspects of leadership practice, and I draw on other sources as well in my analysis (Brookfield, 1987, 1995; Daloz, 1986, 1999; Osterman & Kottkamp, 1993; York-Barr et al., 2001). For example, the principals' stories could be interpreted through the lens of women's development (Belenky et al., 1986; Gilligan, 1982), gender and leadership (Shakeshaft, Nowell, & Perry, 2000), intellectual and ethical development (Gardner, 1983; Perry, 1970), or moral development and exemplary leadership (Kohlberg, 1969, 1984; Sergiovanni, 2000; Sobol, 2002). However, while these frameworks are valuable and could enhance our understanding of particular dimensions of the principals' leadership, I chose Kegan's constructive-developmental theory as the lens for several reasons.

First, it focuses on a person as an active meaning maker of experience, considering both interpersonal and internal experiences, particularly how they intersect in one's work. While other frameworks may address this, it is central in constructive-developmental theory. Second, many developmentally oriented theories focus primarily on children's development and articulate adult development secondarily or in less depth than Kegan's theory does. Third, this theory offers hopeful principles about how to support adult growth so that we can better manage the complexities of 21st-century life, especially in terms of the workplace. Last, it emphasizes that development is *not* the same thing as intelligence and attends to a broad range of aspects of the self. These include the emotional, cognitive, intrapersonal, and interpersonal realms of experience. My primary interest was in learning how these principals support adults' transformational learning, that is, changes in *how* a person knows, rather than in *what* a person knows. It was important that I highlight the developmental principles informing their practices and the supports and challenges that foster growth, making this framework a good fit.

Interestingly, in disseminating this work to the principals in this study, *nearly all* of them wanted to learn more about the ways in which this framework could inform their practices. In fact, when I explained some of the key features of the different ways in which adults make sense of their experiences, many of the principals nodded in agreement. They told me that this framework helped them to understand differences they noticed in themselves and their teachers, gave them a language to talk about these differences, and provided ideas about how to better support growth in their schools. By employing this framework, my learning-oriented model for school leadership makes important linkages between theory and practice.

In this chapter, I present an overview of the theory's (a) theoretical principles, (b) three essential "ways of knowing" that are most common to adulthood, and (c) the central aspects of a "holding environment" (Kegan 1982, 1994). In my writing, I use meaning making and ways of knowing interchangeably to express how individuals make sense of their experiences. A "holding environment" is a context that supports growth. Similar to supporting a child's growth, holding environments offer developmentally appropriate supports *and* challenges to adults who make sense of their experiences in qualitatively different ways. Here, I will describe the characteristics of the different ways in which we, as adults, make sense of our experiences. First, I introduce the concept of transformational learning, because it is essential to the discussion of constructive-developmental theory.

ABOUT TRANSFORMATIONAL LEARNING

As I said earlier, like Kegan (2000), I distinguish between transformational learning—learning that helps adults to develop capacities to better manage the complexities of work and life—and informational learning—increases in knowledge and skills that are also important and can support changes in adults' attitudes and possibly their competencies.[1]

While informational learning is certainly important and needed, my primary purpose in this research was to understand the practices these principals implemented in their schools that were oriented toward supporting teachers' *transformational* learning, as Kegan (1994) defines the concept:

> An *informational* stance leaves the form as it is and focuses on changing what people know; it is essentially a *training* model for personal change. I would contrast this with a *transformational* stance, which places the form itself at risk for change and focuses on changes in how people know; it is essentially an *educational* model for personal change. (pp. 163–164)

Informational learning—new skills and information—increases *what* a person knows, whereas transformational learning changes *how* a person knows, as Kegan (1994) explains. In other words, the adult has enhanced his or her capacities (cognitive, interpersonal, and intrapersonal) to manage the complexities of work.

There is an intimate connection between transformational learning and self-examination (Brookfield, 1987, 1995; Cranton, 1994, 1996; Mezirow, 1991, 1994, 1996, 2000). Increases in developmental capacity broaden adults' perspectives on both themselves and others (Kegan, 1982, 1994). For this kind of change to occur, attention needs to be devoted to both the context and to the ways in which an adult is interpreting his or her experience so that the context can provide both supports and challenges that are developmentally appropriate. In transformational learning, adults undergo a *development* and profound change in the very way they *construct* or *make sense of* experience. This kind of change is at the core of constructive- developmental theory, as Kegan describes it (1982, 1994).

KEGAN'S CONSTRUCTIVE-DEVELOPMENTAL THEORY

Constructive-developmental theories of adult growth and development stem from a 30-year tradition that closely traces how individuals make sense of their internal and external experiences (Basseches, 1984; Belenky et al., 1986; Gilligan, 1982; Kegan, 1982, 1994, 2000; King & Kitchener, 1994; Piaget, 1952).

Basic Principles

The principles of Kegan's constructive-developmental theory are based on two key ideas: one, that people construct—*or actively make sense of*—the reality in which they live (with respect to cognitive, interpersonal, and intrapersonal development) and, two, that people (and their constructions of reality) can *change or develop* over time with developmentally appropriate supports and challenges. The first basic principle of constructive-developmental theory is that growth and development *are* lifelong processes. Development is an interactive process between the person and the environment (Kegan, 1982). In other words, development always occurs in some context. Development or growth, according to Kegan's theory (1982, 1994), is a process of increasing differentiation and internalization; as human beings, we are involved in a process of growth in which we are constantly (and gradually) renegotiating what is *self* and what constitutes *other* (Drago-Severson, in press). A person's meaning system—through which all experience is filtered and understood—is referred to as a way of knowing, a developmental level, an order of consciousness, or a stage (Kegan, 1994).

The second basic principle of constructive-developmental theory is that development involves a *qualitative change* in the ways in which a person makes sense or constructs his or her experience—rather than an acquisition of more skills and knowledge. Crucial to growth, according to this theory, are both the *structure* and the *process* of meaning making. Meaning making is an activity by which the self emerges from being embedded in or subject to and identified with a culture (e.g., its needs, its interpersonal mutuality, or its own authorship and ideology). As the self emerges, it is able to take the previous culture it was identified with as object and *reflect on it.* Put simply, we cannot take a perspective on what we are *subject* to because we are embedded in it and identified with it. It is not separate from our selves. In contrast, that which is taken as *object* can be organized and reflected upon by the self. In other words, what a person can take as object are aspects of our experiences that we can reflect on, look at, be responsible for, and take control of. A person's *way of knowing* dictates how learning experiences will be taken in, managed, handled, used, and understood.

For instance, a way of knowing shapes how a person understands his or role and responsibilities as a teacher, leader, and learner, and how that person thinks about what makes a good student, what makes a good leader, and what constitutes a good employee/community member. A person constructs meaning with the same way of knowing across different domains of life (e.g., work, parenting, partnering), except under extraordinarily rare circumstances (see Kegan, 1994).

People learning this theory often ask whether a higher way of knowing is considered a "better" way of knowing. It is important to consider this question in terms of the "goodness of fit" (Kegan, 1994) or match between a person's way of knowing and the challenges he or she faces. If a person's way of knowing is adequate to meet the challenges or inherent developmental demands of work or life, then it would not necessarily be better to operate from a more complex meaning system (Drago-Severson, Helsing, Kegan, Broderick, Portnow, & Popp, 2001). If that way of knowing is not sufficient to meet those cultural challenges or expectations, then a development in his or her way of knowing would help that individual to better manage the complexities of work and/or life. This in no way means that a person is a better person for having a more complex way of knowing (Drago-Severson, Helsing, Kegan, Broderick, Portnow, & Popp, 2001; Drago-Severson, in press).

Ways of Knowing

Kegan's constructive-developmental theory consists of five qualitatively different systems of meaning making, or ways of making sense of reality.[2] The first of these five systems describes the meaning making of young children, and the last describes a mostly theoretical meaning making system that is rarely found in any population and, if present, has not been detected before midlife (Kegan, 1994). Because of this, I will describe the three qualitatively different ways of knowing that are most common in adulthood: *the instrumental way of knowing, the socializing way of knowing,* and *the self-authoring way of knowing.* Here, I focus on the characteristics of these ways of knowing; however, it is important to note that there are also four identifiable transition stages between each of them (for a full discussion of this, please see Lahey et al., 1988). Moving from one developmental level to another is a progression of increasing complexity in an individual's developmental capacities. Table 2.1 summarizes the essential characteristics of the instrumental, socializing, and self-authoring ways of knowing.

The Instrumental Way of Knowing: A person who has an instrumental way of knowing primarily has a "What do you have that can help me?/What do I have that can help you?" perspective on work and life. A strength of this way of knowing is that the person understands that observable events, processes, and situations have realities separate from his or her own point of view, but understands the world in highly concrete terms. While instrumental knowers are able to take perspective on and control their impulses, they do not have this same type of perspective-taking capacity on their own needs, desires, and interests. Generally, others' interests are important only if they interfere with their own, and the instrumental knower cannot take another's perspective fully.

The Socializing Way of Knowing: A person who makes meaning primarily with a socializing way of knowing has grown to have an enhanced capacity for reflection. Unlike instrumental knowers, socializing knowers

Table 2.1 Stages, Ways of Knowing, and/or Developmental Levels of Kegan's Constructive-Developmental Theory

Stage → / Way of Knowing ↑	Stage 0 *Incorporative*	Stage 1 *Impulsive*	Stage 2 *Instrumental*	Stage 3 *Socializing*	Stage 4 *Self-Authoring*	Stage 5 *Interindividual*
Underlying structure of thinking *Subject* (S): what a person is identified with *Object* (O): what a person can hold out, look at, take a perspective on	S: Reflexes (sensing, moving) O: None	S: Impulses, perceptions O: Reflexes (sensing, moving)	S: Needs, interests, wishes O: Impulses, perceptions	S: The interpersonal, mutuality O: Needs, interests, wishes	S: Authorship, identity, psychic administration, ideology O: The interpersonal, mutuality	S: Interindividuality, interpenetrability of self-systems O: Authorship, identity, psychic administration, ideology
How the self defines itself			Orients to self-interests, purposes, wants, concrete needs.	Orients to valued others' (external authority) expectations and opinions.	Orients to self's values, own internal authority.	Orients to multiple self-systems, open to learning from other people.
Orienting considerations/ concerns			Dependence on rules, decisions are based on what the self will acquire.	Dependence on external authority, acceptance and affiliation are crucial. Self feels responsible for other's feelings; holds others responsible for own feelings.	Reliance on own internally generated values and standards. Criticism is evaluated and used according to one's own personal standards. Concern	Committed to self-exploration. Engaging with conflict is an opportunity to let others inform and shape one's own thinking.

Stage → Way of Knowing →	Stage 0 Incorporative	Stage 1 Impulsive	Stage 2 Instrumental	Stage 3 Socializing	Stage 4 Self-Authoring	Stage 5 Interindividual
				Criticism and conflict are threats to the self.	with one's own competence and performance. Holds contradictory feelings simultaneously. Conflict can be potentially useful and can lead to clarification of issues and more effective solutions.	Conflict is basic to life and opportunities to enhance thinking.
Guiding questions for self			"Will I get punished?" "What's in it for me?"	"Will you (a valued other/authority) still like/value me?" "Will you (a valued other/authority) still think I am a good person?" "Am I meeting your expectations of me?	"Am I maintaining my own standards and values?" "Am I competent?" "Am I living, working, loving to the best of my ability?" "Am I achieving my goals and reaching for my ideals?"	"How can other people's thinking help me to enhance my own?" "How can I seek out information & opinions from others to help me modify my own ways of understanding?"

SOURCE: A similar version of this table appears in Drago-Severson (2002), "Underlying Structure." Row 1 of Table 2.1 is from Kegan (1982), *The Evolving Self* (pp. 86–87).

are able to think abstractly, make generalizations, and *reflect* on their own and others' actions. With this way of knowing, people have the capacity to subordinate their own needs and desires to the needs and desires of others. Socializing knowers orient to their own internal psychological states, feel responsible for other people's feelings, and hold others responsible for their own feelings. However, they are not yet able to have a perspective on their relationships because they are identified with them, so much so that reality is co-constructed. For socializing knowers, others' approval and acceptance is of ultimate importance. Other people, and often societal expectations, are experienced not simply as resources to be used by the self but also as the origin of internal confirmation, orientation, or authority (Drago-Severson, Helsing, Kegan, Broderick, Portnow, & Popp, 2001; Drago-Severson, in press; Kegan et al., 2001a; Popp & Portnow, 2001).

The Self-Authoring Way of Knowing: People with a self-authoring way of knowing have the capacity to take responsibility for and ownership of their own internal authority. They have the capacity to generate (and identify with) their own abstract values, principles, and longer-term purposes and are able to prioritize and integrate competing values. Self-authoring knowers can assess the expectations and demands of others and compare them with their own internal standards and judgment. With this way of knowing, individuals author—and internally generate—their own systems of beliefs or personal ideologies. They have the capacity to reflect on and regulate their relationships. A limitation to this way of knowing is that the self cannot take a perspective on its own autonomy or its own self-system, which manages relationships because it is embedded in its own assertions, theories, ideals, and principles.

Why Ways of Knowing Matter
When Supporting Teacher Learning

Understanding Kegan's theory of constructive-development and the attendant ways of knowing will help readers understand the developmental basis of the principals' practices as well as how teachers and other adults might experience participation in programs aimed at supporting their learning. For example, it is likely that within any school context, adults will be making meaning of their experiences in developmentally different ways. Attention and mindfulness to this kind of developmental diversity can, I suggest, help to make schools even better places of learning. Kegan's theory suggests that teachers at different developmental positions will experience learning opportunities differently—depending on their way of knowing. By shedding light on the unrecognized demands that professional development models or opportunities make on adults' self-knowledge, this theory can inform leadership practices. It is a person's way of knowing that guides how lessons and experiences will be taken, managed, and understood.

In some cases, the professional development models employed in schools may not provide a good match with the developmental level of teachers they are designed to benefit. As Table P.1 shows, assumptions about adults not only drive the models but also, importantly, may inhibit efforts to help teachers benefit from learning experiences. In some cases, teachers may need to have a self-authoring way of knowing in order to participate effectively in implementation. This means that they must be able to *take stands for what they believe in, exercise authority, act upon their values and beliefs, take responsibility for themselves,* and *own their work.* Socializing knowers do not yet have the developmental capacities to do these things; they look to external authorities for answers and solutions.

Constructive-developmental theory provides a new way of thinking about supporting teacher growth. It involves more than merely giving information and/or developing skills (though these are certainly important in today's school world); it also attends to how individuals cognitively organize their experiences and to the ways in which transformational learning can be facilitated. As Kegan and Lahey (1984) have noted, "People do not *grow* by having their realities only confirmed. They grow by having them challenged, as well, and being supported to listen to, rather than defend against, that challenge" (p. 226).

A developmental perspective helps adults in schools move away from labeling teachers on the basis of behaviors (Levine, 1989). It provides a lens through which to view and understand people's attitudes, behaviors, and expectations and helps us to understand how to support and challenge growth for individuals at diverse levels of perception. Principals who are mindful of and attend to this developmental diversity (in addition to forms of diversity such as ethnicity) will be better equipped to support teacher learning.

As Table 2.2 shows, adults with different ways of knowing have qualitatively different capacities for self-reflection and perspective taking when making decisions and when engaging in the collaborative work that is common to professional development initiatives in schools. For instance, instrumental knowers believe that decisions have "right and wrong" aspects to them—with no in-between. When engaging in decision making, these knowers will focus on following the correct steps and rules in order to make the "right" decisions so that they can achieve concrete goals. For them, there is a right and a wrong way to do things. Socializing knowers, when engaging in the decision-making process, need to feel accepted by the group and especially valued authorities within the group, avoid conflict, and look for consensus. They orient toward arriving at one agreed-upon group decision. In decision-making situations, these teachers will look to valued others or authorities for direction, guidance, and validation of progress. For them, decisions are made based upon loyalty or allegiance to valued others. In contrast, self-authoring knowers

Table 2.2 A Developmental Perspective on How Adults With Different Ways of Knowing Experience Different Aspects of Processes Required When Working Together

Way of Knowing ➞	*Instrumental*	*Socializing*	*Self-Authoring*
Perspective on working together	Everybody does their job—and they do it *the right way*.	Forming a group identity with a common, shared goal that everyone is in agreement with.	A complex network of people with differing values, opinions, experiences, and perspectives joining together for a common purpose.
Decision-making skills	Decisions have right or wrong aspects with no in-between or gray areas. There is a right way and a wrong way to do things.	Decisions need group consensus or agreement. It is essential that everyone arrive at a group decision.	Decisions have many possible paths. Making decisions is an exploration of many options. There is not necessarily one "best" decision, but many possible decisions, each one with pros and cons.
Interpersonal skills	Cooperates by arguing or persuading others to agree to the right thing to do and the right way to do it. The right way is dictated by the rules.	Cooperates by trying to build agreement. It is essential to minimize conflict, disagreement, and differences.	Cooperates by ensuring that everyone's voice is heard, regardless of their opinions. Celebrates differences and makes room for all perspectives. The goal is to work toward fair and reasonable compromise.
Conflict resolution and negotiation	Focus is on concrete identification and definition of the conflict, usually on who is right and who is wrong. Watches for who is following the rules and who is not, whether or not one's own concrete needs and goals are being met. Emphasizes meeting one's own concrete needs in a kind of tit-for-tat fairness.	Focus is on acknowledging the existence of and identifying the nature of the conflict and attending to others' feelings about it. Watches for commonalities and places of agreement that can be built on to decrease sense of differences and hurt feelings. Emphasizes loyalty and inclusion of everyone and	Focus is on articulating nature and vicissitudes of the conflict and the surrounding issues. Watches for clear expression and acknowledgment of whole spectrum of issues and disagreement within the conflict. Emphasizes potentially useful nature of conflict and the ways that conflict can clarify an issue and lead to better communication and relationship. Also

Way of Knowing →	Instrumental	Socializing	Self-Authoring
	Challenge is to be able to understand and recognize a more abstract definition and reality of conflict, that there are many ways to resolve it that go beyond rules to taking others' feelings and needs into account as something important in and of themselves.	coming to a mutual understanding and resolution that everyone feels good about. Challenge is to be able to tolerate and accept conflict within a relationship without feeling that it threatens the relationship; to see conflict as a necessary and helpful aspect of relationships and not necessarily something to avoid and get rid of.	emphasizes a resolution that takes into account the diversity of opinions and perspectives and feelings of everyone involved and that will also move the interests of the group forward. Challenge is to see the process itself as the main thing and let go of one's own investment in one's own particular standards for how the process should work.
Communication skills	Communicates by stating rules, opinions, concrete goals, and facts. Not concerned with theories, philosophies, or other people's feelings except as they have an impact on getting the job done.	Communicates feelings and has concern and sense of responsibility for others' feelings and experience. Makes sure everyone understands and agrees with each other.	Communicates feelings, ideas, and philosophies in attempt to express own view within larger group, to explain and understand differences, similarities, and complexities of everyone's perspective.

SOURCE: Adapted from Popp, N. (1998). *Developmental Perspectives on Working Together. The Developmental Skills Matrix*. National Institute for Literacy Equipped for the Future Field Development Institute, Louisville, KY.

believe that there are many paths in decision making. To them, arriving at a decision is an examination of many options—there is no one right decision, and every decision has a set of pros and cons associated with it. Recall that adults with this way of knowing look to their own internally generated set of values when engaging in decision making. Self-authoring knowers are able to hold and coordinate multiple perspectives and to balance them.

While not the focus of this chapter, it is important to emphasize that developmental theory has important implications for understanding the ways in which school leaders' ways of knowing influence how they conceive and enact their roles in support of teacher learning. As Tables 2.1 and 2.2 illuminate, a person's way of knowing dictates how professional development opportunities and lessons will be understood with regard to teacher growth. Simply put, teachers with different preferences, needs, and developmental orientations need different forms of support and challenge in order to participate effectively in teacher learning practices. Next, I discuss the importance of considering the school as a holding environment for supporting teachers' transformational learning.

About Holding Environments

> There is never just a you; and at this very moment your own buoyancy or lack of it, your own sense of wholeness or lack of it, is in large part a function of how your own current embeddedness culture is holding you. (Kegan, 1982, p. 116)

A critical dimension of a constructive-developmental approach is that the exercise and transformation of our ways of knowing always go on in some context, or "holding environment," in Kegan's terms, "the context in which, and out of which, the person grows." In his work with infants, D.W. Winnicott (1965) used the term *holding environment* to describe the unique relationships needed in the psychosocial environment to support infants' healthy development (Drago-Severson, in press). According to Winnicott (1965), these environments needed to both support and challenge an infant's process of growth and development, so that he or she could thrive, in order to be effective. Kegan (1982) extended this usage to a human being's development across the entire lifespan. Both support *and* challenge are necessary for growth.

Attention to schools as holding environments has important implications for leadership practices supportive of adult learning and for the design and implementation of professional development programs. We know that all adults have different needs, preferences, and career phases and that it is crucial to honor these when considering how to best support them in their work and learning. At the same time, since it is likely that in any school context, adults will be making meaning of their experiences with different ways of knowing, it is also important to attend to this type of developmental diversity when considering how to support teacher learning.

Two Key Principles for Shaping Holding Environments: In shaping a holding environment that will best support the learning of teachers with different ways of knowing, there are two principles to consider.

The first principle, similar to what applies when creating a strong learning environment, is that the holding environment needs to offer a healthy mixture of both support and challenge. *Support* can be defined in terms of recognizing and acknowledging and affirming who the person is and how the person is making sense (thinking and feeling) of his or her experiences. *Challenge* can take the form of supportively posing questions to a person in order to gently push the edges of a person's thinking and/or feeling so as to expose the individual to new ways of thinking. These needed combinations of challenge and support bring into being what Kegan (1982) calls the "holding environment."

For example, Table 2.2 depicts helpful challenges to adults resolving conflicts with different ways of knowing. For instrumental knowers, challenging them toward supporting their growth would take the form of asking questions or providing alternative views to help them see ways to move toward a resolution by taking colleagues' perspectives into consideration. At the same time, supports for an instrumental knower would provide a step-wise process for the discussion.

The second principle of shaping a holding environment is the importance of considering the *goodness of fit,* or match, between the holding environment—and its expectations—and an adult's way of knowing. As noted, some types of experiences may place implicit and explicit demands on teachers—demands that exceed their developmental capacities.

For example, if the expectation for participating in shared decision making is that all teachers will be able to *take stands for their beliefs, exercise authority, act upon their values,* and *take responsibility for themselves,* a socializing knower will need to be gently supported and challenged in order to develop these capacities. Since socializing knowers look to an external authority for solutions, gently challenging these teachers to begin to examine what they think and helping them to value conflict would support their growth.

Put more simply, it is important to attend to the implicit and explicit demands of the context as well as the practices employed to support teacher learning within schools. How do these match up with teachers' ways of knowing? What forms of support and challenge might be woven into the design to support and challenge teachers with different ways of knowing?

For instance, as discussed above, if the expectations of learning activities exceed teachers' developmental capacities and if adequate supports are lacking, we run the risk of overwhelming and intimidating them. In contrast, if the program's expectations are too low or do not adequately acknowledge teachers' ways of knowing, this can lead some teachers to disconnect from the experience.

These examples highlight the importance of implementing professional development opportunities that are good fits for teachers with different ways of knowing. These kinds of practices can be robust enough to meet teachers where they are *and* also provide teachers with developmentally appropriate challenges to support their growth—transformational learning.

The Three Functions of Holding Environments: In the classes I teach about leadership for transformational learning, my students (principals, assistant principals, teacher leaders, staff development professionals, and aspiring principals) often ask, "Can a holding environment be a person, a group, or a context?" The answer is yes, yes, and yes—and it can also be a mix of these provided that they offer high support *and* challenge.

A "holding environment" serves three functions (Kegan, 1982, 1994). First, it needs to "hold well." It accomplishes this by meeting people where they are and by honoring how they are making sense of their experiences. Second, when a person is ready, a good holding environment needs to "let go" by challenging learners and permitting them to grow beyond their current meaning system to a new way of knowing. Third, it "sticks around," in order to provide continuity and a context of stability. It needs to remain available to the person as he or she grows, so that relationships and the person can be constructed in a new way. The "sticking around" function may be difficult to provide in some cases for a variety of reasons, one of them including shorter-term professional development programs (Drago-Severson, Helsing, Kegan, Broderick, Portnow, & Popp, 2001; Drago-Severson, in press; Kegan et al., 2001b). However, the practices presented in this book that support transformational learning can be adapted to school contexts, which can then serve as robust holding environments that provide all three functions discussed here.

Constructive-Development Theory: A New Foundation for Teacher Learning

Thinking about development and growth as a movement through periods of stability and change helps in understanding how individuals in schools experience leadership practice aimed at supporting adult learning and other professional development initiatives. Kegan's theory stresses the importance of providing psychological support to the ways in which teachers make sense of their experiences. There is a structural quality to these supports; "they know and hold persons before, during, and after their transitions; they acknowledge and grieve the losses, acknowledge and celebrate the gains, and help the person to acknowledge them himself"

(Kegan, 1982, p. 261). Constructive-developmental theory offers a hopeful and new foundation for considering practices supportive of teachers' transformational learning and development. It highlights the notion that adulthood is not simply an end stage reached in a person's 20s; adults continue to develop as they progress through qualitatively different ways of knowing. The growth processes that schools and teachers try to support in children can continue through adulthood.

CHAPTER SUMMARY

This chapter opened with a discussion of why I selected this particular framework as a lens through which to best understand how the four pillar practices support adult growth and development. I also provided an overview of the key principles informing Kegan's (1982, 1994, 2000) constructive-developmental theory. In particular, I discussed the concept of transformational as opposed to informational learning, and key ideas of constructivism and developmentalism and how they connect to Kegan's framework. I also described the three main ways of knowing that are common in adulthood and presented examples to illuminate why and how ways of knowing matter when considering how to best support teacher learning. In so doing, the examples illuminate the problem that the developmental demands placed upon adults who are participating in some professional development initiatives may be beyond their capacities. Therefore, I introduced key features of creating a holding environment for growth and learning.

In attending to and celebrating ongoing growth and change, we can better support teachers in meeting the complex demands of teaching in 21st-century schools. The practices in this learning-oriented model will enhance principals' capacities to support teachers with a diversity of ways of knowing and will improve the odds that more teachers will feel well held and valued for the meanings they bring to their teaching and learning experiences. Creating these types of supportive learning opportunities may also lead to greater teacher retention, improved teaching, and, I hope, even greater student achievement.

REFLECTIVE QUESTIONS

Please take a moment to think about these questions. They are intended to help you consider ideas discussed in this chapter and can be used for internal reflection or to open up a group discussion.

1. In what ways do any of the practices you named in Chapter 1 serve as a "holding environment" for your own or other people's growth and/or learning?

2. What kind of things, if they were to happen, would better support your learning? What small steps could you take to build these into your practice?

NOTES

1. Some ideas discussed in this section also appear in different form in Drago-Severson (in press).

2. Some ideas in this section appear in different form in Drago-Severson (in press).

3

Principals as Climate Shapers

I think the person who benefits the most [from supporting teacher learning] is the student. If teachers are happy and enthusiastic about what they do and are willing to try new things and are open to criticism, honest criticism, so they can grow, that's what they will model for the children, and that's what learning should be about.

—Sr. Joan Magnetti

Sr. Joan Magnetti, head of Convent of the Sacred Heart School in Greenwich, Connecticut, points to one of the many benefits she sees in her work supporting teacher learning: the connection between supporting teacher learning and supporting student growth and development. Like many of the principals in this study, Sr. Magnetti emphasizes how supporting teacher learning within the school enlivens teachers and students. In fact, creating learning communities in which adults and children can grow has also been linked to increased student achievement (Lieberman & Miller, 2001; Sindelar et al., 2002; Sykes, 1999).

Supporting teacher learning is important to a positive school climate. But how do principals create and grow school climates supportive of teacher learning? In this chapter, I try to answer that question. First, I provide some information from current research on the importance of a positive school climate. I then define the leadership approaches the principals in this study generally practiced to shape school climates that support teacher learning.

LESSONS FROM CURRENT RESEARCH

Research on supporting teachers' professional development indicates that teachers seek collaborative, ongoing, informal, and democratic forums to support their learning (Cochran-Smith & Lytle, 2001; Hargreaves, 1994; Killion, 2000; Sparks, 2000). Because of increasing enrollments, many new teachers need to be hired every year, which can threaten teachers' development to advanced levels because learning initiatives often focus on introducing new teachers to a school. Though the hiring problem is worse in poorer schools, it prevails in the suburbs as well. While many practitioners call for "new blood" in teaching, Chase (2001) maintains that not enough attention is directed toward "holding onto the quality teachers already hired—both the beginning teachers as well as the more seasoned ones" (p. 48). If school districts maintain conditions that threaten teachers' energy and sense of purpose, they will surely end up with vacancies to fill or severely burned-out teachers, he writes.[1]

Similarly, Blase and Blase (1999) describe a questionnaire study of 800 teachers from public elementary, middle, and high schools across the United States who offered their perspectives on what constitutes effective instructional leadership in principals. They identified effective instructional leaders as those who create "a culture of collaboration, equality, and the lifelong study of teaching and learning through talk, growth, and reflection" (p. 18). Furthermore, Blase and Blase (2001) discuss professional development as a tool not only for improved classroom instruction but also for teacher growth and collegial support through teacher-chosen opportunities.

Blase and Kirby (2000) emphasize that adults within the school not only need to feel respected and supported; they also need to feel trusted to make their own decisions for their own professional development. Unfortunately, however, scholars maintain that "compared with the complexity, subtlety, and uncertainties of the classroom, professional development is often a remarkably low-intensity enterprise" (Little, 1993, p. 148). More recently, Little (2000) urges schools to allocate more time for teachers to engage in "critical reflection," "closer collaboration," and to grow a climate that rewards teacher leadership (p. 393). Echoing these sentiments, Greene (2001) views professional development as a way to "plant new seeds" (p. 11).

Blase and Blase (2001) cite Osterman and Kottkamp's (1993) work and advocate for a collaborative approach to teacher learning, because it helps to "develop a culture that supports learning and growth, and facilitate change by virtue of the encouragement and validation of changes that occur" (Blase & Blase, 2001, p. 76). Like Lieberman, Saxl, and Miles (2000), Blase and Blase envision the principal as a facilitator, rather than an authority, of dialogue and reflection. Thus as facilitator, the principal provides resources for effective, collegial work.

In particular, Blase and Blase (2001) list seven assumptions guiding collaborative professional development in creating a climate supportive of teacher learning:

1. The principal must guide or facilitate professional development.

2. All adults can get better in their practice.

3. Change arises when we realize that practice can be improved.

4. Adjusting to change is a complicated, difficult, and emotional process.

5. Teachers are learners who can teach each other.

6. Professional development can take myriad forms.

7. All educators can conduct action research to enhance practice and performance.

Blase and Kirby (2000) stress that in order to achieve a culture of learning, resources such as collegial relationships, time, and appropriate skills are needed to cultivate fertile soil for reflection and self-assessment. I suggest that particular practices, implemented with regard for contextual factors, obstacles, and developmental level, will grow a culture of teacher learning.

The principals in this study echoed these research findings in their beliefs about their roles as climate shapers. They acknowledged various challenges of their work, such as time, resistance, and the complexities of teaching, learning, and leading at the turn of the century. Yet they spoke powerfully about how they support teachers and their learning by shaping school cultures in several ways. For example, they respect and involve teachers in shared decision making; encourage them to offer and accept feedback; invite them to reflect on how they translate the school's mission; and ask teachers to contribute to the school's vision. Next, I highlight (a) the core principles that inform their leadership practices, (b) the challenges they face in supporting teacher learning, and (c) the creative strategies they employ to create conditions supportive of teacher learning.

THE CORE PRINCIPLES THAT GROUND LEADERSHIP APPROACHES

To different degrees, three major principles grounded these principals' leadership practices toward a climate of supporting teacher learning:

1. Sharing and including others in leadership (e.g., seeking feedback, distributing leadership).

2. Building relationships within the school community (e.g., engaging in "conversation," informal gatherings).

3. Embracing and helping people manage change and fostering diversity (e.g., evaluation, celebrating ideas for policy improvement, and implementing changes).

Many of the principals emphasized the importance of "being visible" and of "being in the hallway" through "causal conversations" with adults in the building. In short, many spent a great deal of time building trusting interpersonal relationships.

Challenges to Building Positive School Cultures

Principals in all types of schools reported facing context-specific challenges as they worked to build relational cultures supportive of teacher learning.[2]

The Pressure to Improve Test Scores

Like all of the public school principals and several Catholic school principals in this study, Kim Marshall, principal of a K–5 urban, low-resource public school, discussed one very large challenge he and his school community face: improving test scores. He has implemented several structures to support teacher learning, including building time into the schedule for teacher collaboration, inquiry groups for teachers to analyze student progress, curriculum review teams, and a new literacy initiative. Nevertheless, the school's test scores have stayed "very low." Kim and his teachers experience the schools' testing trends as a significant and predominant concern or as "a matter of life and death, because here are these kids who are taking a test and they won't get a high school diploma if they don't pass."

Avoiding a "One Size Fits All" Model: Attending to Individual Needs

Joe Marchese, principal of Westtown School, a suburban Quaker boarding school in Pennsylvania, highlighted both a key human resource challenge and feature of teachers' individual development when shaping a culture supportive of transformational learning. Teachers are "notoriously isolated," he explained, and their professional development needs are often seen in a "one size fits all" model that doesn't address their real "needs." The administrative layers at Joe's school are fairly thick, yet Joe values consensual and decentralized practices, and he tries to treat teachers as individuals to promote a healthy climate:

What I've learned in [my] sabbatical research is how flat the professional development tends to be. In other words, we tend to have more of a one size fits all, whether you are a first- or second-year teacher, and whether you're a 20-year veteran. The ability to have a sense of camaraderie and a sharing of ideas that can keep you energized and refreshed—as opposed to operating in isolation from other people who you see in the halls constantly, but don't have much interaction—seems to me, a worthy goal.

Strategies for Building a Positive School Climate

All of the principals noted the importance of their role in shaping school climates that support adult learning. However, the manner in which they do so varies, and most combine multiple approaches depending on situational factors and challenges. Those principals in schools with lower resources seemed to talk much more about the importance of climate at their schools. While I am not sure why this emerged, one possibility is that climate might have to make up for other kinds of appreciation that a school could show through financial rewards or a more manageable work schedule. Another possibility might be that in order to work at these schools (especially the Catholic low-resource schools in this sample), faculty might be dedicated to the Catholic faith and more willing to make sacrifices. It could be that this may make the climate of the school more noticeable as a force in the school.

In general, though, the Catholic school principals emphasize visionary or spiritual leadership (i.e., propagating a global direction for the future), cultivating adult learning in relation to the school's vision. Independent school leaders primarily stress instructional leadership (i.e., focusing on good teaching and learning), relying on the flexibility afforded them through their mission to create structures and cultivate opportunities for collaboration. Finally, public school principals tend to employ mostly managerial leadership (i.e., planning, implementing, and organizing with best practices in mind) by using creative strategies to address the financial and structural realities of their settings so that they can focus on instructional leadership.

While almost all of the principals spontaneously voiced their responsibility for a positive school climate, they have different priorities and ways of working to create it (Drago-Severson, 2002; Drago-Severson & Pinto, 2003). For example, several principals conceptualized the school as "a family," while another used the metaphor of a "7–11" store, meaning that community members are there most of the day and know they can get what they need. Nearly all of the principals told me that they wanted their schools to be places where people "want to be" and feel they "belong," are learning and growing, and can have "fun." Building school climate is for most of the principals intimately connected to letting teachers know that they "appreciate them."

Many principals, across school type and resource level, emphasized their roles as "orchestrators," "supporters," "bridges," and/or "encouragers" of teacher learning. Nearly all voiced the importance of "modeling lifelong learning." This, in their view, helps teachers become more effective, increases their satisfaction, supports them in acclimating to change, and decreases teacher isolation. Some of the principals do this by both creating structures *within* the school and supporting teachers as they embark on learning experiences *outside* of the school.

How do principals use resources (relationships, time, and skills) to support the development of fertile soil for reflection and self-assessment—so that teachers can learn from each other, grow, and examine their practice? As I said earlier, obstacles do exist. However, here I underscore *effectiveness* because my intention is to offer practices for building school climate to others.

Finding Time and Money

In Joe Marchese's view, teachers want "extra time" (e.g., a decreased teaching load) more than money so that they can take on increasing leadership roles or professional development experiences. Joe described what is needed to support these aims: (a) "The big thing is to change the mind-set of what professional development means—to see it as lifelong learning," (b) to be able to give people the time to implement forms of collaboration, and (c) to have money to support teachers to take this time. Joe also believes that a positive school climate can be built by treating teachers as individuals, and this can still be done when financial and other resources are lacking.

Informal Structures

During the middle of our interview, Sr. Joan Magnetti,[3] head of the Convent of the Sacred Heart School in Greenwich, Connecticut, a Catholic independent, high-resource school, asked me whether I was "interested only in the formal ways in which [she] support[s] teacher learning" or whether I wanted to learn about the "informal ways" in which she does this. She, like the majority of principals, believes that informal as well as formal efforts serve to build positive school climates. "Being visible" and "having informal conversations with teachers" are two common themes that emerged across all school types and resources levels. After posing this question to me (and after I emphatically stated that my interest is in both of these), Sr. Magnetti discussed her view about the importance of "informal gatherings" and how they build a positive school climate supportive of teacher learning.

Sr. Magnetti thinks that casual "celebrations and dinner parties," such as her school's weekly "TGIF get-togethers," are central to creating a climate where people feel a "sense of belonging." Like many of the other principals in public, private, and other Catholic schools, Sr. Magnetti emphasized the importance of teachers having "fun" together and "bringing people together to reflect as well as to socialize." Nearly all of the principals discussed the ways in which informal gatherings and conversations "in the hallway" with faculty members help to build interpersonal relationships and a sense of community, which they name as critical features in being able to support teacher learning.

Providing Food for Conversations

Sometimes it is challenging for principals to secure needed time for collaboration within the daily schedule. Dr. Mary Nash, principal of the Mary Lyons alternative school in Brighton, Massachusetts, discussed a creative strategy she employs to make time for collaboration and build school culture. For Mary, "treating teachers like adults" is essential. When teachers complained that she wanted them to return from inservice training and give assistant teachers a break (rather than going to lunch), the teachers suggested that Mary provide them with nice lunches in return for their time in these meetings:

> I'll buy them lunch, for example. Like for the literacy training, they were supposed to be released, five or six days last year, half days. And the problem was when they came back and they'd come back at lunchtime, their assistant teachers would have been covering their classes. Were they then going to just sit down and not go into their classrooms? They wouldn't even give the person a break in their class? I said, "That's not right." . . . It was a very, very helpful device because it was a common human need.

When Mary agreed to buy them lunch, the teachers in her school "all appreciated it and they felt like adults," she explained, and she was able to create a context for them to convene.

Creating spaces for teachers to collaborate is a challenge. However, with the institution-wide professional development initiatives at Philips Andover, Barbara Chase has created such spaces around meals:

> The press of time is just so difficult. . . . I think we're always hampered by realizing that people are so busy, and particularly in a boarding school, that it's hard to find the time. . . . When we do [meetings], we usually do it around meals. That seems to work well. We have a special, smallish dining room in the commons where people can go get their trays, but then they can come [back to the dining room] . . . and discuss particular issues.

Providing food for faculty and having conversations around meals are common in the principals' descriptions of how they create a positive school climate for teacher learning regardless of school type or resource level.

Rewarding Teachers in New Ways

Given the scarcity of resources, Muriel Leonard of McCormick School works to reward teachers in new ways. In general, Muriel seeks to build upon teachers' intrinsic motivation for professional development. While the previous school policy had been to reward teachers with stipends for additional work that they do, Muriel was working to change this expectation. Instead of distributing stipends, she invests financial resources into purchasing professional development materials (e.g., books) that the teachers can use collaboratively, because she thinks that these practices help to build a more collaborative culture. In addition, these materials are first given to teachers working most directly on new initiatives, and she has created a common planning time for them to meet and discuss the texts they are reading. However, she also recognizes that teachers can be unwilling to devote more than the already huge amounts of energy they give to doing good work. In response, she has engaged in a creative use of substitutes to give teachers time to collaborate. She describes how this system works:

> I've set up a structure where I'll bring in a group of substitutes, and I try to do this about every six weeks or so, to have extended subject area meetings. So instead of for a period, I might say, "I'm going to bring in five subs. And those subs are going to replace five math teachers. And we'll have a three-hour professional development meeting, in school, on school time." And so, we might start at 7:30 and meet until 10:30.

Honoring Teachers' Strengths and Contributions

Scott Nelson strives to build a positive climate supportive of teacher learning at Rye Country Day School (a preK–12 independent school in Rye, New York) by privately and publicly recognizing teacher accomplishments. For Scott, it is crucial to recognize and voice appreciation for teachers privately. He firmly believes in the practice of writing notes to teachers to recognize their efforts. "The note writing, I think, is invaluable. It's finding the time to do it, and I guess e-mail makes it a little easier. . . . I think it's the kind of thing where you can never do enough of it." Many of the principals voiced this sentiment.

To recognize teachers publicly, Scott created 10 recognition awards, 2 of which go to each of the lower, middle, and upper schools. Two awards also go to the community at large, and the remaining 2 go to the school's staff. The faculty and the staff vote on who is going to receive these $2,500 awards, creating both a sense of community and a feeling of appreciation for the devoted work of several members of that community. These awards are to be used *only* for vacations, which builds a positive climate by providing for the revitalization of community members. While financial security is clearly related to offering these honors, the public recognition and faculty involvement are also important to the positive climate such monetary awards facilitate.

Promoting School Mission

All of the principals serving in Catholic schools—no matter what their schools' financial resource levels are—emphasized their roles as spiritual leaders and their work as climate shapers dedicated to linking professional development to the school's overriding mission. For example, Sr. Barbara Rogers, head of Newton Country Day School of the Sacred Heart, a high-resource Catholic independent school in Newton, Massachusetts, focuses on her role as spiritual leader and understands it as intimately tied to her school's mission, which includes the following core principles: "a deep respect for intellectual values, the building of community as a Christian value, and a social awareness which impels to action."

> [The mission] not just informs my thinking, it is the whole basis of what it is and why I do it. . . . I have a deep sense of myself as a steward of that mission. . . . My real work is about bringing more and more faculty, more and more deeply into an understanding of the total mission of the school.

By focusing on the school's mission and how it comes to life, Sr. Rogers' goal as a spiritual leader is "to make sure that who works here buys into the mission, understands their responsibility for the mission, and mostly loves it." Sr. Rogers builds school climate by frequently asking teachers to reflect on how their teaching embodies or relates to the mission: "We really ask each teacher to write a reflection on how he or she feels they've contributed to each of the goals of the school." In her role as spiritual leader, she emphasizes the value of engaging in "mission-based" inquiry. Not only does this build a positive school climate, in Sr. Rogers' view, but it also helps teachers create their own goals for the next academic year. As a result, Sr. Rogers felt her goal is that "every single person believes that everything we write in our school catalog happens every day."

Sr. Rogers sees part of her role as transferring "ownership of the mission to every adult in the school," and she wants the teachers to share in assuming leadership in it. She explained one of the other reasons why this is important to her: "That's part of treating people as professionals. And . . . sometimes schools don't. And I think particularly in religious schools, Catholic schools, there is a kind of hierarchical nature that does not treat people as adults."

Thus Sr. Rogers builds a healthy school climate by emphasizing her role as spiritual leader, bolstering a mission of active community participation, and demonstrating respect and care for the competencies of the community.

Mission is also an emphasis for Dr. Dan White, head of Seabury Hall, a 7–12 low- to medium-resource independent school in Maui, Hawaii. It is important to note that this school also has had a long and strong affiliation with the church. The school's Episcopal history (and Dan's background as the son of a minister) seem intimately connected to how he enacts his role and builds school climate. Promoting the school's mission is very important, in his view.

Dan sees part of his work as being responsible for discussing the mission and developing the whole person. He stresses the spiritual "aspect of the school, which is actually contained in the mission statement, which talks about causing growth in students in body, mind, and soul." Dan discussed how school climate is improved when adults have occasions to "talk more casually" and "engage in conversations about [their] values." Such "conversations" are "vehicles" for transformational learning, Dan explained. As climate shaper, Dan works to help teachers "do what they love," and he stresses the importance of focusing on the invaluable, internal school resources.

Dan talked about how he gets excited about "building things," and this is part of what he is in the process of doing at Seabury. Financial resources have enabled him and the school to improve their school facilities by restructuring the pillars at the front entrance of the school, which Dan feels "state who we are; there's a suggestion of solidity and permanence, but it's not overstated, it's not overdone." For Dan, the pillars represent an image of the school mission and the type of school climate he is working to foster. He wanted to improve the facilities to reflect the mission's goals of stability and perseverance.

Importantly, the attention to mission occurred even in institutions with no religious affiliation whatsoever. For example, Jack Thompson, who leads Palm Beach Day School, an independent, medium- to high-resource K–9 school in Florida, believes that an independent school setting makes it possible for him to create and enact a vision about how education should be. In his role as climate shaper, Jack strives to provide teachers with opportunities to practice their "profession" and "to do the things [they] want to do." Private schools, he explained, are in a unique position. "In the independent school," Jack shared,

> It's possible to practice what we've all been preaching, what makes good education. And an independent school makes it possible for you to do that. I tell teachers that all the time, we're going to

provide a situation for you where you have a good chance to succeed and to practice your profession and to do things you want to do.

Like other principals, his way of working as a climate shaper is to emphasize the shared bond of community; however, Jack stresses that teachers should not form cliques that might weaken the larger community. To prevent cliques, Jack encourages teachers to talk with colleagues from different grade levels and disciplines. He expects teachers to make a strong commitment to their school and to work more than the minimal hours required to do their work well. In return for their commitment, Jack dedicates himself to supporting his teachers' education.

Valuing and Modeling "Respect for All"

In terms of creating a climate of community, Sr. Judith Brady, a principal of a low-resource Catholic high school located in the Bronx, clearly named "respect for all" as the guiding force in enacting her role as climate shaper. "Respect for all" is displayed on her computer screen so that faculty, parents, students, and visitors to the school can see it, and to remind herself of what she believes is a critical component of her own work and mission. Her hope is that all who see this sign will understand it as the "basis for what we're doing." Sr. Judith emphasizes her role in encouraging teachers to "build on their strengths." This, in her view, will help them to develop curricula and programs that are based in their own areas of expertise. She enacts her role in shaping school climate by encouraging the teachers to embrace policy and programmatic changes and "to do the best with what they have." One of her goals is to "encourage" teachers to "try to open up possibilities . . . individual by individual." She often suggests that teachers sit in on each other's classes and talk to each other about how they teach, in order to learn from each other. While the lower-resource Catholic school principals, such as Sr. Judith, are challenged by lack of human and financial resources that would allow for thicker infrastructure, these principals focus on building positive climate by encouraging teachers to "do the best they can with what they have" and "sharing a common bond of faith."

Growing the School as a Community Center

Gary LeFave, principal of Matignon High School, has served his low-resource Catholic school in Cambridge, Massachusetts, for 29 years, having held various positions ranging from science teacher to department head to curriculum director to assistant principal to school nurse. For the past 15 years, he has assumed leadership as the principal. Gary described part of his role as principal and climate shaper as leaving "things open for people who have ideas that might want to do something," to help them "develop their ideas as opposed to saying no."

His school is relatively small (535 students) and is geared toward preparing students for college. Like one-third of the principals in this study, Gary mentioned that his school has increasingly taken on larger roles in addition to formal education to respond to changes in society, such as the situation of students who do not always have someone at home until much later in the evening. When asked about how he envisions his role in terms of shaping his school's culture, Gary discussed the importance of having the school be a place where people want to be. He explained,

> For the most part, the students that are here wouldn't want to be any other place . . . the faculty work with [the students] to develop. Some of [the faculty] came here as . . . students. . . . I think those are reasons that students find [that they like] being here. . . . It's the things that are in the building that bring them to our school, and I think it's teachers who mentor, not only themselves, but they mentor the students that are here, and help them with problems. . . . This place has become like a 7-11. It's open from early in the mornings. . . . Students start coming here at 6:30 in the morning. . . . I'm here 7, 8, 9 o'clock at night, there's still activities, things going on at the school, with kids still around.

Despite the importance of renovating the school building that is in need of structural repair, Gary, like Sr. Judith, underscored his belief that it is "not what you have but what you do with what you have that is important." Finally—and like three-fifths of the principals in this study—Gary emphasized that his school develops activities that enhance the "sense of community" (e.g., dressing up on holidays and having special make-a-friend days).

Attending to Individual Needs and Values

Barbara Chase, who heads Philips Andover Academy, a high-resource, independent high school in Andover, Massachusetts, promotes a positive school climate by giving teachers flexibility in their schedules, enabling them to pursue vocational and avocational interests:

> We also have a lot of people here who have their own work. We have artists who are working artists. We have two people in the English department who are playwrights, whose plays have been produced on and off-Broadway. We have musicians who really work on their own music. We have math teachers who write textbooks. . . . I think for an institution, somehow to figure out a way to support people in their own work . . . is [important].

The school has a lot of flexibility in terms of employing teachers; some work half-time, for example. The core of Barbara's personal philosophy about shaping school climate is to focus on the development of the entire person. Barbara admits that making these accommodations is not always "easy" and certainly depends on resources.

Encouraging Teamwork

All of the principals promote collaboration and teamwork as a means to a more positive school climate. The public school principals, in particular, underscored the importance of maintaining a climate that associates belonging with collegial inquiry among fellow colleagues, or "neighbors," as Dr. Larry Myatt of Fenway High School in Boston said. He encourages teachers to engage in collaborative inquiry and to build a school culture in which they pursue development internally and externally. Larry stressed that it is important for his faculty to get "out of the box, out of the classroom, out of the school," to broaden their perspectives. While initially resistant to these conversations, teachers at Fenway now look forward to these kinds of opportunities, making ongoing professional growth part of the culture of the school. In his role as climate shaper, he explained that

> Teachers needed to learn how to talk to each other, [and] they had to have structures for that. It had to be made a priority. There had to be a culture established wherein it was okay to talk about practice and okay to talk about your personal perspectives around important curriculum [concerns].

Such conversations, he added, more common now, were "groundbreaking" 20 years ago when he became a principal.

Because of his value for creating a culture of collegiality, Larry has rearranged the school schedule to accommodate and facilitate collaboration among teachers. He intentionally schedules between three and four hours per week for them to work together. Two features are essential to creating a climate of collaboration, in his view: giving teachers the time to talk and helping them learn *how* to talk with each other. The collaborative orientation stands in contrast to focusing on individual personalities, which is a priority of other principals who serve in smaller schools.

CHAPTER SUMMARY

The principals in this study strive to create a healthy school climate by enacting their roles in a way that conveys their care for teacher learning. In fostering a positive school climate, almost all principals discussed the importance of demonstrating respect and care for their teachers through appreciation, involvement in decision making, and thoughtful consideration of the school mission. The importance of school mission is especially noticeable for the Catholic school principals in this sample. While principals in the lower-resource Catholic schools are challenged by fewer human resources, these principals focus on shaping school climate through "sharing a common bond of faith." Independent school leaders also focus on building school climate through cultivating shared values and building an appreciation for community values. For some public school principals with considerably fewer financial resources, a positive school climate is fostered through support for teacher collaboration. All public school principals underscored the importance of maintaining a climate that encourages reflective conversations with colleagues.

Three additional overarching threads are woven into all of the principals' discussions. First, all of the principals in this study believe that school climate is an important ingredient in supporting teacher learning and professional development. Second, all of the principals stressed that they wanted to learn about the findings from this research so that they could improve their own ways of shaping school climate and their own good practices. Last, learning while leading is of key importance to all of them—not only because they have a desire to improve conditions in their own school but also because more than two-thirds reported that it is important for them to "model" a lifelong desire to learn for both teachers and children. Jim Cavanaugh's words resonate with what many of these principals shared:

> Self knowledge is just so important . . . that's crucial to teach a child or a student how to ask, "How do I know what I know? What are my strengths and my weaknesses? How do I build up one and capitalize on the other? What's my preferred learning style? How do I take in information fast? How do I seek out information?" Unless we're explicit about that and we're modeling it ourselves, kids aren't going to learn to be . . . lifelong learners. They're not going to learn to be self-taught.

Modeling the importance of learning while leading is one way that most of these principals build a healthy school climate.

REFLECTIVE QUESTIONS

These questions are designed to assist you in applying the strategies outlined in this chapter to your own context. They can be used for internal reflection or to open up a group discussion.

1. What is your personal vision for shaping a school climate supportive of teacher learning? What are your personal purposes or goals in

growing a healthy school climate? What do you want your school climate to look and feel like for you and your teachers?

2. How do you envision your role as a climate shaper on behalf of teacher learning?

3. How do you enact your role on behalf of your own personal vision?

4. What kinds of challenges or obstacles do you face in terms of creating this type of climate?

5. What kinds of supports exist in your school climate to facilitate adult learning?

6. What kinds of teachers do you think are thriving in your school climate? What enables them to thrive? What teachers do you think need more attention or development, and why?

NOTES

1. I acknowledge Kristina Pinto for her help with creating summaries for some of the articles I collected for this literature review and for her collaboration in thinking through many of the ideas presented in this chapter.

2. Some of the ideas in this section appear in altered form in Drago-Severson (2001, 2002) and Drago-Severson and Pinto (2003).

3. The first time I reference participants in each chapter I use their title (e.g., Dr.). After that, I refer to them by their first name, unless they are clergy (i.e., Sr.), which is how I reference them in all communications.

4

The Impact of Financial Resources on Support for Teacher Learning

Let's face it, money is power in our society. And when you give faculty members a little control over money, they feel energized by it. They feel they have control and power.

—Jerry Zank, Canterbury School

In Chapter 1, I stated that I purposefully selected school leaders who serve in schools with varying levels of financial resources because I was interested in understanding how, if at all, financial resources influenced the ways in which these leaders *can* support teachers' transformational learning. As this chapter will show, the principals in this study experienced different context-specific challenges related to resource levels. Financial resources did present obstacles to principals in lower-resource schools, especially in terms of not being able to fund teacher attendance at conferences and graduate education or provide stipends. However, many of the practices they employ for teacher learning demonstrate creative strategizing within financial constraints. My intention is to highlight the financial challenges these school leaders face and to illuminate their creative strategies for teacher learning.

It is widely recognized that financial resources are a major influence in programs that support teacher learning and that with higher salaries, stipends, or other financial inducements, teachers can better develop their instructional skills (Darling-Hammond & McLaughlin, 1999; Drago-Severson & Pinto, in press; Elmore & Burney, 1999; Killion, 2000; Sparks, 2000). Elmore Burney (1999) found that budgets for professional development typically include allocations for salaries and professional development materials, yet schools lack funding for principal-teacher collaboration during the school day. While acknowledging the challenges of acquiring money to support professional development, these authors (1999) contend that committing resources to a few professional development priorities and to showing the relationship between changes in teacher practice and student achievement are keys to effective professional development.

In this study, the schools' locations on a continuum of financial resources variously influence the types of initiatives the principals employ to support teacher learning. As stated earlier, in Chapter 1, the standard for determining low-, medium-, and high-resource levels was to first report (a) a school's annual operating budget (for Catholic and public schools) or (b) a school's endowment (for independent schools) (see Table 1.1). Second, I assessed how each school compared with other schools of the same type (i.e., independent, Catholic, or public) to determine whether it was low, medium, or high in financial resources. Last, during interviews, I asked principals if they would categorize their schools' resource levels relative to schools of the same type in a similar geographic location.

All of the principals in this study reported that supporting teacher development and learning is a "high priority" and that financial resources influence the ways in which they were able to do so. For this reason, this chapter provides a crucial foundation for considering the four pillars discussed in later chapters.

CHALLENGES POSED BY LIMITED FINANCIAL RESOURCES

The school leaders identified a number of challenges posed by varying levels of resources in their ability to create a climate of professional development. Some of the challenges include providing adequate compensation for teachers, allocating resources from very tight budgets to professional development, prioritizing their programs, and identifying resources for different types of initiatives. I discuss each of these below.

Providing Adequate Teacher Salaries

Owing to increasing enrollments and teacher retirements, schools must hire many new teachers every year (Johnson et al., 2001). Yet the problem is not only attracting new teachers but also retaining those already in the profession. Offering incentives and school environments that focus on teacher and student learning is one way to improve teaching and create lasting, positive change (Darling-Hammond & McLaughlin, 1999). National Education Association President Bob Chase (2001) cites a 50% turnover rate in some schools as teachers are increasingly migrating from poor and minority schools to the suburbs. Though this problem afflicts poorer school districts more often, it is also an issue in the suburbs. High rates of teacher turnover are particularly evident in private and Catholic schools, where on average teacher salaries are lower than in public schools (Virginia Education Association, 2000). The turnover rate for public school teachers is 12%, whereas the rate for Catholic schoolteachers is 18%.

While many schools call for "new blood" in teaching, Chase (2001), like Elmore and Burney (1999), Johnson et al. (2001), and Darling-Hammond and McLaughlin (1999), maintains that we are not paying enough attention to "holding onto the quality teachers already hired— both the beginning teachers as well as the more seasoned ones" (p. 48). Meager salaries are one primary reason for the difficulties of attracting and retaining teachers (Darling-Hammond & McLaughlin, 1999; Pappano, 2001). Schools with low salary scales find it difficult to attract and retain high-quality teachers and must often hire beginning teachers, who then leave after gaining a few years of experience. In schools with high turnover rates, professional development initiatives must attend to training and supporting new teachers.

Teacher Turnover and Teacher Retention

Similar to the national research trends, the three Catholic school principals with lower resources explained that teacher turnover and providing teachers with adequate compensation were their greatest financial concerns. For example, Deborah O'Neil, principal of St. Peter's Catholic elementary school in Cambridge, Massachusetts, explained that the younger faculty bring new innovations to the school, but she regrets that they leave after a few years because of lower pay. She said,

> I have a teacher who's leaving us and going into a public school setting, and making an $18,000 salary increase. . . . He's going to a fantastic suburb . . . that pays its teachers very, very well. I [also] have a teacher who left the front door of this building and walked into the front door of a public school building, two blocks away, at a $13,000 salary increase. [We] can't compete with that.

Deborah estimated that to maintain a full time staff of 13, she has hired about 35 teachers in 8 years.

Sr. Joan Magnetti heads the Convent of the Sacred Heart (preK–12) School in Greenwich, Connecticut, a high financial resource level school. She acknowledged that more pay attracts a wider pool of more qualified, more appropriate candidates. In discussing how she invests money and time in important interests, Sr. Magnetti explained how she prioritizes training people who are not members of the Sacred Heart community to help them understand the mission. In doing so, people learn about the school's mission and have the chance to infuse its guiding principles into their teaching practices and school life.

Seeing the mission of the school as "catchable," she believes that many lay adults in the school could easily assume the suffix "religious of the sacred heart" because they live the mission so well. Greater financial resources enable her to pay these experienced teachers reasonable salaries as they help new teachers reflect on how they are enacting the school mission in their practices. This, in Sr. Magnetti's view, fosters a deep understanding of the mission in all of her teachers.

Unlike Deborah and Sr. Judith Brady, who lead financially strapped schools and whose faculty leave for higher pay in public schools, not all principals who provide modest salaries find turnover problematic. For example, despite his modest pay scale, Gary LeFave, principal of Matignon High School in Cambridge, Massachusetts, did not mention turnover or inadequate salaries as major concerns. In fact, on average, his teachers have been teaching at Matignon for 12 years, and several have been teaching there for more than 30 years. He allocates $200 stipends to teachers who have additional extracurricular responsibilities, but he believes rewards come from sources other than money. The rewards for teaching at the school are "intrinsic," and teachers "feel part of a community" by "doing good work."

Expectedly, none of the principals in the middle- or higher-resource schools in this sample described teacher salaries as an issue in attracting and retaining teachers. However, several independent school principals have focused on raising faculty salaries in recent years and increasing funding for teachers' professional development.

Budgeting for Teacher Professional Development

A *New York Times* analysis of how the city's 32 community school districts have allocated money in the last four years shows sharp disparities in the districts' spending choices. And it suggests that money spent on aides and administrators does less to improve student achievement than money spent on books, teacher training and other instructional categories. (Wyatt, 2000, B6)

All of the principals, across school type and financial resource level, discussed the importance of allocating adequate funding in their schools' professional development budgets. Financial resources are especially important to them in terms of more traditional types of professional development:

1. Financing teachers' attendance at conferences

2. Hiring substitutes to cover classes while teachers engage in professional development activities

3. Being able to subsidize teachers' graduate coursework

All of the principals in this study devote energy to securing resources to better support teacher learning. These efforts echo recent research results: When principals provide basic resources such as time, educational materials, and financial resources in a timely manner, they encourage and support teacher growth (Blase & Blase, 2001; Darling-Hammond & McLaughlin, 1999; Elmore & Burney, 1999). Notably, in schools where financial resources are scarce, principals are not able to allot much funding to supporting these traditional types of professional development. However, in all of these cases, the principals voiced a desire to be able to do so in the future.

Benefiting From Discretion Over Resource Allocation and Hiring

Dr. Mary Nash both founded and leads the Mary Lyons School, an alternative elementary school for children with special needs in Brighton, Massachusetts. She acknowledged benefiting from a great deal of discretion over issues of funding and hiring, though, notably, her situation differs from other public school principals' circumstances. She explained,

> Essentially, the school department said to me, "You have a blank check. Figure it out. And build us programs where we can put these kids." . . . I needed to be able to convince the school department to put the money into my account at the school in a lump sum without [strings attached] . . . and this was a very new concept, very scary to the central office.

Like Mary, most public school principals in this sample warned that the central office administration can easily grow isolated from daily classroom practice. Furthermore, when central office administrators serve separate functions, principals can encounter unresponsive bureaucratic systems when they try to make change.

Allocating a Percentage of the Budget to Professional Development

Many of the principals serving in lower-resource public schools and high-resource schools spoke similarly about needing a percentage of their operating budget for professional development. In other words, dedicating funds, whether large or small, exclusively for professional development demonstrates that teacher learning is a priority. For example, resources clearly are important to the initiatives that Dr. Jim Scott can undertake at the Punahoe School, a high-resource, independent school in Honolulu, Hawaii. He wants to allocate 2% (or more than $1 million) of the school's total operating budget for professional development. Having so much money could lead to a kind of traditionalism at some schools. Yet because Jim believes the school should not grow complacent with current or long-standing practices, he searches for ways to improve. As a result, the school offers many unique professional development opportunities, including a sabbatical program and international travel.

Harnessing Additional Resources for Professional Development

Like several principals in medium- to high-resource schools, Dr. Sue David asserted the importance of funding less conventional professional development, recalling,

> When I came to [the school], there was very little money available for professional development for teachers. It was a pittance. And in conjunction with that, there was an attitude that there was not much beyond the school gates of interest. So, I'm sorry to say at that point there was a kind of provincialism . . . And [I] went about garnering more resources for professional development so that there would be a larger pot of money for faculty who would then be stimulated, hopefully, to take advantage of opportunities that I learned about or that they learned about.

After raising "a very handsome pot," Sue holds a great deal of power in terms of the distribution of this money among teachers because there is no faculty development committee at her school. One of her less traditional developmental strategies is that her teachers "pursue their own goals," not just her own agenda.

Sharing the Professional Development Budget With Faculty

Sr. Barbara Rogers, head of the Convent of the Sacred Heart (a high-resource Catholic, independent school in Newton, Massachusetts), spoke a great deal about harnessing resources for things the community really believes in, and she, like others in the study, decided to share the budget with the faculty so that they would understand "where we were." Sr. Rogers believes it is important for the school community to be aware of the budget so that collectively they can decide on how to invest funding. In her view, this is a way to demonstrate respect for adults within the school, to engage in shared decision making, and to support learning.

Sr. Rogers is very proud that she hasn't denied any faculty requests for funding in recent years. However, she emphasized that money should not "define the school." Nevertheless, Sr. Rogers, like many of the principals, described her efforts to raise money to increase faculty salaries and opportunities for faculty development. Sr. Rogers seemed quite pleased with her fundraising efforts, which have enabled the school to pay for "100%" of the faculty's request for summer learning opportunities.

Establishing Priorities for Limited Resources

While all of the principals, regardless of resource level, fund some professional development initiatives, more than half of them stressed the importance of directing funds to a few key priorities. Rather than allocate professional development funds equally to each department, some of these principals prefer to fund particular departments annually as needed. In their view, they serve the department with the greatest need, expecting that different departments will receive funding each year.

Inviting Teachers to Establish Priorities

For example, Jerry Zank, head of the Canterbury School in Fort Myers, Florida, contended that articulating specific programs for professional development enables him to secure funding from donors and illustrate results:

> Donors . . . will say, "We really want to improve the quality of instruction at Canterbury. Do you have a program [we can donate to?]" I said, "You could make a donation to a summer grant program." It works that way, because it isn't like sort of in the general hopper of school funds. . . . It works with donors. It's concrete, it's specific, it has visibility, and it's programmatic. It's written up, and it isn't just a whim of the headmaster.

In Jerry's view, teachers need to be part of decision making when it affects them and the school community. Rather than making independent decisions about which department or program should be allocated money, he works collectively with a faculty development committee to set annual priorities for budget allocation. Jerry believes this shared decision-making process empowers the faculty.

Like Jerry, Dr. Jim Cavanaugh of Watertown High School emphasized that it is important to prioritize how they invest the professional development budget and "fight off other initiatives" that might distract them from professional development. Dr. Larry Myatt, principal of

Fenway Pilot High School in Boston, also recognizes the need to prioritize professional development spending. Although he thinks he and his school could improve a lot of things, he feels good that they are attending to "bigger and more important things." For example, Larry and the school prioritized allocation of larger chunks of time each week for teachers to collaborate on reform efforts, such as the new student advisory board and core curriculum.

Using Funding to Hire Additional Staff

The public school principals demonstrated a slightly different way of framing financial concerns. For example, principals in four of the public elementary schools in this sample described the importance of hiring additional staff to keep the student/teacher ratio low, and help teachers work with the youngest children or allow them to attend to those with special learning needs. In many cases, hiring additional staff means the principals have to make difficult decisions about their priorities.

Joe Shea, principal of Trotter Elementary School in Boston, decided to use money from the Boston Plan for Excellence (1999) to hire a paraprofessional for every kindergarten class, in which there are 22 to 25 students, to increase time spent on learning in the classroom. Before hiring paraprofessionals, Joe observed the classes and noticed that students were "interrupting the teacher in instructional time, 50% of the time." Joe felt that adding adults to his classrooms would enable teachers to implement their professional development training, for example, on issues of literacy.

CREATIVE STRATEGIES FOR COPING WITH LIMITED FINANCIAL RESOURCES

The range of financial resources and their effect on professional development seem largest among the independent and lower-resource Catholic schools in this sample. However, even in lower-resource schools of different types, the principals work creatively within their places on the financial resource continuum to create climates supportive of teacher learning. A critical finding of this research is that even in schools with low resources, principals find creative initiatives that do not require extensive financial resources to support teacher learning. While the previous section illustrated how principals use funds, this section highlights the different lower-cost strategies that leaders employ.

Encouraging Faculty to Write Proposals

All of the principals in the higher-resource schools (across school type) believe faculty proposal writing for enrichment and professional development opportunities powerfully facilitates teacher learning. Several of the principals in financially resource-rich independent schools recently implemented in-school laptop training programs that give computers to teachers for classroom use. The programs also train teachers (e.g., from fellow teachers, alumni, and/or outside experts) to improve use of technology in their classrooms, enhancing students' and their own learning. In many of these cases, teachers and school principals cowrote proposals to finance these programs. For example, faculty members on a technology committee at Rye Country Day School developed a long-range plan for integrating technology into the school. After the board of trustees accepted their plan and its cost, the faculty members wrote a grant to the Edward E. Ford Foundation to subsidize it.

Dr. Dan White, head of Seabury Hall (a 7–12 low- to medium-resource independent school in Maui, Hawaii), happily shared that he funds his faculty's professional development proposals with a donor gift allocated for teachers' professional development. "Seabury," Dan explained, is "blessed with a trustee who looks after the well-being of the school, and several years ago she set up an endowment for faculty professional growth." Every year, Dan designates $20,000 to $25,000 from this endowment, or "lifeblood," to support proposals from faculty members.

During the summer of our interview, Dan approved and funded 23 of the 25 proposals for professional development, and the 2 proposals he did not fund were applications to support master's degrees outside of education. While Dan cannot always finance attendance at national conferences on the mainland, he gladly finances proposals for attending and presenting at the Hawaii Association of Independent Schools conference and an annual writer's workshop in Maui. Dan sees faculty proposals and funding them as an important "incentive" and an opportunity for growth.

Traveling for Development

Sr. Barbara Rogers spoke excitedly about a schoolwide professional development event for a group of faculty who will travel to Israel with her for a "learning" and a "tremendous community-building" opportunity. It will be, she said, "incredibly demanding intellectually because we'll have to do a great deal of reading" in advance of the trip. Sr. Rogers also emphasized how this opportunity will put everyone in deeper touch with the school's mission.

In contrast, the Catholic school principals with lower resources emphasized that they struggle with lack of funding for this kind of teacher learning. Instead, they can only "encourage" teachers to engage in it—without school funds. Four of the principals in lower-resource schools explained the benefits of schoolwide professional development events for the entire school community, including teachers, the principals, and also administrators in most cases. They participate in conferences or travel to other schools to learn about a particular program, model, or initiative. In all of these cases, the principals value the shared experience as a source of reflection.

For example, Deborah O'Neil, mentioned earlier, principal of St. Peter's School in Cambridge, a low-resource Catholic school, has a meager annual budget for teachers' professional development. Normally, she divides this funding to support several small initiatives, but last year, she and the entire faculty invested their entire professional development budget in one activity. They traveled to a National Educators Catholic Association Conference in Washington, D.C., and closed the school during the week of the conference, sacrificing part of spring vacation to eliminate the need for substitute teachers. Deborah believes that while this initiative drained their professional development budget, it enhanced the growth of the whole school community, carrying them through the year. In particular, it catalyzed yearlong dialogue groups for the teachers, in which they discussed implementation of new pedagogical ideas from the conference.

Locating Grants From Outside Sources: A Low-Cost Learning Initiative

Because many low-resource schools cannot offer internal funding, grant writing is an important low-cost learning tool when faculty solicit funding from outside sources. Gary LeFave explained that introducing technology across the curriculum has been one of the particularly important initiatives at Matignon Catholic High School. To develop and use software to help them teach specific subject matter, teachers write proposals for what Gary refers to as "mini-grants" from the archdiocese of Boston. Funded proposals support classroom use of software and technological instruction of other faculty. These teachers, Gary explained, have eventually become the school's technology committee, which makes decisions about technology-related issues. Notably, teachers' proposals for technology grants must specifically pertain to the education of both faculty and students, as opposed to word processing or e-mail.

Kim Marshall proudly shared that the Mather School is the "third best school in Boston" in terms of raising money. Kim devotes much time to grant writing because the additional financial resources help him to develop corporate and university partnerships, such as his school's school-university partnership wherein they developed a social competency program. Grants also enable him to compensate teachers for their time spent in professional development activities and partnership work. Grant funding has also made it possible for him to purchase materials for the professional development library, pay teachers to attend literacy training workshops, and furnish additional instructional materials needed to better support teacher learning. He believes that grants help him and his teachers to build partnerships and improve education within the school with regard to both teacher learning and student achievement. Children of poverty can succeed, Kim emphasized, if the "right combination of factors" are present in a school.

Instituting Sabbaticals

Like other high-resource schools in this sample, Jim Scott's school offers learning opportunities that include international travel and exchange programs, opportunities to teach or take courses online, and visits to other schools to learn about programs of interest. While Jim's school can afford these programs, some also reflect his priorities. For example, he believed that a very popular sabbatical program was too "isolationist," benefiting one teacher but not necessarily others in the school. Therefore, he wanted to institute an in-house sabbatical for teachers to serve as researchers and consultants on the school's key areas of need. While Jim has the resources to institute these sabbaticals for the entire year, other schools with fewer financial resources might provide teachers with release time to research issues of significance to the faculty.

For example, Sr. Judith Brady, principal of St. Barnabas High School, a low-resource Catholic school in the Bronx, New York, released the teacher who helped her develop the school's new Medical Horizon program with local hospitals to investigate similar programs at other schools. This teacher also conducted research on components of programs at several local hospitals to benefit student learning in hospital internships.

At Convent of the Sacred Heart School in Greenwich, Connecticut, teachers with six or seven years of experience working 80%-time or more are eligible to write proposals for a sabbatical, to be taken during the academic year or summer. Teachers who write proposals must explain how the sabbatical will "expand their own education," "enhance the school," and reflect the goals of Sacred Heart education. Sr. Magnetti expects anyone on sabbatical to assume leadership in sharing their learning with other teachers. One science teacher recently took a sabbatical to learn about advances in molecular biology at Albert Einstein hospital. The teacher then returned to share her learning with the entire community, including setting up a program for students. She was then appointed to a new position, curriculum coordinator.

In several lower-resource schools, principals have developed creative strategies (grant writing, partnering with businesses, etc.) to garner funding so that teachers can receive training in technology and literacy. Once teachers are trained in specific areas, they then assume leadership in training others in the school.

Harnessing the Power and Generosity of Alumni

Across school types, principals emphasized the role of alumni. Notably, however, alumni from all of the Catholic schools with lower resources actively support their alma maters, offering their expertise (and in most cases, funding) *to support teacher learning.* Gary LeFave, like other Catholic school principals, gratefully acknowledged the generosity of Matignon alumni, who donate money, services, and time. Gary explained that because of an alum's generosity, the school is now "wired" so that all teachers have computer access.

Building Partnerships

Across school type and resource level, the majority of principals emphasized the importance of various forms of partnerships. Principals reported that the additional resources have moved their school from being underresourced to having "adequate" resources.

Significantly, all of the public school principals stressed how partnerships with businesses, universities, and other community organizations have fostered teacher learning opportunities. For instance, these partnerships include new teacher training programs (e.g., literacy initiatives, Japanese models of learning and teaching) and providing more time for teacher collaboration by placing more adults (i.e., paraprofessionals) in the classroom. Partnerships, as Larry Myatt's said, help to provide "time," "psychic space," and "the physical space" needed to engage in learning and supporting teachers in their "good work."

Many principals emphasized how partnerships with local universities and community businesses support teacher learning. Dr. Jim Cavanaugh indicated that Watertown High School in Massachusetts benefits from many different kinds of partnerships and connections, and he credits this to his school's geographic proximity to partners. Larry Myatt, principal of Fenway Pilot High School, commented that he "learned early on the power of collaboration beyond the building." He explained that the school has developed relationships with partners such as Facing History and Ourselves, Harvard Medical School, and the Urban-Suburban Collaborative. These and other organizations are "pretty skilled at coming in and adding energy to the mix." Through the partnerships, he learned that collaborations with partners couldn't always take place after the teaching day ended, and his school community benefited by altering "structures and schedules and priorities in order to accommodate them."

The Fenway partnership with Harvard Medical School focuses on both student *and* teacher learning. This partnership aims to develop HIV and AIDS curricula, mentors students of color who are interested in medical careers, and introduces medical school faculty to Fenway faculty to jointly develop diagnostic case studies. Larry explained,

> They come in with ideas that we didn't plan on and we say, "Oh, gee, that's even better than what we had in mind—let's can our stuff, and let's get them in here really heavily for the month

before science fair so they can help us work with kids on control and variable."

Partnerships between Fenway and the medical school and other organizations "wax and wane," Larry said, depending on the school's needs.

The Graham and Parks Alternative School also partners with other institutions or organizations for professional development. Principal Len Solo attributes this to his own and his teachers' "initiative." For instance, Len and his teachers used a National Science Foundation grant to develop a partnership with Boston and Cambridge public schools, MIT, and Harvard's Graduate School of Education. "Over the last five years," Len said, "we've just evolved more and more. We started with student teachers, evolved to interns . . . and then on to site supervisor [for graduate students from local universities], and [to teachers teaching] graduate courses." He believes that the school's partnerships with universities support teacher learning and the learning of partners from the universities because everyone shares expertise. For example, teachers from Len's school teach courses at local universities, share their practical knowledge with professors, and work collaboratively with universities to develop new programs (e.g., in technology).

In addition to the financial benefits of partnerships, principals with rich connections to partnering organizations described how such affiliations enhance teacher learning by bringing more adults into classrooms. The additional "pair of eyes" invigorates school culture and bridges worlds by "sharing resources." Principals reported that such partnerships revitalize faculty, free up time for teachers to collaborate, and create contexts where teachers reflect on their practice.

Visiting Other Schools

Many principals also strongly encourage teacher visits to other schools and other classrooms in their own schools. With this low-cost strategy, teachers "look beyond" their own schools and classrooms. Similarly, several principals encouraged teachers to serve on accreditation teams, which consist of teachers and school administrators who visit and evaluate other schools and their programs. These opportunities broaden perspectives and promote reflection on new programs and practices—both of which support teacher learning.

Bringing in Reform Experts for Conversations

Many principals support teacher learning by bringing in instructional or school reform experts (Drago-Severson, 2002; Drago-Severson & Pinto, 2003). Principals described successful outside experts as those who serve as long-term consultants and coaches to teachers and who do not deliver onetime lectures. For example, Kim Marshall, principal of the Mather School in Dorchester, Massachusetts (a low-resource public school), creatively employs a "bartering" arrangement with a university. University teachers come to his school to work with teachers, and in exchange, he travels to the university to share real-life school and leadership expertise with students. The Mather School holds a professional day each year, during which consultants talk with faculty on particular topics.

Mary Newman, head of Buckingham, Browne, and Nichols, preK–12, believes that such consultants really "vitalize" school communities.

> It's that link with the university . . . with people who are really involved in studying and asking the difficult questions . . . that [link] begins to change a fabric and alter a culture so that everybody is always thinking about what they can do and what they can do better.

Mary echoed what other principals said about the importance of these relationships and connections; many work to maximize a location near universities, museums, and other educational resources.

CHAPTER SUMMARY

In this chapter, I discussed the financial resource challenges that these principals encounter and how they influence leadership practices for teacher learning. In discussing their efforts to support a climate of continuous teacher learning, these principals named several important context-specific challenges, including school size, mission, student population, teaching staff, their own past experiences, and school location. But by far the most common challenge cited, across all school types and economic levels, was resources—*financial, human,* and *time.*

Depending on school context, principals referred to the challenges of working with younger faculty who may leave after a short time. In the low-resource Catholic schools, principals cited limited financial resources as their greatest challenge, such as teacher turnover owing to low salaries. In the schools with lower financial resources, providing teachers with adequate salaries is a concern. Across school types, principals reported that allocating a portion of the school budget to professional development is a priority.

In addition, I highlighted many of the principals' creative strategies for promoting teacher learning with minimal financial resources. I provided examples of the strategies that these principals employed to harvest needed resources to implement practices that clearly support teacher learning. These include inviting faculty to write grant proposals, making use of alumni, building partnerships with organizations, and visiting other schools. Principals, in many cases, work to develop partnerships because they revitalize faculty, free up time for teachers to collaborate, and create contexts for teachers and partnering organizations to learn from one another.

The great majority of these principals develop creative strategies to support teacher learning as they move toward achieving their goals. The types of initiatives that the principals employ to support teacher learning are differently influenced by their schools' locations on a continuum of financial resources. However, a critical finding of this research is that even in schools with low financial resources, principals use creative initiatives that do not require high financial resources to support teacher learning.

In summary, these principals, who serve in low-, medium-, and rich-resource schools, work creatively and differently to support teacher learning effectively—despite the financial nature of the challenges of leadership in the 21st century. In the following chapters, I discuss the practices these principals employ to support teachers' learning and how they are implemented in different school contexts. I also point to developmental principles informing these efforts that can support teachers' transformational learning, and devote special attention to a developmental framework for understanding how adults make sense of their experiences.

REFLECTIVE QUESTIONS

These questions are intended to assist you in applying the strategies outlined in this chapter to your own context. They can be used for internal reflection or to open up a group discussion.

1. What are two ways in which financial resources present obstacles or challenges in terms of supporting adult learning in your context?

2. What are your personal priorities or goals for supporting your own or other people's learning in your school? In what ways do financial resources influence your efforts to achieve these goals?

3. What creative strategies for coping with limited financial resources do you or others employ in your school context?

4. After reading this chapter, what are two practical ideas or creative strategies that you have learned about that you would like to implement in your school? What steps could you take to pilot your ideas?

5

Teaming

Learning Opportunities for Individuals and Organizations

This chapter illuminates how the principals in this study practice teaming to promote personal and organizational learning. Through examining examples of professional partnering and collaboration, I discuss their understanding of this practice and highlight the adult learning and developmental principles informing it. These examples include curriculum teams, literacy teams, technology teams, and team teaching. Many of the principals organize their schools for teamwork, finding that the practice opens communication, decreases isolation, encourages collaboration, and creates interdependency.

Many of the participants in the study also employ teaming to share their leadership and strengthen the implementation of change. Teaming represents one way they invite and encourage the participation of community members in collective inquiry. Since many of the principals are active members of various teams in their schools, teaming serves as a context for both teachers' *and* their own learning.

After presenting theoretical perspectives on teaming adults in schools as professional development, I provide specific examples of how principals implement this practice in their respective organizations. This chapter closes with a case of how one principal employs teaming to make a collaborative decision, support teacher learning, and develop ways of knowing.

ABOUT TEAMING

Teaming in the Literature

Theorists contend that teaming is crucial to opportunities for critical reflection and examination of assumptions and practice. It can take several forms, such as placing more than one teacher in a classroom, pairing veteran and novice teachers, or inviting teachers to work collaboratively on subject-related or administrative issues. Researchers argue that teaming reduces teacher isolation, creates innovation, builds capacity, and establishes knowledge-based management systems (Fullan, 2003; Hannum, 2001; Little, 2000, 2001; Pappano, 2001; Rogers & Babinski, 1999).

Teaming practices have been shown to cultivate fresh avenues for teacher collaboration. For example, researchers emphasize the importance of creating contexts for teachers to dialogue and reflect (what I call "collegial inquiry") through mentoring, action research (investigating issues related to their practice), and curriculum design (Miller, 2001; Stokes, 2001). Teacher learning in these practices occurs through collaboration, which has benefited schools across contexts, regardless of affluence and ethnic diversity (Sparks, 2000). As York-Barr and colleagues (2001) write, "Sharing responsibility for group learning and working together enhances effectiveness."

Researchers also cite teaming as an opportunity for meaningful reflection. In a qualitative study on teacher reflection, Kruse (1997) builds upon the work of Dewey (1910/1991, 1915/1944, 1938/1974), Athey (1970), and Kolb (1984). Their research suggests that experience provides the basis for learning and that reflection upon this experience is essential to the learning process. Kruse (1997) found that teachers who engaged in reflection and collaboration reported improved efficacy in their practice, seeking out innovations for new pedagogy. They also reported more ownership in their classrooms and increased ownership of their schools' missions.

Another way teaming contributes to a culture of adult development is by challenging teachers to examine their assumptions and practice (Schön, 1987). Kruse (1997) discovered that teachers who treat relationships with other teachers as resources more readily "seek other ideas and opinions concerning expert practice" (p. 57). Identifying multiple sources of knowledge enabled teachers in that study to reference a broad knowledge base to change their practices and make future decisions (Kruse, 1997). This is often lacking, however, because school staff often do not have adequate opportunities to reflect on their assumptions about practice. Using teaming for "unfreezing" assumptions provides a space for transformation.

Many figures in school reform advocate creating opportunities for teacher teams because they initiate systemwide change, encourage instructional innovation, *and* empower teachers (Meier, 2002; York-Barr et al., 2001). Recently, schools have concentrated on technology as a tool to enhance teacher and team collaboration and engagement in professional discourse (Lampert & Ball, 1999). Furthermore, teaming can be a developmental mechanism because it cultivates an individual's skills for dialogue and discussion, builds leadership, and contributes to school growth (Senge et al., 1994). Teaming as a developmental mechanism is explored further below.

Research illustrates the importance of building a culture of a community of inquiry to enhance the professional context of school (Cochran-Smith & Lytle, 2001; Elmore, 2002; York-Barr et al., 2001). Friedman (1997) maintains that teaming makes sense only if it involves a shift in how teachers and principals think about their work: "This shift involves regarding teams as the primary unit of teaching practice and as a means of linking instructional and structural change within schools" (p. 335). Friedman believes schools must be ready to operate in states of uncertainty, which is logical, because teaming challenges the status quo of traditional pedagogy.

Teaming is certainly not without challenges, however. Weiss and Cambone (2000) found that teams of teachers engaging in shared decision making with principals can actually alter the balance of power and engender initial teacher resistance and conflict. However, they assert, "conflict need not be all bad," since it is a signal that "people are confronting serious issues and beginning to 'unfreeze' obsolete ways of work" (p. 377).

While theorists have identified a number of teaming's benefits, as well as the challenges it poses, the findings of this study indicate that a school's culture and context must be considered when establishing collaboration among teachers. This chapter explores how teaming serves as a practice that supports teacher learning. While most of the principals in this sample may be unaware of the developmental basis of teaming, the ones who employ it believe these practices effectively support teacher learning because they can "see" differences in the teachers.

A Developmental View of Teaming

Despite the challenges teaming can pose, several principles of constructive-developmental theory (Kegan, 1982, 1994) can help in understanding how a team approach ultimately supports transformational learning. Developmentally speaking, learning to understand and appreciate others' perspectives can assist individuals in managing situations that require multiple perspectives. Participants can release themselves from embeddedness in or identification with their own perspectives and an inability to comprehend other people's meanings. Most important, articulation of a perspective might afford greater opportunity for people to reflect upon ways of knowing. (See Chapter 2 or the Glossary for definitions of transformational learning and the three basic ways of knowing.)

The context of working with colleagues in teams can challenge participants to consider new ways of thinking and acting. In this way, teaming can potentially provide a safe "holding environment" (Kegan 1982, 1994) in which participants take risks and collectively explore multiple perspectives. Adults with different ways of knowing, however, will experience teaming in different ways. And the extent to which individuals are able to benefit fully from this practice depends on their developmental levels and appropriate supports and challenges for growth within this context. Table 5.1 illustrates how teachers with different ways of knowing might make sense of engaging in teaming.

As Table 5.1 illustrates, individuals with a self-authoring way of knowing have the capacity to take responsibility for their work and consult

Table 5.1   How Adults With Different Ways of Knowing Experience Teaming

Way of Knowing	Experience of Teaming
Instrumental knowers	Working with a team can supportively challenge these knowers to think differently about not only their own but also other team members' perspectives on teaching practice, students' work, proposals for change, the school culture and/or mission, and other issues discussed in team meetings.
Socializing knowers	Working with a team, for these knowers, can serve as a safe context for learning about other colleagues' experience, practices, ideas, and perspectives as well as their expertise. A team context could serve as a place in which they have the opportunity to broaden their own perspectives by learning from valued colleagues, who they would look to for approval and acceptance of their own ideas.
	As long as all team members share a similar outlook, which in their view protects relationships with other team members, differences of opinion are okay. These knowers rely on absence of conflict to feel safe and comfortable taking risks in this context.
Self-Authoring	Teaming for these knowers serves as a context in which they learn from other people's perspectives, outlooks, and opinions about teaching, practice, and school improvement. Teachers with this way of knowing will use the learning, ideas, and information gleaned from other team members to help themselves in their own self-understanding and improvement. These teachers internally evaluate suggestions, ideas, and perspectives offered by fellow teammates; and, if they assess them to be desirable, they will integrate these new ideas with their own. Unlike adults who are socializing knowers, these knowers experience conflict as a natural part of working in teams and learning from others.

their own set of guiding values. Self-authoring knowers are more likely to welcome opportunities that enable them to take a stand for what they believe (or what they disagree with) within interpersonal situations. Team members with this way of knowing might feel best supported if others encourage them to assume more responsibility and leadership within the larger school organization.

On the other hand, teachers with a socializing way of knowing do not yet have the capacity to fully own their work and their beliefs. These individuals still look to external authorities for solutions to problems, and while they know when they have done something well, they *rely on others* to affirm their actions and views. Team members might help them to think through the challenges of implementing new teaching practices, serve as mentors and guides, or aid them in seeing themselves as specialized experts.

Thus from a developmental perspective, the team structure can provide a safe context within which to voice and share one's thinking. In doing so, teaming holds the potential for supporting transformational learning. Teaming can be a context for testing new ideas and ways of acting as colleagues collaborate over time. In essence, teaming holds the potential to help all adults improve their capacities to handle the complex responsibilities of professional and personal life.

WHY PRINCIPALS SUPPORT TEAMING

Nearly all of the principals in the sample employ teaming. They reported that it helps teachers—and others, including themselves—build connections with one another and decrease feelings of isolation. Teaming also helps them to share leadership. In teams, they encourage members to articulate their perspectives and share information and expertise. Thus teaming, as a developmental initiative, holds the potential to help both team members and the school community.

The principals discussed three underlying reasons for using teams: including others in leadership, building community, and unfreezing assumptions to benefit from change and diversity of perspectives. In about half of the schools, principals believe teaming offers potential for the entire community to consider and deliver more informed and effective decisions. More than half of these principals explained that they often ask for input and assistance from different teams before making any major decisions. Teaming is thus an essential part of their communities, enabling team members to share information and expertise with the larger community.

Beyond fostering shared leadership, more than half of the principals believe teams build relationships based on communication and collaboration. For example, in many cases, faculty teaches in teams. About half of the principals explained that adults from different organizational levels and with varying subject expertise team up to focus on school outcomes. These include curriculum teams, diversity teams, and technology teams. One of the key benefits of teams is reduction of teachers' and principals' isolation.

The third reason principals gave for using teams was to unfreeze assumptions and promote inclusion of diverse perspectives. Many said that teachers working in teams benefit from diverse points of view when considering important changes in the school. Teaming also helps individuals manage and acclimate to change because it encourages them to share ideas for change efforts, articulate goals, and be accountable for meeting them. Several principals, for example, shared stories about how teams present views that sometimes challenge well-established school norms and practices. This, in many cases, has spurred the principals and their school communities to reevaluate the challenged norms, and together they have worked to invent and/or implement strategies for change, such as literacy programs or technology initiatives.

Table 5.2 summarizes the reasons why the principals see teaming as an essential practice and gives specific examples of how teaming has been

Table 5.2   Teaming: Reasons Why Principals Employed Teams and Their Practical Applications of This Practice

Teaming	*Examples*
Principals' philosophies and espoused beliefs	• Sharing and including others in leadership • Building relationships • Embracing and helping people manage change and fostering diversity
Examples of teaming practice	• Inviting adults into conversations; requesting feedback on ideas • Principals and teachers, principals and board members, educational and administrative teams work toward strategy development & shared decision making • Teacher teams (e.g., in/out of classrooms, regarding curriculum, ministry teams at Catholic Schools, and visiting other schools) • Research/study/book groups • Faculty development committee teams (medium- and high-resource schools) • Department meetings • Developing partnerships with universities, businesses, and community organizations

used in their schools. In many schools, teaming has been employed extensively, while in a few of the schools, principals are beginning to employ teaming more frequently as a practice supportive of teacher learning.

EXAMPLES OF PRINCIPALS' USE OF TEAMING

Many principals said that one of the main ways in which teachers teamed up is to teach together. Others discussed how teachers team together to form book clubs, study groups, or research groups. Across the sample, principals specifically mentioned teaming teachers so that they can visit each other's classrooms and in some cases visit other schools regularly to improve their practice. Many principals value teaming for curricular issues in particular. While most of the high school principals, across school type, discussed teaming within departments, the elementary and middle school principals mostly pursue teaming within grade level. This seems to correspond logically to the structure of most primary and high schools.

Across the sample, nearly all of the principals also named cross-functional teams as "critical" opportunities to broaden everyone's perspective and to share decision making. For example, principals and teachers from different grades evaluate curricula across grades, or teachers and administrators develop standards and schoolwide policies. Several principals also discussed the great benefits of teaming teachers and other adults within the school with outside partners, such as universities, museums, and research centers.

Next, I present specific examples of how these sorts of teams work, from the perspectives of the principals in the study.

Receiving Feedback: Learning From Multiple Perspectives

Dr. Sarah Levine is the former head of Belmont Day School and also of Polytechnic High School, a high-resource, K–12 independent school in Pasadena, California. Like many of the principals, she employed teaming as a way for teachers to give feedback on her ideas and gain diverse perspectives. Sarah summarized her thinking about the importance of a trusting relationship with team members:

> The ability to tolerate and even invite disagreement and confrontation is important, I think. It's too easy to . . . want people near you to agree and support. A key to good leadership is finding people whom you can trust enough so that they can disagree and confront you in a way that's not ultimately threatening.

Sarah's experience of diversity resonates as a core theme across the principals in this study. She sees the practice of inviting adults to team as essential to leadership and as an opportunity to support teacher learning and growth.

Strategy Development and Shared Decision Making

The majority of the principals reported that teaming creates a context for shared decision making and respect for teachers' perspectives.

Dr. Jim Cavanaugh, principal of a medium-sized, public high school in Watertown, Massachusetts, provided the example of his high school's leadership team, which has met for several years. This is a cross-functional team composed of 16 members, including Jim, teachers, specialists, and other administrators from various areas. The team's goal is to "build a collaborative learning community for the school," Jim explained, and at the time of our interview, they were focusing on informing lesson design with evaluations of student work. The team uses a protocol of questions to assess student work, which Jim calls "designing with the end in mind." He stated that this team's work would further the school's goal of designing lessons that strengthen student learning. He considers this team to be an opportunity for teachers to assume leadership roles and reflect on their practice and school issues. Jim believes teaming and the collaboration it engenders will further many school goals and also promote school safety.

Joe Shea, principal of Trotter Elementary School in Boston, consciously resists imposing demands upon his teachers without their approval: "None of this top-down stuff." Joe, like more than half of the principals in this sample, stated that he wants to hear from all sides before making decisions. In addition to working closely in teacher-teams, cross-functional teams, such as the early literacy collaborative and assessment teams, enable him to garner multiple perspectives to guide decision making. While he occasionally must make the final decision, teaming gives teachers a voice in his resolutions.

The teachers at Dr. Mary Nash's special needs (alternative K–8 public) school feel that teams should make decisions when a student can no longer be helped by the school. She explained,

> One of the things that the teachers have asked me to do is never make a decision on my own, whether or not it's time to let go of a kid. . . . And we only made one decision like that, but it had a big effect on the whole faculty, and they came to me and they said, "It's not right. We need to make those decisions together as a group."

Mary implemented "service team meetings," which meet in the morning every day before the official school day. The purpose of these meetings, Mary said, is to counteract the students' tendency to "split the adults" and to provide opportunities for teacher learning. Adults meet to discuss how they can work with particular children or issues that arise, and they benefit from other team members' perspectives. Mary explained that this helps to reduce isolation.

Teaching in Teams

One common application of teaming is pairing teachers together to teach. For instance, principals team associate teachers (graduate level educators at nearby colleges) with experienced teachers at their schools throughout the academic year. The principals explained that team teaching sometimes serves different purposes. In a few cases, principals reported that team teaching is a vehicle for allowing one teacher to attend to the class while the other collaborates with colleagues. In general, these teachers alternate teaching the same class at different times. On the other hand, in close to half of the cases, team teaching is an opportunity for true collaboration among teachers. It provides an ongoing opportunity for each to strengthen teaching practices through dialogue and questioning assumptions and practices. Sometimes team teaching involves coteaching. At other times, one teacher teaches and the other observes and often videotapes the lesson so that both teachers can examine practice.

Discussing Curriculum and Student Work

Several principals believe teams allow teachers to give and receive input on curricular matters and assessments of student work. Across school types, the principals emphasized how teaming helps to improve conditions for individual students. Jim Cavanaugh stated the benefits of having teachers team up to review student work:

> [Working with others in a team] can be a gentle process, it's not criticizing the teachers, and it exposes so much when you have five or six pairs of eyes looking at a piece of work and ask[ing] questions. . . . They ask clarifying questions, and then they ask . . . questions that make you think about what you did and how you set the lesson, or you set the task as well as what the student has done.

Teaming enables Jim and the teachers to ask "questions that make you think about what you did," which strengthens instruction across the school.

Similarly, the Trotter School in Boston has biweekly grade level team meetings for teachers. Principal Joe Shea explained that these teams meet for 90 minutes and serve as forums for teacher collaboration. Teachers plan together, assess student work, develop rubrics, and discuss teaching and students in their classes. In addition, the teachers alternate directing these grade level meetings, taking on leadership for their own class planning and practice.

At St. Peter's School, a Catholic K–8 school in Cambridge, Massachusetts, Deborah O'Neil's teachers meet regularly to discuss children who are getting help from the special education teacher. Deborah believes that teams provide teachers with important opportunities to learn from each other. Working with teachers in teams has challenged everyone in the school to attain "a higher level of thinking and acting."

Across all school types and resource levels, teachers regularly work to evaluate and improve curricula. Kim Marshall's public, low- to medium-resource Boston elementary school provides an example. One of his projects focused on having teachers examine the MCAS (i.e., Massachusetts' standardized assessment of students' learning) guidelines and standards to develop a rubric of the skills that should be taught in each grade. Teachers formed committees to examine the test and "walk backward" through the grades until they developed guidelines. After engaging in reflection and dialogue, teachers could begin to focus on how they would teach these content areas and skills.

Scott Nelson, head of Rye Country Day School in Rye, New York, also uses teaming for curriculum design. "Being involved in curriculum development and the design, development, and implementation of programs" supports both teacher learning and school development. "The technology initiative," as he calls it, was developed by a faculty team. "Bringing people together" to think through funding, teacher training, and integrating technology in the school is a tremendous learning opportunity for teachers, in Scott's view.

Most of the opportunities for teaming at Dr. Sue David's (a pseudonym) high school seem to focus on curriculum writing or rewriting. The history and English departments stay on campus at the end of the school year to update their curricula. The English department also started to plan a writing-across-the-curriculum program. Sue believes it is important to provide teachers with a stipend for working during their vacation. She explained that she wanted to

> Acknowledge that they're giving up a valuable week of vacation time in the summer to stay together as colleagues and think through changes in the curriculum. And I think I upped that stipend recently to $800. But the point is to say, "Your time is valuable."

Sue believes that these weeklong meetings are ways for teachers to be more productive and focus in more depth on "serious transformational change that you're trying to achieve."

Engaging With Outside Experts

Across all school types, nearly all of the principals value having teachers visit other schools in teams. Through teaming, they believe, teachers can broaden perspectives, discuss their learning, and inform their practice at their own schools. For instance, Annenburg funds enabled Muriel Leonard's school to participate in a whole-school change program. At the

McCormick Middle School in Dorchester, Massachusetts, Muriel hired a "whole-school change coach" and a "content coach," who provide outside expertise on school restructuring and literacy, respectively. They serve on various cross-functional teams and also support individual teachers by teaching and modeling new pedagogical practices. The whole-school change coach participates on the instructional leadership team—the "central brain" of the school, as Muriel calls it. Teachers from each of the six disciplinary clusters (e.g., math and social studies), a literacy specialist, the assistant principals, and Muriel are also members of this team. They examine student work and make leadership decisions about important school issues (e.g., "What kinds of instruction strategies need to happen in order to address . . . this particular area of the curriculum?").

Similarly, members of the science department at Joe Marchese's school have developed a tradition to "close down" for a day to visit another school. Akin to the challenges identified by Weiss and Cambone (2000), some teachers complain about having to go. But, Joe explained, "They all come back feeling charged up about what they've seen, because they have some points of comparison." This comment indicates that despite initial resistance, individual science faculty benefit from learning about multiple points of view.

The Punahoe School in Honolulu, Hawaii, also teams by inviting a team of teachers from the Gardner School in Indianapolis to teach summer school with the Punahoe teachers. Principal Dr. Jim Scott hopes that the teachers on this team will share what they learn with other schools and bridge with other independent and public schools. He explained,

> And so that's part of what I'm saying to the faculty all the time, that you're not just a teacher here, you are an educational leader. And part of leadership is taking risks and trying on things and reflecting upon them.

Establishing Faculty Development Committee Teams

Nearly all of the independent schools and two of the higher financial resource Catholic school principals in this sample discussed the benefits of having a faculty development committee and/or a faculty steering committee. These cross-functional teams are composed of teachers (and in many cases administrators), and they engage in setting priorities with school principals. In all cases, the faculty development committee teams solicit and evaluate faculty requests for financial support of their professional development.

At Palm Beach Day School, the professional development faculty committee volunteers to identify "processes or even places and things to do. In some cases, places to go, but I think even more significantly, ways to do it within the resources we have." Principal Jack Thompson supports their recommendation to make professional development part of the teacher contracts. The team's membership and chairmanship rotate, and Jack believes the group has "generated a better understanding of what everybody's doing."

When the school engaged in a study of residential life at Westtown, Joe Marchese created a steering committee. Given the mission of the school, Joe explained, "There's already a sense of great collaboration with it being a Quaker school." While making decisions by consensus could have created problems, they produced a document that was accepted in 45 minutes. Reflecting on this, Joe said, "There's so much collaboration and so much decision making on the part of faculty that one of the difficulties in a Quaker school that operates by consensus is, what's the role of the principal? What's the role of the leader?"

Developing Partnerships With Other Organizations

Many of the principals believe teams and networks with other organizations outside the school or district support teacher learning and organizational learning. For instance, teachers from the Buckingham, Brown, and Nichols School in Cambridge, Massachusetts, team with professionals at the Museum of Science in Boston to "infuse our school with new ideas and opportunities for learning for faculty as well as for kids." This type of team, Mary Newman stated, provides important opportunities for all involved. Both students and faculty travel "back and forth" between the school and the museum to learn from museum professionals.

A CONTEXTUALIZED CASE: A CROSS-FUNCTIONAL TEAM OF TEACHERS, ADMINISTRATORS, AND STAFF

Dr. Sarah Levine, former principal of Belmont Day and Polytechnic schools, used teaming extensively.[1] Lower-school faculty taught in teams, and graduate level educators from a nearby college were teamed with different experienced teachers each semester to fill a degree requirement. In addition, teachers, administrators, and staff worked together on teams in developing and writing the "self-study" document presented to the evaluation committee for accreditation.

Sometimes, in Sarah's experience, teams of teachers and administrators worked together to achieve school objectives. One team of teachers and administrators worked for several months to develop a new schedule with larger blocks of time for each subject area in the school day. Another team of teachers and staff worked to upgrade computer systems and to improve instruction. Yet another team organized a "language arts night" at which they presented the school curriculum to parents. In each of these teams, individuals developed and implemented ideas through shared inquiry and distributed responsibilities for various tasks. This teamwork, in Sarah's view, built interpersonal relationships and created opportunities to learn about one's own and others' thinking.

One year during my research, the school was searching for a new director of admissions. One of the applicants under serious consideration was an African American individual whom Sarah considered well qualified for the position. Although diversity was one of this school's core values, and the school had increased diversity, no one in administration belonged to a minority.

In making the decision about hiring a director of admissions, Sarah worked closely with the following teams: administrative and educational teams (composed of administrators and division directors, respectively), board members, and faculty and staff teams. Each of these teams interviewed candidates and shared with Sarah and other teams their perspectives about candidates' strengths and weaknesses. "Community support" was needed to make a collaborative decision, and Sarah wanted as many "voices" as possible in the decision-making process.

The teams debated the characteristics needed by the appointed person and discussed who appeared to best meet requirements. They then shared their views with Sarah and other members of the leadership team (i.e., upper- and lower-school directors). During a final selection meeting, each team member presented his or her favored candidate and explained why that person would be the better fit for the school community and the position. After team members had presented their top choices, the team took a few moments to reflect on notes that had been displayed on the chalkboard describing the top choices. They then engaged in dialogue in order to come to consensus. During the discussion, two team members who initially favored different candidates changed their minds about who would be best suited for the position. The community decided to hire a well-qualified candidate who happened to be African American. Sarah said that it was important for community members to support the decision to select a certain candidate over others. In Sarah's view, working with various teams helped make this decision a shared one, which was well supported by the entire community's learning and growth.

Teaming in this school allowed team members to articulate their thinking and to support others'. Developmentally speaking, adults also challenged each others' thinking as they worked together over longer periods of time in a process of inquiry about the hiring process. On many occasions, individuals encouraged teammates to consider alternative ways of thinking about the hiring process. This example highlights the ways in which teaming worked in one school context and how it supported teacher learning.

CHAPTER SUMMARY

This chapter illustrates some of the ways in which many of the principals implemented teaming. The principals in this sample involve teachers, administrators, and staff in teaming to facilitate teacher learning and to increase the effectiveness of their schools. They view teaming as a practice that results in the following benefits:

- Enhances teacher learning and growth
- Improves instruction and schoolwide decision making
- Decreases teacher isolation
- Helps adults acclimate to change
- Encourages pedagogical innovation
- Empowers teachers
- Develops skills for dialogue and reflection
- Builds leadership capacity
- Contributes to the growth of the learning organization

Developmentally speaking, teaming serves a number of important purposes, including creating a safe environment for perspective building, taking risks, and considering new ways of thinking and acting. Teaming is a robust practice that supports and challenges adults, regardless of their ways of knowing, in ways that facilitate learning and growth. I also discussed the reasons why the principals believe teaming allows for shared leadership and community building and helps teachers and themselves to better manage change. Most of the principals, across school type, stressed the importance of open and honest communications when working in teams and of the need to give attention to each member's ideas and concerns in order to cultivate this practice. In addition, the principals indicated that the practice of teaming helps adults to manage and acclimate to change by reducing teacher isolation and providing a context for collaboration. The principals reported that participation in various types of teams creates opportunities for regular discussions about student progress.

In this chapter, I have presented examples of different types of teams that principals in this sample have established in their unique school contexts. Departmental teams are prevalent in high school settings, whereas grade level teams are popular in the elementary schools. Also, cross-functional teams are important contexts for jointly exploring ideas and perspectives, collaborative decision making, and supporting teacher learning. The chapter's concluding case illuminated how one former principal employed teaming to make a collaborative decision, support teacher learning, and develop ways of knowing.

REFLECTIVE QUESTIONS

We learn by conversing with ourselves, with others, and with the world around us. (Harri-Augstein & Thomas, 1991, p. 3)

The following questions are offered to assist you in applying the strategies outlined in this chapter to your own context. They can be used for internal reflection or to open up a group discussion.

1. What kinds of teams are in place at your school? How do you think they work to support teacher learning?

2. What do you see as the benefits of inviting teachers to form and work in teams—for yourself and for your teachers?

3. What, if any, are the constraints in helping teachers to work in teams, given your school context?

4. How do you think teachers in your school are experiencing the practice of learning in teams? How do you experience such learning?

5. Knowing what you now know about adults who make meaning in different ways, how might you embed different structures within teams to help support adults with a diversity of ways of knowing? (You may want to review Chapter 2, visit the Glossary, or look ahead to the tables in the final chapter.)

6. What are two practical ideas for teaming that you have learned about and would like to implement or encourage in your school?

NOTE

1. This case is adapted from Drago-Severson (1996).

6

Providing Leadership Roles

Opportunities for Leadership and Learning

By providing leadership roles, I mean giving other people the primary responsibility and authority for doing some work or making a change. . . . Because although people would keep me informed, they would primarily do [the leading] on their own.

—Dr. Sarah Levine, Belmont Day School

In this chapter, I discuss how the principals in the study understand the practice of providing adults with leadership roles and how this practice can support transformational learning. I describe how they believe these roles invite teachers to share ownership of authority. I use "providing leadership roles" rather than the commonly used term "distributive leadership" because of the intention behind these roles, which is to not merely distribute leadership duties. In contrast to assigning tasks, "providing leadership roles" offers supports and challenges to the person who assumes such a role so that he or she can grow from them.

Across all school types, principals, to different degrees, presented examples of how teachers assume leadership as curriculum developers, leaders of groups within and outside of the school, or school administrators (e.g., department chairs). This leadership, they believe, builds community and promotes change. Providing leadership roles is undeniably related to the practice of teaming detailed in Chapter 5. For example, working in teams affords opportunities for various individuals to assume leadership roles. In this chapter, however, I focus on the benefits of promoting the development of leadership.

After presenting theoretical perspectives on providing leadership roles in schools as professional development, I provide specific examples of how principals implement this practice in their respective institutions. This chapter closes with a case of how one teacher has assumed a role as an administrator while continuing to teach.

ABOUT LEADERSHIP ROLES

Research shows that inviting teachers to assume leadership within their schools is one practice that supports teacher learning.

Theoretical Principles of Providing Leadership Roles

Discussing the Institute for Educational Leadership report on teacher leadership, Zehr (2001) advocates increasing leadership opportunities for teachers in schools. Zehr contends that in many districts, the only accessible leadership roles for teachers are in administration, activism, or teachers unions. However, he also argues that principals should support teacher leadership in the areas of curricular development, budgeting, and selection of administrators.

Similarly, Leithwood and colleagues (1997) advocate for creating school conditions that support teacher leadership. In their study comparing teacher and principal leadership, teachers had the strongest influence on school planning and structure, while principals had a great impact on school culture and mission. In particular, they highlight the benefits of teacher leadership, including building democratic workplaces, increasing teacher satisfaction and professionalism, increasing effectiveness, and promoting collegial interaction (Leithwood & Jantzi, 2002; Leithwood et al., 1997).

To facilitate leadership within schools, Blase and Blase (2001) maintain that principals need to develop teachers' skills as data collectors, decision makers, and problem solvers. Principals also need to create opportunities wherein teachers can dialogue with each other and administrators. In particular, this dialogue must build upon teachers' expertise in their disciplines and pedagogy.

While leadership roles have many benefits, Zehr (2001) found that some schools that afford decision making to teachers have encountered resistance from school boards, administrators, and legislators. Moreover, Leithwood and colleagues (1997) discovered that time constraints, funding shortages, and the absence of training often impede teacher leadership. In addition, they pointed to "cultures of isolationism" that are oftentimes prevalent in schools that "inhibit the work of teacher leaders with their teaching colleagues" (p. 6). To ensure more positive outcomes, school leaders need to cultivate support from teachers, parents, and school board representatives (Darling-Hammond, 1999; Lieberman & Miller, 2001; Zehr, 2001). Positive outcomes are supported when school leaders approach challenges collaboratively by inviting teachers into leadership roles and sharing responsibility (Rallis & Goldring, 2000).

A Developmental View of Providing Leadership Roles

Providing leadership roles for teachers fosters reflective practice that supports adults in developing the capacity to better manage their work. When serving in these roles, teachers have the opportunity to share their own thinking, learn about the perspectives of others, and reflect on their own assumptions. Dialogue offers a chance for others to challenge one's thinking in ways that might support the reshaping of assumptions and practices.

Leadership roles can serve as a context of growth, a "holding environment" (Kegan, 1982, 1994). In other words, a leadership role can provide a space where individuals are supported and challenged by others as they articulate their own thinking and reflections in an open way and listen to and learn from other people's perspectives. Moreover, risk taking supports greater self-authorship, especially in an independent task or project. Yet how teachers in leadership positions view support, challenge, and risk will be experienced in qualitatively different ways, depending on how the teacher in a leadership role makes meaning of that experience. Principals who understand a developmental perspective may better support teachers in pursuing leadership roles.

Table 6.1 highlights how adults with socializing and self-authoring ways of knowing tend to make sense of the leadership experience.

As Table 6.1 illustrates, people with a self-authoring way of knowing have internal standards that guide them through the decision-making process. To support people with this way of knowing in a leadership role would be to provide them with freedom and authority to carry projects to completion, offering feedback as they evaluate their work and discussing the feedback with them.

Support for teachers with a socializing way of knowing should encourage their independence and consultation of their own developing internal standards in making decisions. It is key, though, that principals *explicitly* acknowledge the steps needed for this shift, for example, openly recognizing teachers' perspectives when they voice them and encouraging them to share more of their thinking. If a teacher has not stated that he or

Table 6.1 How Adults With Different Ways of Knowing Experience Leadership Roles

Way of Knowing	Orientation to Lead Role	Supports	Challenge (Growing Edge)
Socializing knowers	• Need to feel safe and comfortable asking questions, asking for help and guidance when they are unsure about what to do in situations. • Conflict is experienced as a threat to the self. • Approval of others is of utmost importance. • Authorities and valued others are sources of knowledge and informed opinions about decisions. • Need authority to confirm and accept one's self and one's own beliefs. • Emphasis on loyalty and all group members coming to a shared understanding or solution.	Authority and valued others confirm, acknowledge, and accept these knowers' selves and their own beliefs.	• Gently encourage person to look to oneself and one's own views when leading and making decisions; • To construct one's own values and standards rather than co-construct them with other valued authorities; • To tolerate and accept conflict, conflicting points of view on an issue, or solutions without feeling that it threatens the interpersonal relationship; • To see conflict as part of interpersonal relationships rather than something to avoid.
Self-authoring knowers	• Understand varying perspectives as informing decision making and the self. • Conflict is experienced as a natural part of dialogue that can inform a decision-making or other process. • Internal focus on own value generating system when making decisions. • Capacity to listen and attend to new ideas and points of view, multiple diverse perspectives on a situation, and to challenge new perspectives without having one's self be at risk. • Focus on solutions that include a diversity of points of view and that will move the team's interests and goals forward.	Providing learning opportunities to consider and benefit from diverse points of view; contexts for analyzing and critiquing proposals and/or ideas; opportunities to explore their own self-determined goals.	• To be able to let go of one's own investment and identification with one's own standards and values—or to set them aside—and embrace/acknowledge values of others that may be in opposition to one's own; • To embrace/accept different approaches to the process of exploring a problem or solving it that may not be aligned with one's own way or approach.

she is ready to assume leadership, a principal's support may or may not be perceived as helpful.

Providing teachers with leadership roles is a robust practice that can support and challenge teachers with different ways of knowing and provide holding environments for growth. Also, a leadership role can serve as a holding environment for a teacher who is making the transition between a socializing and a self-authoring way of knowing.

WHY PRINCIPALS WANT TO PROVIDE TEACHERS WITH LEADERSHIP ROLES

More than half of the principals serving in different school contexts reported that leadership roles provide transformational opportunities to teachers and themselves. In their view, people develop from the experience of being responsible for an idea's creation, development, or implementation. Most of the principals believe that leadership roles also foster relationship building, help adults to acclimate to change, and ultimately enhance school climate (see Table 6.2). According to these school leaders, a leadership role is an opportunity to raise not only one's own consciousness but also the consciousness of a group.

Table 6.2 summarizes why the principals see providing leadership roles as an essential practice and gives specific examples of this practice in their schools.

Shared Responsibility for Work and Direction

One of the primary ways leadership roles are crucial for teacher learning is through a shared responsibility for the direction of the school. Leadership roles for teachers include the following:

- Facilitating department or faculty meetings
- Sharing expertise with faculty in their own schools or at other sites
- Leading steering teams or accreditation committees
- Overseeing mentoring programs

In most of these roles, a faculty member takes responsibility for seeing a proposed idea through to implementation.

Dr. Jim Scott supports teachers in leadership roles by conceptualizing the school as a "learning laboratory." Teachers, in his view, should have a sense of "ownership about the entire enterprise," meaning the entire school. Their leadership of committee work, implementation of changes, and research, for example, allow them to make decisions that shape the direction and climate of the school. Like many other principals, Jim explains that teacher learning needs to be "driven by the faculty" themselves.

Table 6.2   Providing Leadership Roles: Reasons Why Principals
Employed This Practice and Its Practical Applications

Providing Leadership Roles	Examples
Principals' philosophies and espoused beliefs	• Sharing and including others in leadership • Building relationships • Developing a positive school climate
Examples of providing leadership roles	• Teachers and staff share knowledge and expertise • Teachers become administrators or team leaders/dept. chairs, deliver workshops • Leaders in technology • Experienced teachers mentor associate teachers (graduate students, interns) • Teachers have authority for decision making (ownership) and for their own work • Teachers are members of accreditation teams, lead roles in self-study • Teachers deliver workshops (outside of their own schools and/or at conferences) • Teacher involved in evaluation of other teachers • Teachers develop expertise (through sabbaticals or training) and teach others • Developing partnerships with universities and/or businesses • Developing courses to teach graduate students on-site

Sr. Barbara Rogers points out that teachers who initially may not embrace such roles ultimately feel satisfied after assuming leadership:

> Sometimes we ask people to do things that they're delighted to do, and sometimes we ask people to try things that make them very nervous to do. And often the person at the [end of it] will say, "I never thought I would love this so much." But our job is to imagine possibilities for people.

Distributed Leadership

Beyond sharing responsibility, the principals strongly believe in a model of distributed leadership. Nearly all of them connect inviting teachers into leadership roles as an important part of their leadership philosophy.

Jack Thompson believes it is critical for teachers to feel that the school supports them in developing their own ideas for their professional development. He explained, "The most effective professional development in my experience has been when you can engage a significant and substantial group of faculty in the process." He has found that ideas for learning and professional development will more likely succeed if they do not come from him. Jack believes that the "reason we're successful and contemporary and still working well" is that teachers have taken charge of coming up with their own ideas for their learning and improvement.

Similarly, Kathleen Perry of Lake Worth Community High School encourages many different teachers in her school to participate in leadership roles, so that "it's not the same people all the time who are taking advantage of" these opportunities. She also encourages other teachers to take advantage of the expertise of the leader, urging fellow teachers to "sit down, one on one . . . [and] talk to" the person with the lead role. She feels that teachers assuming these roles could be "brutally frank" and "tear apart" new ideas for change. Thus she does not look only for agreement when distributing leadership because of the "danger of . . . being blindsided" later by unexpected criticisms.

Most of the principals pointed out that leadership roles take large and small forms. Many also explained that, often, leadership roles help teachers see beyond their own classrooms, departments, and fields of expertise. In addition, the principals recognized that teachers are at different places in their own lives. Finally, most stressed that some teachers prefer their specific roles as teachers and would not like to step beyond these types of leadership roles. As a result, many principals create alternative options for leadership roles. Next, I discuss the specific ways principals provide leadership roles for teachers.

EXAMPLES OF PROVIDING LEADERSHIP ROLES

The following range of examples reflects the principals' belief that it is important to offer an array of opportunities to fulfill their commitment to sharing leadership.

Sharing Knowledge and Expertise: Knowledge-Based Management

Across school types, principals remarked that teachers learn when they share their expertise within and outside of the school. These roles allow teachers to direct their own learning, promoting "self-discovery."

Sr. Joan Magnetti emphasized how "teacher initiative is a big thing." In fact, Sr. Magnetti told me that teachers would feel stifled if she did not support them when they want to create new courses or implement new ideas. These, in her view, are leadership opportunities for growth and learning.

In more than half of these schools, principals encourage teachers to deliver presentations on their work at national and regional conferences. They believe this supports teacher learning because teachers can broaden their perspectives by sharing and learning from others in their fields. Even the work of developing the proposal, in their view, fosters the development of certain abilities or skills. Jerry Zank is one such principal. Encouraging teachers to write proposals and deliver presentations supports "self-reflection and self-education." In Jerry's view, learning occurs when "we become active and engaged in a project, when we own it, when it is ours. That's what really gets our juices going—when we talk to others about it, that's where you get the development."

The teacher coordinators for the Trotter School's literacy program are trained at Lesley University. In Principal Joe Shea's view, they gain significant leadership and learning by training other teachers in this program, observing, and being observed as models. Joe referred to the coordinators as "lead" teachers and underscored that this type of leadership is now welcome as part of the culture of public schools.

Many principals reported that faculty-led workshops within their own schools provide a way of sharing ideas and broadening perspectives. The principals also stressed that teachers often do this less formally, such as when they want to share a book with others. This also occurs when faculty share learning from conferences with an entire group of colleagues.

For example, Dr. Sue David explained that faculty have smaller leadership roles by sharing their summer activities with each other at the start of faculty meetings. Teachers also assume leadership roles on the school's diversity committee, which attends a "People of Color" conference and shares its experience with the school. These teachers help the community develop "a common basis of understanding" in terms of diversity in their institutions.

Taking Leadership Roles in Larger Projects

Across school types, principals explained that teachers also assume leadership roles by instructing teachers, coaches, and coordinators, which also serve as rich contexts for their own learning.

At Graham and Parks School in Cambridge, Massachusetts, a half-time literacy teacher is leading an assessment program. Len Solo explained that the teacher in this leadership role has trained all of the other reading teachers "how to do [individual assessments in reading and writing] and how to score [them]." At Len's school, teachers also have leadership roles in training each other in different ways of teaching writing. He explains,

"We have created a lot of very expert people here and then we call upon them to help ourselves internally."

Authority for Decision Making

Across all school types, close to half of the principals explained that teachers assume leadership by developing and implementing new models for practice. For example, Mr. Scott Nelson of Rye Country Day School discussed how a physical education teacher at his school assumed a leadership role in starting a new program called "Hoops for Hearts," which combined science and physical education. Scott emphasized how this teacher became a "model for other [teachers] to follow," a leader in his curricular field.

At Sr. Joan Magnetti's school, Convent of the Sacred Heart, teachers research and determine evaluation models that they feel will best support their own growth. The school set up a task force composed of teachers and found that many teachers prefer department heads to conduct evaluations. Some teachers don't feel that their peers will provide good feedback other than "Everything you're doing is really good." However, Sr. Magnetti believes that involving peers in evaluations will provide teachers with learning opportunities as they assume leadership roles. The teachers who have leadership roles in this research are now reevaluating this system.

Leading Accreditation

Close to half of the principals, across school types, reported that they encourage teachers to serve on accreditation teams. This provides leadership roles as teachers visit and assess other schools and their programs. Serving on these teams promotes individual teacher learning as well as school learning because they bring back new ideas and, in turn, generate new ideas with faculty. Dr. Dan White of Seabury Hall School, like other principals, shared, "I've made known, statewide, that I like to have my teachers involved in accreditation teams because I don't think that there's any better way to have teachers understand what other schools are like, and how good Seabury is."

A CASE STUDY: SHARED LEADERSHIP–PETER'S STORY

Here, I present an in-depth case of a teacher, Peter (a pseudonym), who assumed a leadership role. I also describe the efforts of the school principal, Dr. Sarah Levine, to support his learning and growth in this role.[1]

Sarah selected Peter to be interim upper-school-division director, after consulting with the lower-division director, Betty, in making the choice.

Peter, a talented and well-respected teacher, had eagerly pursued the position. Peter's new duties included communicating with upper-school faculty to learn of their concerns and feelings about issues and keeping the educational team informed about those concerns and feelings. He shared his thinking with the educational team (composed of Sarah and the two division directors) as to how the upper-school faculty might respond to specific changes under consideration and implemented policies accordingly. He also taught one class each day. It was important to Sarah that the division directors stay in touch with faculty needs and communicate them to her openly. However, because Peter was finding that his new responsibilities were demanding more time than he had, for the first few months, Sarah allowed him to miss many meetings of the educational team.

Airing Problems

Several months into Peter's appointment, Sarah opened an educational team meeting by sharing the agenda. After mentioning several items, she invited the two division directors to "chime in" to add to the agenda. They all talked for a few minutes about whether it would be more helpful to talk first about "the nitty-gritty" specifics or more general ideas. Peter and Sarah both preferred to talk about specifics.

Looking uncomfortable and a little nervous, Sarah opened by explaining that she did not like the way the educational team was working together this year. Sarah said that she appreciated Peter's feeling overwhelmed by the amount of work he had. She and Betty had been doing all they could to help him, but she felt that Peter's "overload" was causing her to rely too much on Betty. Sarah concluded by saying that it was not fair to Betty that she needed to lean so heavily on her, since Betty had too much work of her own. She and Betty could no longer "cover" for Peter. They told him that they needed to know "what was going on" with him.

Peter said that he was having trouble "staying above water" because the position had too many responsibilities. After listening to Peter for some time, Betty and Sarah asked questions seeking to better understand Peter's needs. Peter responded cooperatively while continuing to restate his feelings about working "so hard."

Several times during the meeting, both Peter and Betty interrupted each other. When Sarah brought specific examples of unsatisfactory interactions among teachers to Peter's attention, he defended himself. He believed that these situations were Betty's responsibility and not his, and Betty felt "misunderstood" by him. Sarah said that each division director was responsible for certain tasks, and making sure teachers worked together was one such duty. It was up to them to work effectively with all teachers so that the community could grow.

Sarah was puzzled that the two previous upper-school directors were able to fulfill more responsibilities than were asked of Peter. She reminded him that he had been relieved of some teaching duties to serve as division director. He interrupted, saying that although the previous director managed the work, he did not want to be as "stressed out" as she had been. Peter reasserted his confidence in his ability to do the job and emphasized that he was still learning, as this was his first year. Sarah said gently, "I know you're working hard. I don't want you to work harder. I want you to work *smarter*." After taking a deep breath, she said firmly that she and Betty could no longer take on Peter's work in addition to their own.

"I hear what you're saying," Peter said to Sarah, "but it is not so easy for me to translate it into action." Sarah then offered several suggestions, based upon her own experiences, about how he might better handle his workload: "Do all of your written work at home. Use your down time to talk with teachers and keep in touch with issues, and be in the loop. Get to know the kids more." Sarah also acknowledged that Peter had to learn how to say no to others' requests. At the end of the meeting, Sarah reminded Peter that she supported him and firmly advised him to make changes in his working style. Sarah also suggested that the three of them meet with the school psychologist for assistance with working out their communication difficulties.

As mentor, Sarah invested time and effort into guiding Peter through his difficulties. Following the meeting, she took several steps to seek him out and provide support. She checked in first thing the next day and continued to communicate about his progress and further strategies in person and via notes. Knowing that community support was important for Peter's success, Sarah also alerted the community about his situation. She asked other administrators to encourage and support him during "a rough time."

Immediate Outcome

A few weeks later, Sarah conducted Peter's performance evaluation. In addition to discussing performance issues in the meeting, Sarah explained in some detail how she saw his responsibilities changing in the next academic year. While his abilities had improved, being an administrator would not be any easier than it had been this year. He would have more teaching duties (two classes of 20 students each), and Sarah would have less time to mentor him because of her involvement in a capital campaign. Moreover, because the current educational team had fallen short of some expectations, more changes in structure and responsibilities were anticipated.

Sarah gave Peter some time to consider their conversation and to decide for himself whether to continue administrative work along with his teaching responsibilities. A few days after the performance evaluation, Peter met briefly with Sarah. He had carefully weighed all she said and wanted to continue as division director. Sarah offered Peter a contract for the following year, and Peter signed it.

By encouraging teachers and administrators to take on more authority and responsibility, Sarah wanted to provide support and challenge to help them manage their work. Sarah faced tensions as she tried to help Peter become more successful, while not abandoning her responsibilities to other teachers.

Sarah's Perspective on the Leader's Dilemmas

Providing leadership roles involves more than just inviting people to assume those roles and leaving them to do so alone. Much more is often needed for individuals to develop their leadership potential. Sarah was aware that even with a holding environment, development for those in transition is complicated because people grow at different rates and require different supports and challenges. Because of competing commitments, demands of the role, and variation in individuals' ways of knowing, sharing leadership inevitably creates dilemmas for school leaders as well as for people assuming new roles.

Getting the Work Done While Also Providing Support

As school head, Sarah's chief objectives were to get the school's work done and to provide the best education possible for the children there. She saw herself as "ultimately responsible" for the organizational effectiveness of the school. If others with leadership roles were not performing up to standards, Sarah believed their deficiencies affected her performance as school leader and the performance of the entire community. Sarah viewed the educational team meetings as a way to share and include others in her leadership. Thus balancing her own values, supporting Peter by relieving him from some meetings, and keeping the educational team's communication open created a dilemma for her. Sarah concluded that she might have to forgo the product and ally with the process of development.

Stretching Competencies

In sharing her leadership, Sarah held very high performance and growth expectations for herself and others. Sarah was able to successfully handle a multitude of tasks in different domains in a way that made it all look easy. "Expectations are a great motivator," she once said. "When we know someone believes in us, we work hard to live up to those beliefs." Sometimes, however, she acknowledged that she worked too hard.

Sarah also expected a great deal of others and encouraged them to stretch their competencies. She wanted Peter to broaden his leadership potential in his new role, and she expected him to succeed. Though always supportive to Peter, Sarah also appeared to have doubts. Were the demands of being a school director and an excellent teacher too much for him? How could all the work get done without compromising her own standards and adult development in this community?

Ensuring Future Success

Sarah saw Peter as a gifted teacher and would not have been disappointed if he had decided to return to full-time teaching duties. Although some might interpret her stances as a no-confidence vote for Peter as an effective upper-school director, Sarah was sincerely concerned with doing what was best for him.

Sarah put her theory about conflict management into practice at the meeting. She appeared to share her concerns openly, listen attentively to Peter, and ask questions that might help both of them better understand his experience. Her questions also helped her better grasp the assumptions guiding his way of knowing, so that she could assess where further development and improvement were needed. In follow-up interactions, Sarah seemed to support Peter, though in her view, mistakes were an opportunity to learn.

Sarah and Peter agreed that in the following year, Peter would again serve as both teacher and upper-school division director. In continuing to support Peter's development, Sarah believed she was doing what was best for Peter *and* the school. Sarah inevitably continued to be concerned about how Peter would fare in the year to come and how well the school's mission and objectives would be fulfilled. Nevertheless, she remained committed to supporting adult development, while acknowledging that the process would never be easy, readily quantifiable, or its results immediately visible.

Peter's View of the Transition

About two months after the difficult educational team meeting described earlier, Peter talked with me about his new experience as an administrator. Three themes surfaced during this conversation. First, Peter showed appreciation and gratitude to Sarah for the leadership role and for supporting his decision to succeed in his new post. Second, he shared a value for communicating openly and directly with members of the school community, even though he occasionally found it hard to practice. Finally, he exhibited pride in working with a community of adults who also demonstrated a commitment to adult growth and development.

Peter believed that Sarah had offered him the leadership role because she believed he was capable of growing into the job. "If Sarah hadn't been a person who was open for people to learn, she would never have trusted me with the position." He also felt fortunate to work with Sarah and said that he had learned a great deal from her, including how to mentor faculty, give negative feedback constructively, and focus on school mission while juggling duties. Peter's learning seemed to mirror Sarah's own mission and values.

For Peter, as for Sarah, open communication was crucial: "If you lose that, you lose everything, or you've really dug a hole for yourself." Although Peter still sometimes found it difficult to give direct feedback, especially giving "hard news," he knew directness would build respect. He acknowledged that he still needed to "work on" this ability. He told me that he recently had to deliver "hard news" to a colleague. Instead of taking responsibility, he "sort of blamed it on Sarah" by telling his colleague that Sarah had told him to give the news. Reflecting on that situation, Peter explained how he would handle things now:

> Even if you're dealing with somebody who's your friend, when you need to tell him hard news, you have to set him down and present the hard news and let the person know that you are open to discussing how the decision was made.

Peter appeared to be leaning toward taking more responsibility for delivering clear but empathic feedback. This is developmentally significant, since he was now able to have a broader perspective on his relationships with teachers and to act on his thinking differently. He seemed to be making meaning as self-authoring knower.

Peter believed that the trust he had developed with upper-school teachers made a difference in his relationships with them as their administrator. He worked "really hard" at establishing "good rapport" with his teaching colleagues. He said that he likewise received a great deal of support from them. He believed that fair and direct communication were key to that rapport and mutual support.

Peter said that the work of being an administrator included "dealing with differences of opinion." Both he and Sarah held "strong opinions" and respected each other's differences. Peter also discussed Sarah's belief in the importance of a shared mission at the school. He was aware of the need to be a "learner" in order to succeed in the school culture. He said that in his work as an administrator, he, like Sarah, worked to support and encourage adult growth.

When asked about his leadership style, Peter said he would like to get to a point where he could have many issues to handle and give each of them "equal billing" and "importance." He saw himself with an approach different from Sarah's, whom he saw prioritizing issues according to their importance. When asked whether he thought he was learning in his leadership role, Peter answered: "Oh, most definitely. I hope, even if I become head someday, I hope I never get to the point that I think I know it all." One of the best parts of working in the community, in Peter's view, was that everyone was growing. "One of the things I love about my position here, and about a lot of the people here, is that we're all in different stages of growth, but I don't think anybody feels that they want to just be stagnant here." Though acknowledging that he still found aspects of his new role "hard," Peter said, "I do feel, personally, that I'm still growing. And that's what I want to be doing. That's the most important thing."

Developmental Lessons

Similar to other principals, Sarah believes one of her biggest challenges as head of school involves giving someone negative feedback; it is uncomfortable and potentially painful for the recipient. Sarah wanted Peter to know that she recognized his hard work, but she also wanted him to know that he needed to become more effective. In this situation, for Peter to "work smarter," he had to grow into making meaning with a self-authoring way of knowing. He would not succeed by looking to external authorities for what he *should* be doing. Recall that a self-authoring knower has the developmental capacities to assess a situation and look internally to decide what needs to be done in order to "work smarter."

With this way of knowing, Peter would be able to look to himself, and his *own* values and standards, to decide what had to be done. Sarah gently challenged Peter's thinking by suggesting that he occasionally withhold help from colleagues, especially when he was sacrificing his own efficiency. By suggesting that Peter set boundaries in his work with others, she challenged his thinking in the context of their interpersonal relationship, thus creating a "holding environment" (Kegan, 1982).

Sarah also supported and gently challenged Peter's leadership by encouraging him to own his work. First, she created a safe context in which she asked questions that invited Peter to reflect more deeply upon his current way of making meaning. By inviting him to consider alternative ways of behaving, she challenged his current way of thinking. Then, by offering concrete suggestions based upon her own experience, she guided him to view and execute his work in a broader context.

CHAPTER SUMMARY

This case illustrates how Sarah supported and "held" Peter as he assumed his leadership role. She was able to build community while supporting him in effective transition to his new role. Throughout the transition, she demonstrated support for Peter's growth, while also being firm and direct in her communications. Sarah and the school provided additional support and challenge when a teacher was not fully ready for a particular leadership role. Over time, the school community began to view Peter as a leader. The case highlights Sarah's and Peter's rewards and unforeseen struggles, describing how she negotiated the demands of supporting a teacher and attending to the needs of the whole school. In so doing, it illustrates how principals can tailor support and challenge to individual needs, because people with different ways of knowing experience these roles in developmentally different ways. The case also shows how these roles can serve as a context for growth.

Inviting teachers to assume leadership roles is one of the four practices the principals in this study employ to support teacher learning. Most of the principals explained that these roles serve as a context for giving teachers the opportunity to run with their ideas. When inviting teachers into the roles, several said that they focus on individuals' strengths and areas for growth as they encourage them to assume greater authorship and responsibility. Another group of principals in this sample feels that faculty members should select teachers for leadership roles. In addition, most principals in this study work to enable teachers to implement their own ideas for improvement and encourage teachers to present them to their colleagues. Adults in these roles have opportunities to reflect on their own assumptions, convictions, and practices. Examining assumptions is essential for the development of lasting change and new practices, because it can lead to reframing prior ways of seeing and interpreting experience.

Inviting others into leadership roles is one way these principals share leadership and ownership of ideas and promote individual and organizational growth. The majority of the principals reported that leadership roles encourage faculty to share and expand their perspectives. In most cases, teachers who assume leadership roles are able to share their expertise, present new ideas, and attend to others' concerns about the proposed ideas.

Two threads—one practical and one developmental—seem to run through the process of providing leadership roles. First, many of these principals reported that teachers in leadership roles share leadership, power, and decision making with them. Second, these roles serve to create "holding environments" (Kegan, 1982, 1994) for growth.

REFLECTIVE QUESTIONS

Please take a moment to write about these before turning to the next chapter. These questions can be used for private reflection or for a group discussion.

1. How does the "holding environment" you or others provide at your school support teachers with different ways of knowing as they assume leadership roles? What kinds of supports and challenges exist in the context?

2. How do you think that the "holding environment" could be reshaped, if it should, to accommodate particular teachers at your school?

3. What kinds of leadership roles do you invite teachers into at your school?

4. What do you see as the benefits and challenges for teachers in these roles?

5. In what ways does this chapter and/or developmental theory help you to better understand how teachers with different ways of knowing might experience leadership roles within your school and within their classrooms?

6. In what ways, if any, do Sarah's dilemmas resonate with you?

7. How are teachers supported and challenged in your school in leadership roles?

8. After reading this chapter, what are some additional supports and challenges you and/or others in your school might provide?

NOTE

1. This case is adapted from a case that I presented in Drago-Severson (1996).

7

Collegial Inquiry

A Practice for Talking and Thinking About Practice

Schools are social places. Although too often educators think and act alone, in most schools colleagues do share daily events. Stories told in teachers' lounges are a potential source of rich insight into issues of teaching and learning and can open doors to professional dialogue.

—Hole & McEntee (1999, p. 36)

"Collegial inquiry" is an example of a larger developmental concept known as "reflective practice," which can occur individually or in groups. I define collegial inquiry as a shared dialogue in a reflective context that involves reflecting on one's assumptions, convictions, and values as part of the learning process. According to the principals in this study, collegial inquiry can facilitate both teacher learning within a school and the growth of the institution. The various forms collegial inquiry takes include public discussion and private reflection, collaborative goal setting and evaluation, and engaging in conflict resolution.

In this chapter, I briefly describe the theoretical foundations of collegial inquiry in professional development and adult development research, highlight why principals value collegial inquiry, and provide examples of how it has functioned in their schools. I close the chapter with an in-depth case study of how one school leader employs collegial inquiry with her teachers in the annual process of goal setting.

ABOUT COLLEGIAL INQUIRY AND REFLECTIVE PRACTICE

Theoretical Principles of Reflective Practice

> Many of us recognize that as adult educators we are also adult learners, and that engaging in critical self-reflection about our existing assumptions, values, and perspectives can further prompt our development. (Taylor, Marienau, & Fiddler, 2000, p. 317)

Reflective practice is another tool identified by school leaders and theorists as a practice that supports teacher learning (Rasmussen, 1999; Schön, 1987). The central goal of reflective practice is improving one's teaching—which includes attention to the emotional and intellectual well-being and growth of the teacher (Brookfield, 1995; Osterman & Kottkamp, 1993). When adults engage in reflective practice, they become aware of their own and others' assumptions and behaviors. "In many ways," Brookfield (1995) writes, "we *are* our assumptions. Assumptions give meaning and purpose to who we are and what we do" (p. 2). Assumptions are the *big Truths* we hold. We do not question them—nor do we question how they guide behavior—because they are taken-for-granted beliefs about how the world works. We *assume* them to be true.

Brookfield (1995) asserts that examining and modifying assumptions promotes growth. Similarly, Osterman and Kottkamp (1993) contend that reflective practice increases awareness and that this is necessary for behavioral change. However, identifying problems is not an easy task, because the assumptions that inform and direct our behavior are not easy to articulate. Once a problem is identified, Osterman and Kottkamp (1993) suggest that we can gather information about it from multiple data sources and envision solutions by "stepping outside the action to observe it critically and to describe it fully" (p. 24). These authors suggest that this description should incorporate both cognitive and emotional aspects of behavior.

Collegial Inquiry in the Professional Development Literature

Killion (2000) maintains that "most teachers construct knowledge from their experiences, often sharing this private knowledge with no one" (p. 3).

Therefore, she recommends organizing professional development around analysis of current practices because it fosters teachers' use of research in their teaching. Rogoff and Lave (1984) point out that it is critically important to consider the role of context in supporting cognitive growth in this endeavor. Creating a context wherein teachers are encouraged to engage in reflection promotes (and models) risk taking and can support transformational learning.

It is generally accepted that professional development in the 21st century must center on creating opportunities for teachers to examine and reflect on their practice and how it can be improved to better support student achievement (Ball & Cohen, 1999; Darling-Hammond, 1998; Elmore & Burney, 1999; Hawley & Valli, 1999). Recently, however, Cochran-Smith and Lytle (2001) point to the divergent assumptions guiding the "new visions of professional development" and the various ways in which these assumptions translate to practice (p. 46). These authors, among others (Darling-Hammond, 2003; McLaughlin & Zarrow, 2001), advocate for a "knowledge-of-practice" approach infused by its core concept of "inquiry as stance" on teaching (Cochran-Smith & Lytle, 2001, p. 48). This approach supports teacher learning by focusing on teacher knowledge, teacher practice, and the relationships between the two to build a culture of inquiry. It attends to the individual and collective growth of teachers and is based on the philosophy that learning is a lifelong process. Cochran-Smith and Lytle (2001) contend that this stance holds greatest promise for realizing the democratic purpose and practices of professional development in this century.

Among others (Becerra-Fernandez & Stevenson, 2001), Neuman and Simmons (2000) emphasize that school leaders must distribute leadership, but they warn that simply delegating tasks constitutes "responsibility without authority" (p. 10). Instead, they advocate that school leaders distribute leadership by involving teachers in reflective practice to develop a shared mission. This call, like that of Cochran-Smith and Lytle (2001), requires flexibility in leadership, innovative approaches to problem solving, collaborative decision making, and constant experimentation (Hackney & Henderson, 1999).

Blase and Blase (2001) highlight the principal's role in building an organizational structure grounded in teacher reflection and shared governance: "The principal's role becomes one of communicating, coordinating, fostering mutual problem solving, and providing resources for effective work" (p. 77). Establishing structures for discussion is a crucial step that helps teachers become more invested in inquiry and the shared governance process (Blase & Blase, 2001; McLaughlin & Zarrow, 2001). The "structures" that Blase and Blase (2001) recommend include providing opportunities and adequate time to meet, ensuring inclusion of faculty and staff in shared decision making, and participating as an equal player in the shared decision-making process.

According to Blase and Blase (2001), teachers also reported increased motivation when participating in reflective practice. Another benefit they cite is an increase in teachers' sense of ownership—at both the group level and the individual level—in terms of processes and outcomes. Last, they note that teachers expressed a greater sense of professionalism, experiencing more respect and trust in their ability to participate in reflection and decision making.

A Developmental View of Collegial Inquiry

Collegial inquiry is a developmental practice that holds the potential to provide a supportive, safe environment for individuals to develop greater awareness of their beliefs and assumptions and to reflect with others in ways that may allow them to envision alternative ways of thinking, acting, or behaving. Encouraging this practice helps create a space that serves as a holding environment. Inevitably, though, people's different ways of knowing influence how they will make use of and experience the practice of collegial inquiry (see Table 7.1).

As Table 7.1 shows, instrumental knowers in a discussion might focus on concrete goals and guidelines, as opposed to abstract purposes, whereas socializing knowers, who seek to gain approval from authorities and to meet their expectations, will likely defer to authority figures before voicing their own stances. Self-authoring individuals, however, will be able to consider others' perspectives in relation to their own preestablished ideas. A more complex discussion of the implications of different ways of knowing within collegial inquiry is undertaken in the case study later in this chapter.

By supporting the person's meaning making and appropriately challenging his or her way of knowing, I suggest that collegial inquiry can support a person's growth to a more complex way of knowing and can support development beyond self-authoring. By participating in the reflective discussion demanded by collegial inquiry, teachers are invited to listen actively to the intersections of multiple perspectives, including theoretical, political, and emotional. Over time, conflict and contradiction may yield solutions and lead to the development of a different way of knowing. To make the most of conflict, awareness of inconsistencies in one's own perspective helps in being able to seriously consider new and divergent ideas.

Thus from a developmental view, collegial inquiry provides a safe context within which to voice one's thinking, to challenge participants' assumptions, and, ultimately, to create opportunities for individuals to shift in their thinking and assumptions (i.e., act upon or test new ways of knowing).

Table 7.1 How Adults With Different Ways of Knowing Experience Collegial Inquiry

Way of Knowing	Supports	Challenges (Growing Edge)
Instrumental knowers	• Establishing step-by-step guidelines or rules as to how to engage in discussion. • Sharing the concrete details of their practice and whether it is "right" or "wrong." • Engaging with others in conversation is supportive when it provides them with concrete advice, skills, and information about practice, for example. • Colleagues are experienced as resources with information and skills. • Providing clear descriptions of ways to proceed with conversations and/or reflective writing. • Addressing concrete needs for improving practice (e.g., learning better skills or more effective rules to follow).	Thinking differently—and more abstractly—through discussion and reflection about their own practice and other people's practices and to understand and evaluate themselves through another person's point of view.
Socializing knowers	• Meeting the expectations of valued others and evaluating *themselves* based upon what these other important people think of their ideas. • Acceptance from colleagues will help these knowers feel recognized and safe in taking risks and sharing their own perspectives. • Evaluate their practice through writing. • Sharing their own perspectives in pairs or smaller groups of colleagues before sharing their perspectives with larger groups. • Differences of opinion will be experienced as being okay as long as colleagues remain connected and the interpersonal relationships are not jeopardized.	Developing their *own* beliefs and values independent of what valued others think they *should* be thinking or doing; becoming less dependent on the approval of others.
Self-authoring knowers	• Learning from the *process.* • Learning about their own capabilities and competencies. • Evaluating and critiquing their own practices, decisions, vision, and internally generated standards within the larger context of the school. • Emphasizing becoming more competent and extending one's own options in order to achieve their self-determined goals. • Inviting these knowers to create some of the structures for how to proceed with the process of collegial inquiry (i.e., allowing them to demonstrate some of their competencies and providing some freedom within the structure of group conversations). • Conflict is experienced as a natural part of dialogue that can help the group arrive at better solutions, more effective practice, and/or ideas for implementation.	To be able be less invested in their *own* identities, standards, points of view, and to become more open to and welcoming of standards, values, and points of view that are directly opposed to their own; to experience *themselves* as being process driven.

WHAT PRINCIPALS LIKE
ABOUT COLLEGIAL INQUIRY

The principals in this study explained three underlying reasons for using collegial inquiry: it helps them to include others in leadership, it helps to manage change, and it emphasizes the value of learning from diverse perspectives.

For the principals, collegial inquiry is a way to share power with teachers by asking for honest communication of their ideas for change, school practices, curricula, and policies. Engaging in honest conversations about new ideas and proposed school changes enables teachers to gradually adjust, because these conversations provide a context for teachers to voice concerns and feelings about the impending changes and help principals to appreciate and learn from the teachers' perspectives. In several cases, principals reported that collegial inquiry helps them address conflict around policy, interpersonal, and instructional issues with teachers, which is beneficial regardless of whether outcomes align with expectations. The principals also said that collegial inquiry fosters diversity, thereby strengthening interpersonal relationships. As a practice that helped participants learn from each other's perspectives, it increases community ownership and paves the way for more successful implementation of proposed changes.

Table 7.2 summarizes the reasons why the principals see collegial inquiry as an essential practice and specific examples of how it is used in their schools.

Table 7.2   Collegial Inquiry: Reasons Why Principals Employed This Practice and Its Practical Applications

Collegial Inquiry	Examples
Principals' philosophies and espoused beliefs	• Sharing leadership • Building relationships • Embracing and helping people manage change and fostering diversity
Examples of collegial inquiry	• Free writing in faculty meetings and brainstorming before discussions • Asking for feedback on practices and/or engaging in dialogue about ideas • Journal writing and sharing of thinking; reflection after community events • Goal setting with principals and fellow teachers • Engaging in discussion for conflict resolution

Collegial Inquiry	Examples
	• Engaging in reflection related to classroom practices and student work • Engaging in writing and reflection for the school's self-study • Thinking together about altering curricula or practices and/or developing assessment • Conceptualizing and writing proposals and/or articles • Reflecting on philosophical questions related to practice, mission, and/or testing • Proposal writing (for grants, new programs, sabbatical, graduate study) • Reflecting and creating critical inquiry in faculty meetings • Sabbaticals, in and out of house

EXAMPLES OF PRINCIPALS' USE OF COLLEGIAL INQUIRY

There's nothing like putting together good educators and having them talk with each other about what they're doing. . . . You get a lot of synergy out of that. (Jerry Zank, Canterbury School)

The examples in the following discussion are grouped into four broad categories that highlight the ways in which the principals employ collegial inquiry: reflection through writing, through dialogue and feedback, through decision making, and through serving as key consultants and/or researchers.

Reflection Through Writing

Whenever I begin to think about something differently, the first thing I do is try to clarify my own thinking. I find writing a powerful tool for this purpose. Although time is precious and writing hard, the benefits almost always outweigh the difficulties. (Dr. Sarah Levine)

A common theme that emerged from these principals, across school type, was that writing is a tool for their reflection and clarification of ideas.

The writing often takes the form of "free writes," journal entries, or proposals for their teachers and their own professional development or some other area of interest.

Free Writing

Free writing is a practice that invites people to respond in writing to a question, a sentence stem, or a quotation by writing their unedited thoughts in reaction to the prompt. When free writing, a person is to write down exactly what he or she is thinking, giving no attention to self-censoring, grammar, or syntax. The main idea is to think freely on paper. For example, in the belief that improved thinking can be facilitated through writing, discussions about writings, and shared reflection, at the beginning of a meeting, Dr. Sarah Levine, former head of Belmont Day and Polytechnic Schools, would invite group participants to reflect privately by writing responses to a question. During one faculty meeting, Sarah asked every teacher and administrator to write about "What do I think about being evaluated?" Upon completion, Sarah invited people to share some of their thinking and writing and remarked, "We had a great discussion about people's fears and hopes about the evaluation process." Sometimes, after a few minutes of writing, ideas or key concepts were noted on a pad of paper attached to an easel located in the front of the room. After several minutes of such sharing, the community would discuss, debate, support, and challenge the ideas, issues, and concerns expressed.[1]

Journal Keeping

Another form of writing principals named was journal keeping. Sarah, like other principals in this study, also thought it important that she, the teachers, and administrators model the value of journal writing and sharing for the children: "The message that our work merits reflection and that writing is important is a good thing for kids and for us [adults] too." Teachers are able to discuss important and sensitive personal and professional issues in these contexts.

Proposal Writing

At all of the independent schools in this sample and many of the public and Catholic schools, teachers reflect through proposal writing. For instance, the principals ask teachers to write proposals to apply for funds to support their professional development, stating that doing so encourages them to clarify ideas and take responsibility for asserting their own needs. For example, Dr. Sue David (a pseudonym) stated:

Each year in late March, I send a letter to the entire faculty, asking them to apply for professional development funds by a particular deadline. And that gets them to think about what they want to do over the summer or to plan ahead in the next academic year.

Dr. Mary Nash, principal of the Mary Lyons Alternative (public elementary) School, also employs the practice of writing to facilitate reflection. At one point, a teacher requested that she be moved to a different class, and Mary told her why that move would not be possible. But to encourage reflection, she invited the teacher to write a proposal and clarify her reasons for wanting to switch classes. The teacher wrote "the finest 16-page presentation" and convinced Mary to make the switch.

Reflection Through Dialogue

Throughout the interviews, these principals discussed reflective practice in two different, yet complementary, ways. At times, they used the term *reflective practice* to refer to teachers knowing why they are doing what they are doing in their classrooms. This seemed to refer to the need for teachers to have a sense of *purposefulness* about their teaching and a devoted attention to what works for their students. In other words, they need to be able to articulate these purposes for others.

At other times, many principals employed the term to refer to teachers'—and their own—*awareness* or *mindfulness* about themselves as teachers.[2] In this case, reflective practice was understood as a questioning and learning tool for reflecting on what works well in their craft and what does not. Many topics for reflection arose out of teachers' own practice in the process of engaging in dialogue, including the following:

- Developing accountability systems
- Integrating innovations
- Developing strategies to assess student work and measure achievement
- Developing a shared sense of purpose within a school
- Improving teaching quality and the professional development for teachers

For example, Dr. Larry Myatt, principal and founder of the Fenway pilot high school in Boston, explained that creating spaces for teachers to engage in meaningful dialogue about their practice is vital to supporting teacher learning. "Getting people out, out of the box, out of the classroom" is important because it helps with "unpacking our own baggage." Teachers, Larry explained, were initially sometimes resistant to some of these conversations about curricula and other school issues, but now they look forward to them. Larry discussed how this has helped the school culture develop in terms of both purposefulness in their teaching *and* mindfulness of themselves as educators. Larry pointed out that "helping them to learn *how* to talk" is an essential ingredient in collegial inquiry.

Like Larry, Dr. Jim Cavanaugh, principal of Watertown high school, emphasized that "being reflective about your practice is the key." For Jim, this is the ultimate way to raise student achievement. Rather than putting themselves on "automatic pilot," teachers need to ask themselves and each other about how they know that students have learned (or have not learned) something, which is a "deep question." In his view, this changes the focus from "covering the material" to making "student learning and performance the priority." Jim feels that teachers—and all adults—need to have self-awareness, which he sees as developing through the process of dialogue.

Curriculum Development

Mrs. Kathleen Perry explained that teachers engage in the dialogue necessary to reflective practice by developing curricula during full-day seminars. Kathleen emphasized how dialogue helps teachers to reflect on their practice (in terms of *purposefulness*) and how it helps them develop a heightened *mindfulness* about what works well for them. Teachers have one day in every nine weeks to discuss curricula, during which time they dialogue about what is working for them and the difficulties they encounter.

Similarly, at Punahoe School teachers engage in both *purposeful* and *mindful* collegial inquiry as they map the curricula. The purpose of curriculum mapping, Dr. Jim Scott explained, is "to uncover some of these differences [in teaching and implementation] and promote an environment for discussion." He hopes that dialogue about curriculum mapping will help teachers learn about "inconsistencies" in their teaching and guide them toward change. He described how he has worked to help faculty strive toward "unfreezing of some of the old assumptions about, 'we can't do this, can't do this.'"

Faculty Meetings

Many of the principals encourage dialogue by using faculty meetings differently. Instead of focusing on nuts-and-bolts-type issues, they engage teachers in discussion about larger, more important issues. Some of the principals reported that they also invest time in faculty meetings in developing strategies for improvement or implementation of new ideas. About one-third of the principals indicated that they would like to move more of the routine information that is shared at faculty meetings to other vehicles for communication (e.g., e-mail) so that they can devote more meeting time to "issues of substance."

Dr. Dan White of Seabury Hall in Maui, Hawaii, explained that these reflective conversations help faculty—and him—to better understand students' needs. For example, one year, the Life and Development Committee sensed that there was a problem with how much homework students were receiving. At the start of the next year, he explained, a faculty meeting was devoted to reflecting on questions related to what should be the right amount of homework assigned to the kids, and they engaged in discussion about this issue. Dan also felt that there may be times when teachers have to cut some "slack" for kids who have a crisis at home. He hopes that such conversations will broaden teachers' perspectives about various student needs.

Sr. Joan Magnetti of the Convent of the Sacred Heart School in Greenwich, Connecticut, said that she includes the entire school community in some faculty meetings to reflect during the school's quinquennial self-study. Sr. Magnetti explained that the purpose of the study is to heighten community *awareness* of the school mission, such as,

> How well are we doing in making sure that that mission is alive and palpable and not just a nice thing that sits on the shelf? . . . If we really want to look at issues of racial diversity, well, why? What's the benefit of just having more Hispanic and black children? How are we educating all together? . . . How do we deal with difference and prejudice in the larger world? What is it in our system that's warm and inclusive, and what of it is not? And how do we get over dealing with kids who have a lot of money and some kids who have no money?

Sr. Magnetti emphasized that this dialogical process involves faculty, alumnae, parents, kids, faculty, secretaries, maintenance people, trustees, and administration "to make sure that we follow through on fine-tuning and strengthening the way in which we carry [the mission and its development] out here."

Conflict Resolution

Several of the principals encourage collegial inquiry to resolve conflicts, build awareness, and sharpen teachers' sense of purpose. For example, Sr. Barbara Rogers wants teachers to reflect on the ways in which they support or challenge America's consumer culture, that is, the high value many people place on acquiring possessions. She provided an example of athletics, where teams often want to have jackets to demonstrate their pride. When I asked her how she made sense of this, she explained,

> One of the hardest things is to get a coach to understand is "Yeah, [asking students to purchase team jackets] might be a great idea, but

it might not be really something that everyone on the team can do. . . ." So we're participating in this culture that we really want to stand in opposition to. . . . But how do we raise their level or awareness about . . . we don't need one more sweatshirt, one more jacket.

This is one example of how Sr. Rogers intentionally creates spaces where the community engages in shared dialogue as they work to resolve conflicts. Such conversations, in her view, help the community to develop greater awareness of how their thinking and actions align with the school mission.

Reflection Through Decision Making

Several school leaders feel that explicit conversations about decision-making processes (e.g., mission and school goals) could transform their communities.

For example, Ms. Mary Newman, head of Buckingham, Browne, and Nichols K–12 independent school in Cambridge, told me that dialogue and reflection are natural processes by which the school community makes shared decisions (e.g., about practice and its connection to the school mission) because they have been used since the school's inception a century ago. From Mary's perspective, her teachers, administrators, and staff "are always asking the tough questions of ourselves" when engaged in shared decision making. In fact, Mary believes that there are times when people need to learn to take a rest and appreciate what they have accomplished because "everybody is always thinking about what they can do and what they can do better."

Dr. Jim Cavanaugh of Watertown High School shared the complexities of needing to make decisions about faculty evaluations while building an atmosphere of trust. Like Jim, his coordinators of various disciplines (e.g., technology) and two assistant principals also evaluate teachers and provide written narratives of evaluation. They engage with teachers in collegial inquiry toward shared decision making as part of this practice. The school, Jim explained, is now restructuring this process so that teachers are even more involved in making decisions about the areas of focus for evaluation. This has helped the school to shift from formative and summative evaluations (the old way of conducting evaluations) to a new model—where Jim and each teacher decide on "two or three areas that we agree mutually, the teacher and I, we'll focus on."

Reflection Through Serving as
Key Consultants and/or Researchers

Internal and external sabbaticals and workshops were named by close to one-third of the principals as important opportunities for teachers to engage in collegial inquiry—and then to share their thinking with the broader school community.

While creating opportunities for teachers to engage in reflective practice, Dr. Sue David also encourages teachers to leave the school campus for professional development. For Sue, this promotes "empirically testing, if you will, the validity of your own educational philosophy or pedagogy or ideas."

Dr. Mary Nash described an important learning event at Mary Lyons School in Brighton, Massachusetts. As a team of researchers, she and the teachers flew down to New York to visit a school with a well-developed literacy program to better understand that model and to develop their own. They debriefed in the airport cocktail lounge, discussing the things that they saw that they liked and wanted to try. These conversations about their research continued throughout the year and served as rich contexts to carefully examine practice, make improvements based on research, and support teacher learning.

At Dr. Jim Scott's school, the Punahoe School, teachers engage in collegial inquiry as they conduct research on their own and other schools' practices. Jim explained that teachers "can apply for learning fellowships, which allows them to teach with a reduced class load and meet together to try and implement change based on research and study they have conducted." Upon completing their research, they share what they have learned with colleagues and with Jim, and together they translate results to their own school programs. One of Jim's hopes is to encourage teachers to reflect more on global education and instructional technology, and he hopes to send teachers to "different parts of the world together, and to reflect on . . . how it may affect the curriculum."

Jim is also entertaining the idea of instituting an "in-house sabbatical." For example, he would like a teacher to investigate software and recommend programs that would be useful to the school. Jim sees in-house sabbaticals as opportunities for a person to be "a thinker, reflector, reader, traveler."

DEVELOPMENTAL BENEFITS OF COLLEGIAL INQUIRY

Engaging in collegial inquiry helps teachers explore and challenge their own and others' thinking through writing and/or discussing of ideas, premises, or assumptions. Engaging in this practice provides a structure for reflection, problem solving, decision making, and development.

The principals in this sample prioritize the development and learning of those around them. While nearly all value both support and challenge, 16 said that sometimes they tend to put more emphasis on the "challenge" side of the learning and development equation than on the "support" side (this, they explained, was especially true in their early years as leaders). Prioritizing time needed for teachers to collaborate reflectively within the school is important to the majority of these principals.

A CASE STUDY: USING COLLEGIAL INQUIRY IN COLLABORATIVE GOAL SETTING AND EVALUATION

The more I have learned about how adults grow, however, the more respect I have for the complexities of growth. (Dr. Sarah Levine, Polytechnic School)

In this section, I will describe how Sarah Levine engaged in the process of collegial inquiry in goal setting and evaluation with the teachers, administrators, and staff at the Belmont Day School.[3] I also discuss how developmental theory informs the practice of collegial inquiry, by illuminating the ways in which people with different ways of knowing may experience and make sense of this process.

The Goal-Setting and Evaluation Process

Each fall, Sarah asked faculty, administrators, and staff to write and submit two personal and two professional goals related to "the areas of teaching and support for the school community." Sarah was interested in having teachers become more involved in the larger community of the school and to assume greater leadership in the classroom. For example, as part of the goal-setting process, Sarah encouraged teachers to form and to join action research groups wherein they investigated questions related to their practice. She also supported staff members in leading groups wherein they shared their personal and professional expertise (e.g., poetry-writing seminars, dance, and knowledge of using computer application programs).

Each faculty and staff member chose three evaluators to assess his or her performance in meeting-stated goals. These evaluators could be colleagues, administrators, division directors, or Sarah herself. Sarah thought it important that adults feel comfortable with their evaluators and that accepting responsibility for choosing their own evaluators might help them to feel empowered.

In addition to the three evaluators, throughout the year Sarah often talked informally with community members about their goals and asked them what support they needed from her or others in order to achieve their goals. She also provided support to faculty by periodically observing their teaching and offering both written and verbal feedback. Occasionally, she invited the school psychologist to observe teaching in order to incorporate yet another perspective. Sarah also enlisted the two division directors in providing support to teachers with respect to their goals for improving their teaching and new curricular ideas.

In the spring of each year, Sarah met with every adult to talk about progress during the past year and about areas for growth in the coming year. In preparation for the annual goal-setting and evaluation meetings, Sarah asked all teachers, staff members, and administrators to write self-evaluations of their goals and the progress they had made in meeting them. She also conferred beforehand with the division directors about teachers' progress and used these comments to inform her discussions with them. Sarah's aim in these sessions was to provide teachers with helpful feedback; however, she acknowledged that doing so was "hard, and this is where development comes in too, because people hear feedback really differently. Their tolerance for negative feedback is very different." Sarah intended to create a context within which she and a community member could productively reflect in a way that was "mutually support-ive" of their interests and needs. She believed that her "ability to see the boundaries of other people" gave her "more resources for helping" others in this process.

Teacher Responses to the Process

Several teachers spoke about how the above process was inspiring to them and stimulated them to take the process more seriously. One teacher felt that Sarah's sharing of her own ideas had "made people stop and think about what their goals are, what their aims are, and share them with others." Another teacher, Paul, said that he appreciated Sarah's informal observa-tions in his classroom, as well as her feedback. Although he acknowledged that the process of setting and reviewing goals was important and thought-provoking, he believed that Sarah should invite teachers to help shape the goal-setting process instead of designing it herself. He wanted to have some "input" about the format and the types of goals discussed. In his view, Sarah "set up the format, and we were told how we were supposed to do it." Another teacher, who had been at the school for more than a decade, said that the format of goal setting seemed to affect how some teachers experi-enced the process. In his view, some misunderstood the process as a require-ment merely to list all the things that they did at the school.

Several teachers felt that the personal goals they set needed to be in some way aligned with the school's larger mission. One teacher said that there were times when his personal goals were in "conflict" with the larger community goals. For example, at times, he believed that his ideas about the role of parents in the school were in conflict with those of most com-munity members, and he questioned the degree to which academics were the focus in the early grades.

Some teachers experienced the process of goal setting and evaluation as challenging, yet supportive; others felt that Sarah was encouraging them to take on goals too challenging for them. One teacher said she believed some teachers would prefer not to engage in the process at all.

Developmental Lessons

Sarah's stated intention was to provide a collegial exploration in a reflective context; however, the ways in which community members experienced this process were diverse. Some individuals experienced collegial inquiry as a welcome gift, whereas others experienced it as difficult or threatening. Based on the ways in which teachers experienced collegial inquiry differentially, I suggest that differences may have been due to the way in which they were making meaning of the implicit and explicit demands of the process. Of course, there could be alternative reasons for this, such as a personality clash or stress.

For example, Sarah's role as a critical friend who offered both challenge and support may have been experienced quite differently by people at different developmental levels. How might the goal-setting process be a challenge for a socializing knower or a self-authoring knower?

There are several reasons why goal setting might be difficult or challenging for a socializing knower. For socializing knowers, approval from others (authorities and valued colleagues), acceptance, and being liked are critical to the cohesion of the self. Acceptance from Sarah (who would likely be considered an external and valued authority) would be important for teachers with this way of knowing. For teachers with a socializing way of knowing to be invited into a goal-setting session and asked to share their goals with Sarah (the external authority and boss), a developmental demand may have been placed upon their way of knowing that they could not yet meet. They may not yet have developed the capacity to look to an internal set of standards (or authority). Their concerns about the interpersonal relationship would be far more important; they would look to Sarah, the authority figure, to suggest goals. Take the case of a socializing knower who, instead of stating goals that she thinks would be appropriate for herself, formulates goals that she thinks Sarah would support, feel good about, and with which Sarah could easily agree. In another case, if a socializing knower were invited by Sarah to revise his goals, he might interpret such an invitation as meaning that his goals were somehow inadequate or wrong; the invitation could be seen as a rejection of his goals. He might think that Sarah expressed disapproval of him and not merely of his goals.

The opportunity to formulate appropriate goals might be beyond the developmental capacity of a socializing knower. However, with appropriate supports and challenges to the way socializing knowers make sense of experience, the goal-setting context might very well serve as one that helps them come to a new relationship to their own thinking (that is, from being identified with aspects of their thinking to being able to look at these aspects or take a perspective on them and evaluate them). Support for people with this way of knowing might take the form of encouraging them to look at themselves, first, in order to formulate goals in a supportive context of colleagues before writing up their goals. Socializing knowers might best be supported in their development if they were explicitly encouraged to talk through the goals *they* would like to achieve in the coming year.

A self-authoring knower would be more aware of his or her own theory of teaching and might feel much more comfortable articulating and making those assumptions known. Self-authoring knowers have the capacity to reflect internally and appeal to an internal system in developing and presenting goals. They might be more friendly and open to making their assumptions known, even assumptions that were hidden or unknown to them prior to collegial inquiry making them more apparent.

Kegan and Lahey (1984) state that self-authoring knowers are primarily concerned with their performance at work. They are no longer subject to (identified with) interpersonal relationships but can now take a perspective on them. A self-authoring knower now has his or her *own* set of internal standards, which are the source of evaluation. With this way of knowing, individuals have the developmental capacity to critique and evaluate their own goals and progress toward them. A limit to the self-authoring way of knowing is that it may be difficult to hear alternatives or consider them as being acceptable alternative goals for one's self. For example, a person may have a set of goals he believes to be best for himself. While engaging in the collegial inquiry process with someone making meaning in this way, Sarah would support the person's growth by suggesting alternative goals to consider or by asking questions about how he came to decide on those goals. She might also invite the person to elaborate on his existing theory about his work or pose challenging questions that ask him to reconsider alternatives.

However, such a teacher (or administrator) might experience Sarah's suggestions offered in the spirit of inquiry as threatening. He may feel that he is being *forced to adopt* a goal that is not aligned with the way he wishes his system to run. Support for self-authoring knowers might take the form of inviting them to test alternative, competing ideas. If, after testing them, they find that the alternatives did not work for them, they may well return to prior goals or ways of behaving.

Developing Others as Leaders

Sarah seemed to be aware that her own development and way of knowing was important to how she would support others in the goal-setting and evaluation process. She developed the following "hypothesis":

> To support other people's growth most effectively, you [the leader] have to be at a least a stage apart, a half-stage apart from where they are so your developmental growing doesn't always bump up against theirs.

Michael McKibben and Bruce Joyce (1986) argue that environments need to be directed just above the level at which a person functions most comfortably. Kegan's theory (1982, 1994) suggests that it is important, first and foremost, to determine how a person is making sense of his or her experience; and then it becomes important to facilitate growth toward a more complex level of development. The learning environment must be a context supportive of growth; it becomes a "holding environment" for growth.

Sarah's knowledge of the developmental needs of adults seemed to inform her interactions with members in this process by

1. Offering different supports and challenge to individuals who were setting goals

2. Seeking to create holding environments that would be developmentally appropriate to adults with different ways of knowing

For example, she encouraged certain community members who appeared "ready" to take on different types of organizational goals to "stretch" themselves. She encouraged others to focus on personal goals or classroom-related goals that were more appropriate for them. I suggest that Sarah was providing teachers with the opportunity to actually name aspects of their own thinking, a space for them to be *in relationship to their thinking*. The goal-setting and evaluation process seemed to offer an opportunity for individuals to *alter* their thinking and test new ways of thinking. However, it is equally important to emphasize that this process should be more "self-regulating" because taking greater responsibility in the process may have been experienced as a *developmental demand*, which may have been beyond some members' developmental capacities.

Supporting people in their current ways of knowing was important to Sarah. These supports for developing capacities, in Sarah's view, included accepting people as they were, listening closely to the ways in which they were experiencing their work and achievement of their goals, and finding ways to appropriately challenge their thinking. Sarah's understanding of individuals' needs, developmental theory, and human resistance to change seemed to inform how she engaged in a process of support and challenge.

Summary

Constructive-developmental theory offers a powerful lens with which to better understand the process of collegial inquiry; it informs thinking about how best to create a context supportive of development. Sarah appears to have focused her efforts on providing effective and appropriate holding environments of challenge and support. Sarah, like other principals in this sample, valued creating opportunities that would support the growth and development of the adults within the school.

As shown, teachers' reactions to Sarah's work with goal setting indicates that they had varied ways of making sense of the goal-setting process. Sarah seemed to appreciate the ways in which developmental theory can inform understanding about how to support teacher growth. Sarah's leadership work, like that of other principals in this sample, was in a very real sense designed to acknowledge more than merely *what* adults know; it was also a leadership supportive of transformational learning.

CHAPTER SUMMARY

For the most part, the principals in this study believe that schools run best when the teachers have a voice in sharing leadership, shaping the community, and promoting change. They use collegial inquiry to invite teachers to reflect upon the school's mission, practices, and proposals for change. Sharing perspectives and listening to others is a way of encouraging adults at school to work together and to assume shared responsibility in shaping the school community.

The examples I discussed earlier and the case study illustrate how collegial inquiry provides a context within which the teachers can reflect together while learning more about their own assumptions. By asking questions and by listening carefully, these principals create contexts within which teachers—and they themselves—come to better appreciate the diverse perspectives of colleagues. Sharing perspectives about curricula and proposed changes are ways to openly communicate. Collegial inquiry helps teachers and principals to better understand the reasons why some advocate strongly for certain changes in curricula or schoolwide change, and also the reasons why others appear to resist with conviction.

By employing collegial inquiry, the principals work to build a community in which members are encouraged to bring their contributions to the dialogue. Diversity of perspectives, they explained, is an opportunity for learning as well as for individual and collective transformation.

REFLECTIVE QUESTIONS

Please consider how constructive developmental theory may play a critical role in how teachers engage with collegial inquiry as you respond to the following questions. They can be used for internal reflection or to open up a group discussion.

1. What are two practices you employ to help teachers reflect on their teaching? On schoolwide issues?

2. What do you notice about the various ways in which teachers are able to participate in these reflective conversations?

3. How do you think teachers with different ways of knowing engage in practices involving collegial inquiry at your school?

4. How do you employ writing as a tool for reflection?

5. How do you think that teachers select and evaluate criteria for their annual goals? How would they do this if they were socializing knowers? What might matter most to them?

6. How do you think teachers with a self-authoring way of knowing select and evaluate criteria for their goals? What might matter most to them?

7. Whose evaluation matters most when teachers with different ways of knowing are invited to revise their goals? What is at stake for individuals (with different ways of knowing) as they engage in collegial inquiry?

NOTES

1. This example is discussed in different form in Drago-Severson (1996).
2. I acknowledge Deb Helsing for her help in thinking through this idea.
3. A version of this section appears in different form in Drago-Severson (1996).

8

Mentoring

A Powerful Means of Facilitating Learning

In this chapter, I discuss how the principals in the study understand the practice of mentoring and how it can support teachers' transformational learning. Across school types and resource levels, these principals believe mentoring invites teachers to share leadership and helps them to manage change. The various types of mentoring programs they have implemented include pairing experienced teachers with new teachers, pairing teachers with deep knowledge of school mission with other teachers, and pairing experienced teachers with local graduate student interns. When I refer to "mentees," I include teachers at any stage of their careers, not only interns or inexperienced teachers.

Mentoring is necessarily related to providing teachers with leadership roles and collegial inquiry. As with these other practices, many principals remarked that mentoring is a reciprocal learning opportunity, meaning that mentees *and* mentors reap benefits from mentoring, because both learn as a result of the relationship. Acting as a mentor is a leadership role, and mentoring creates opportunities for perspective broadening and examination of assumptions. However, mentoring is distinct in three ways. First, mentoring allows for leadership roles that are less public and formal, offering leadership opportunities to those who might prefer a more private setting. Second, mentoring is often used to introduce new members of a community to the school, to foster their belonging and ownership of the mission in a social and less pedagogical setting. Third, mentoring typically operates in one-on-one relationships, versus collegial inquiry, which primarily occurs in groups. As a paired rather than group practice, mentoring seems to offer a more personalized learning option for individuals in terms of their ways of knowing, the specific material they seek to learn, and their personal needs.

ABOUT MENTORING

Research shows that creating opportunities for teachers to become mentors within their schools is a practice that supports teacher learning (Saphier, Freedman, & Aschheim, 2001). Several researchers see mentoring in particular as one means of addressing the teacher attrition problem. Mentoring that pairs experienced teachers with new and also seasoned teachers helps to make both feel "more comfortable and personally connected" (Pappano, 2001, p. L6).

Theoretical Principles of Mentoring

Although mentoring is arguably one of the oldest models for human development, research has only recently begun to address it as a model for supporting teacher learning within schools (Saphier et al., 2001; Wollman-Bonilla, 1997). The professional development literature commonly defines mentoring as the relationship between an experienced or veteran teacher and a less experienced one, with the former offering support and advice, curriculum help, and guidance in classroom management (Fagan & Walter, 1982; Galvez-Hjornevik, 1986; Kram, 1983; Saphier et al., 2001; Wollman-Bonilla, 1997). Whether participating in a formal or informal mentoring program, a mentor is traditionally conceived as a friend, a guide, and, above all else, a teacher (Collins, 1993; Levinson & Levinson, 1996; Merriam, 1983). Through this relationship, the (usually) younger mentees are expected to become more autonomous (Kram, 1983), more comfortable in their work life (Little, 1990), and more reflective (Darwin, 2000) and to learn skills to enhance their teaching.

One common belief is that mentoring skills can be taught through training (Fagan & Walter, 1982; Saphier et al., 2001), which occurs in the context of a personal relationship (Daloz, 1983, 1999; Killion, 2000; Merriam, 1983). Many suggest that mentoring works best when a proven veteran teacher is assigned a newer teacher who has a similar teaching assignment (Compton, 1979; Wollman-Bonilla, 1997). Others claim that the mentoring relationship works well when the two have similar philosophies of teaching (Huling-Austin, Barnes, & Smith, 1985) or are the same age, gender, position, and confidence levels (Hunt & Michael, 1983; Levinson & Levinson, 1996). Still others claim that the success of the relationship does not depend on a personality feature or common background, but rather on the ability to work together (Otto, 1994). Most recently, a track record as a successful teacher, a commitment to mentoring, and "a communication style that adapts to individual differences" have been identified in successful mentors (Saphier et al., 2001, p. 32).

As I said earlier, Killion (2000) points out that teachers generally construct knowledge from their experiences and rarely share this "private knowledge" with anyone (p. 3). This knowledge, she explains, stems from asking themselves questions about their classroom experiences. Killion believes that professional development programs can encourage this kind of analysis in a context of collaboration, to break teacher isolation. She emphasizes how the practice of mentoring can enhance reflection and learning. Beginning teachers, she explains, benefit from mentors who share teaching tools and research, and who articulate their own experiences with implementing these tools and research.

While mentoring clearly supports relational growth, we need a better sense of how different mentoring programs work, how teachers experience them, and how school context can enhance these relationships.

A Developmental View of Mentoring

Mentoring is a practice that, by its very nature, can build greater capacities to manage the complexities of work and life. As found in this study, both mentors and mentees are often invited to share their reflections. Dialogue on classroom practice, improving skills, or expressing vulnerabilities is inherent to this practice. Over time, this dialogue offers an opportunity for *both* participants to challenge their thinking, reshape their assumptions, and grow to more complex ways of knowing. As both participants better understand the values they bring to the teaching process, mentoring can support transformational learning.

Daloz applies Kegan's constructive-developmental theory (1982, 1994) to mentoring and suggests that the relationship can provide a "holding environment" for transforming ways of knowing. Daloz (2000) argues that the mentor acts as a bridge in that he or she must support the mentee's current meaning making while providing the necessary challenges and continuity for development. Support, as Daloz (1986) explains, is "the activity of holding, of providing a place where [a person] can contact her need for fundamental trust, the basis of growth" (p. 215). Mentors can provide trust by attending to mentees' meaning making, expressing positive expectations, advocating for the mentee, and creating a safe space for growth (Daloz, 1983, 1999).

It is important to recognize that the mentoring relationship may be influenced by both partners' ways of knowing. This developmental mindfulness can help in understanding how mentees will experience the advice and guidance based on their way of knowing, as well as how mentors may make sense of the experience. As such, the mentor relationship has the potential to enhance the development of both individuals (Drago-Severson, 2002; Kram, 1983).

Principals who understand mentoring from a developmental perspective may be better able to support teachers in their mentoring practices. Table 8.1 highlights how mentees with socializing and self-authoring ways of knowing may make sense of the mentoring experience. As Table 8.1 shows, socializing knowers first and foremost seek approval from important others, such as mentors. Rather than viewing the relationship as an opportunity for critical feedback, socializing knowers may believe it is an arena for positive reinforcement. They may thus feel threatened if the feedback is perceived as critical or negative.

Also recall that socializing knowers are not yet able to take a perspective on the interpersonal relationship. If invited to express a point of view, they will look to their mentors for the "right" opinion and adopt it. Mentors working with colleagues with this way of knowing can, first of all, explicitly validate their points of view. In addition, it would be wise to gradually encourage mentees to look internally for what *they* believe before sharing one's own perspective as mentor. The mentoring relationship could likely provide a safe context in which socializing knowers feel accepted and comfortable in expressing themselves, enabling them to ask questions and take greater risks.

Helping mentees with this way of knowing to increasingly see themselves as authorities will facilitate growth. Kegan and Lahey's (2001) work highlights the importance of "ongoing regard," where statements of appreciation and admiration shape development. Such a context holds opportunities for supporting adults with *all* ways of knowing, but especially socializing knowers.

Teachers who are self-authoring knowers would likely feel supported if a mentor provided feedback on performing their work more effectively. Because a person with this way of knowing has the capacity for self-evaluation, a mentoring relationship can be an opportunity to improve performance with external help and criticism. Self-authoring knowers have the capacity to reflect on multiple perspectives simultaneously. Achievement for achievement's sake, as opposed to others' approval, is more important to them, and their performance will be measured against internal standards. They will understand mentoring as a context for collaboration with another person to improve and to grow.

Conflict and difference of opinion will be experienced as a natural part of the relationship in service of bigger goals, such as improving thinking and practice. Because self-authoring knowers want their own self-systems to run smoothly, challenging them to consider disparate perspectives will challenge them and support their growth.

Mentoring, like the other three pillars, is a robust practice in that it can support and challenge teachers with different ways of knowing and provide holding environments for growth.

Table 8.1   How Mentees With Different Ways of Knowing Experience Mentoring

Way of Knowing	Supports	Challenge (Growing Edge)
Socializing knowers	• Explicitly acknowledge others' beliefs and points of view. • Confirming and accepting these knowers' selves and their own beliefs. • Feeling known and accepted.	• Looking to oneself and one's own views in the relationship. • Constructing one's own values and standards rather than co-constructing them with mentors. • Tolerating and accepting conflict, conflicting points of view on an issue, or solutions without feeling that it threatens the mentoring relationship. • Separating one's own feelings and responsibilities as distinct from the mentor's feelings. • Separating one's own feelings and point of view from one's need to be accepted by the mentor.
Self-authoring knowers	• Providing opportunities to demonstrate one's own competencies. • Learning about diverse points of view. • Creating spaces in the mentoring relationship for analyzing and critiquing one's own work. • Providing information and practices that help teachers improve and move forward with their own self-determined goals.	• Letting go of one's investment and identification with one's own understanding, or strategies without feeling internally conflicted. • Setting aside one's own standards for practice and/or values and opening up to other people's values. • Acknowledging values of others that may be in direct opposition to one's own. • Accepting mentor's different approaches to the process of exploring a problem.

WHAT PRINCIPALS LIKE ABOUT MENTORING

> I love mentoring people. So I think mentoring, for me, it's like teaching. You know, it's learning more about yourself by working with other people. (Barbara Chase, Philips Andover Academy)

Nearly all of the principals discussed how they benefit from the help of mentors in their own professional development. Many principals in this study echoed Barbara Chase's view (above) about the importance and growth-enhancing benefits of mentoring.

Almost all of the principals in this study have mentoring programs at their schools. Most programs are voluntary for teachers. However, in the Boston and Florida public schools, all first-year teachers are assigned mentors. All of the principals' programs are at different stages of development, and almost all principals want to improve existing programs or, in cases where a program did not exist, build one. The programs varied in purpose, including

- Exchanging information
- Providing emotional support to new *and* experienced teachers
- "Mission spreading" to supporting graduate student interns

Most often, experienced teachers volunteer or are "encouraged" to participate as mentors. As I will describe, principals select mentors according to different criteria, including understanding of the mission, teaching experience, disciplinary focus, and/or other nonacademic characteristics.

These principals reported that mentoring provides opportunities for transformational learning to both teachers and themselves. Most principals in this study also use mentoring to share leadership, strengthen relationships within their schools, and help adults to manage change and diversity. Two major reasons why the principals value mentoring programs are that they provide a mechanism through which teachers of all levels of experience can support each other and through which they can share their expertise. Mentoring serves as a context for individual and shared reflection, which they name as essential to supporting teacher learning. As Table 8.2 shows, across all school types and to different degrees, principals implemented mentoring practices in a variety of ways, for several different purposes. However, in almost all cases, the principals explained that mentoring supports both the mentor's and the mentee's learning in important ways.

There are three lessons that emerged from the principals' practices of mentoring. First, as mentioned, almost all of the principals discussed how their own mentors contribute to their self- and leadership development and personal lives. Second, they spoke less about this initiative than the

Table 8.2   Mentoring: Reasons Why Principals Employed Mentoring and Its Practical Applications

Mentoring	*Examples*
Philosophy (espoused beliefs)	• Sharing leadership • Embracing and helping people manage change and fostering diversity • Building community

Reported purposes and selection criteria	• Mentoring (multiple purposes)
	  - The *purposes* of these programs vary and range from:
	    mission spreading to exchanging information to providing social or relational support to new teachers and/or staff.
	  - *Selection criteria:* Mentors are selected according to different criteria including:
	    knowledge and understanding of the mission, teaching experience, disciplinary focus, and/or other characteristics (nonacademic).

Examples of mentoring	• Mentoring: pairing experienced teachers with new teachers or teachers who are new to the school. • Experienced teachers who are familiar with the mission are paired with new teachers or teachers new to the school to help them understand the mission. • Experienced teachers mentor intern teachers (graduate students, interns); intern teachers and practicing teachers are paired to help interns learn about teaching and culture of the school. • Mentors teach other teachers to become mentors.

other three practices described in prior chapters. While I did not probe them about it, I do not believe that the time spent discussing this practice reflects the worth they see in it. In fact, the third finding that emerged is that each principal who mentioned mentoring wanted to learn how other schools use it and how developmental principles inform the practice of mentoring. I hope that this chapter is helpful to them and others in their efforts to support teachers' transformational learning.

EXAMPLES OF MENTORING

The following range of examples reflects the principals' belief that an array of mentoring opportunities is important, and it demonstrates their commitment to helping adults build community, in addition to supporting individual's growth.

Pairing New and Experienced Teachers: Sharing Expertise for Growth

In most of the schools in this sample, principals encourage more experienced teachers to share their knowledge with teachers new to their schools or in other disciplines. Mentors have particular areas of expertise, such as disciplinary knowledge or understanding of the school mission. There are two types of mentoring programs in this category. One focuses on supporting new teachers, who are either recent graduates or midcareer professionals entering teaching. The second type of program consists of pairing teachers with varying levels of experience.

Programs for Beginning Teachers

Mentioned earlier, the sample's Boston and Florida public schools require all first-year teachers and occasionally teachers who are new to the school to work with a mentor. Mentors in these leadership roles were often described as guides, coaches, and, in many cases, as learners.

At Lake Worth Community High School, in Lake Worth, Florida, principal Kathleen Perry shared that all teachers new to the county must participate in the Employee Support Program (ESP). At her school, the program centers on a team approach and involves support groups as well as pairing new teachers with volunteer mentors, or "buddy" teachers.

In general, department chairs match the "buddy teachers" by similar disciplinary expertise. In Kathy's view, these relationships help to "decrease isolation" and provide important opportunities for growth. At Lake Worth, the team approach allows for support from a variety of individuals and learning from diverse perspectives on particular issues. These teams consist of individuals across domains, including teachers within and outside the mentee's discipline, an administrator, a department chair, and the technology coordinator. Support, in this case, quickly reaches across areas to include the mentee in the school community.

The team approach enables new teachers to have close relationships with their "buddies" while also benefiting from the teachers who visit their weekly meetings and demonstrate lesson planning or teaching tips. In fact, for the first seven weeks of the academic year, new teachers meet individually with all members of their teams and participate in "new-teacher support groups." These serve as contexts for teachers to "get to know each other" and engage in dialogue about practice.

Employing a team approach to mentoring at Lake Worth, Kathy explained, helps to share information, broaden the perspectives of all involved, and offers support to all teachers—both "new and seasoned." These relationships help to foster a sense of belonging and decrease feelings of isolation. Teachers discuss their expectations, share strategies that work or do not work, and develop a sense of their shared experiences.

Sr. Judith Brady of St. Barnabas High School recently started a mentoring program. It has two components, a "support group" for younger and new teachers, and a pairing of new teachers with more veteran faculty. The purpose of this program, Sr. Judith stated, is to provide a context in which she and more senior teachers share experiences and expertise with new or younger teachers. Sr. Judith facilitates the weekly support groups for new teachers and explained that she initially focused on "sharing information." She reported shifting her focus, however, to asking more questions, such as, "Are there any things that you would like to share with each other?" This creates more opportunities for learning because it emphasizes teacher needs, she explained.

In addition to the mentoring support group, new and younger teachers are paired up with more veteran teachers. This is done even if the more senior teachers have been at the school only a short time, due to teacher turnover and lower financial resources. Sr. Judith feels that if she "can get the right people connected, they can help each other." She also mentioned that the younger teachers "are more geared to working across department lines and more apt to want to do that." In light of this, mentees are often paired with more senior teachers who teach in different disciplines.

Sr. Judith decided to implement the mentoring program because she wanted teachers to talk more with each other. She admitted that on "some days [teachers would] probably be glad for a little isolation," but she still believes that communication is important for new teachers because "we have a school community, and yet much of what you do as a teacher is out there with the kids."

Programs Employing a Staff Developer

At principal Len Solo's Graham and Parks school in Cambridge, Massachusetts, a staff developer mentors *all* teachers regardless of their levels of experience or expertise and meets with individual teachers, for example, for reflective conversations and setting goals. As Len explains, the staff developer visits classrooms and gives teachers "feedback . . . a shoulder to cry on, somebody to hold your hand. Somebody to help with resources."

Len described this mentoring relationship as "one of a kind" in that the staff developer knows the teachers, kids, parents, and various school programs. During the year after this research, Len said that the staff developer invests half of her time teaching teachers "how to be mentors," and he hopes that this will evolve into a buddy system.

Programs Making Use of Computer Mentors

The use of computer mentors is a progressive form of mentoring in this sample. Jack Thompson recently implemented such a mentoring program at Palm Beach Day School. A group of twelve faculty, whom Jack sees as "clearly in a different league" with respect to their computer expertise, mentor fellow teachers and administrators at the school. The mentors offer assistance one-on-one and to groups of teachers. The individual and group components are both important, Jack explained, because they help teachers feel more comfortable admitting when they are "confused" and asking for help. In a large group, he shared, many feel reluctant to ask questions that would demonstrate a lack of understanding. But he also believes that the group gives "a sense that someone else is working with you on this, to share and so forth."

While Jack admitted that this new program "doesn't work perfectly," he also emphasized how the "individualized education" works to support teacher learning in a variety of ways. The computer mentors

> Sit with you and determine where you were, where you reasonably wanted next to be. And take you there. . . . I might just want to learn how to better use the e-mail with the rest of the world. You might want to find out if there's a more competent, comfortable way you could use it with your fourth graders, because . . . they know more than you do right now . . . . They're not going to be upstaged by the kids.

These mentoring relationships serve as a context for teachers to learn about both computer skills and themselves, Jack emphasized. He shared an example about how one senior teacher had difficulty using computers and therefore did not use them in his classroom. However, the mentoring program has enabled him to increase his knowledge and to integrate them into his classroom. After participating in the program, this teacher gave a speech to the faculty about how computers would revolutionize teaching.

Thus not only do the mentor teachers share their expertise, but their colleagues can learn from one another. Jack explains, "Just the consideration of an idea and the reasonable rejection thereof is personal development, I think." In Jack's view, mentoring also influences classroom practice. As he said,

> If you feel more computer competent, you'll feel better about yourself personally, and professionally. And does it effect the classroom? Sure it does . . . especially if it's a classroom-oriented thing.

Spreading the School Mission

All of the Catholic school principals emphasized that mentoring helps to spread the school's mission, in addition to the benefits identified earlier in this chapter. The supportive context of mentoring relationships between new teachers and those with deep knowledge of the school mission enables both to reflect on the school mission and its practice. As with the other school types, mentoring programs are in different stages in the Catholic schools. The two programs I discuss here are at different phases of implementation.

The mentoring program at Cardinal Newman High School in West Palm Beach, Florida, still in its early stages, is an outgrowth of an existing state certification program for new teachers. In the state certification program, new teachers are paired with administrators. In the mentoring program, teachers are paired with each other. John Clarke sees his new mentoring program as serving five purposes:

1. To welcome new teachers into the "Newman Family"

2. To share the school mission with them

3. To help new teachers enhance their skills

4. To provide a supportive context in which they can share their questions and reflect with more experienced faculty

5. To create a structure for new teachers to meet colleagues socially (because many teachers move from out of state)

John explained his purposes:

We want something where if a teacher has a question and they may not feel comfortable coming to the principal because they may feel well . . . that [they] should already know this, they can go to their buddy teacher, their mentor, their big brother, big sister. We haven't worked out terminologies yet, but we're kind of settling in on "mentor." They can go to them and say, "Listen, I'm not sure about this. . . . What do you think?"

In addition, John explained the social function of the program: "When the new teacher comes in [to the school] there's someone that they can call . . . [a] friend. And that person can introduce them to all the things that go on that we don't cover in a faculty meeting." The interpersonal relationships inherent in mentoring, he said, help to "pull" new teachers "into that larger family spirit here." In turn, the experienced teachers learn from the new teachers, who bring new ideas, new teaching methods, and more experience with technology to the school.

At Cardinal Newman, teachers either nominate themselves or are "invited" by the administration to be mentors. When I asked how mentors are paired up with new faculty, John said that he works closely with the "guidance personnel." If the guidance personnel feel that a person who has not volunteered would be helpful in a particular area, they will encourage the person to become a mentor.

When matching mentor-mentee pairs, John shared, "We look at it individually and . . . make that decision." I asked whether he considers age when selecting teachers to be mentors, and he replied, "No. . . . Really it's more a question of wisdom." Additional characteristics that are considered when pairing teachers are disciplinary similarities and background (e.g., they attended the same college). They also ask the new teachers whether there is an established teacher with whom they want to work, such as a person with whom they have already established a relationship.

At Convent of the Sacred Heart School, Sr. Magnetti has recently implemented a mentoring program, led by two teachers with a deep knowledge of the school's mission. When a new teacher, staff member, or maintenance person enters the school, he or she is assigned a mentor. This program is oriented toward helping new people understand the mission so that they can keep it alive. Since Sr. Magnetti believes that the mission is "catchable," she emphasized that others can spread it. In fact, she talked about how some lay people in her school understand the mission so well, they could easily be of the religious order.

The most important criteria for selecting mentor teachers, Sr. Magnetti explained, is "to choose people who we know really get it about Sacred Heart education. They have a heart for it, they have a sense of what it's about." Faculty who "live the goals" of the school and Sacred Heart Network are paired with new faculty members. Mentors help new community members "reflect" on the goals and "how they implement the goals in their classrooms or their work." For Sr. Magnetti, reflection is a key component of mentoring and "a big part of keeping the mission alive." She believes that this often involves examining beliefs and bringing them into line with actions.

Sr. Magnetti described the initial phase of the mentoring program as "a little weak," because it sometimes can be more of a passing down of shared histories and traditions. She wants the program to grow to be one where teachers have more opportunities for reflection on "the present reality." She would like teachers to be constantly reassessing and looking for ways to grow, apply the mission, and/or find new areas for improvement.

Mentoring Graduate Student Interns

[Graduate interns are] interesting people, and they help us with all their brains and energy to have a better conversation about our own teaching. [There is great] value of being a cooperating practitioner. (Dr. Larry Myatt, Fenway Pilot High School)

Across school types, a common practice that the principals reported was mentoring graduate student interns from local universities. This practice is especially prevalent in the public schools. Many of the principals commented about how "geographic location" is a valuable resource, meaning that being located near universities enhances teacher and organizational learning. For instance, Mary Newman of Buckingham, Browne, and Nichols in Cambridge, Massachusetts, commented on how her school's location enables her teachers to mentor graduate student interns from several local universities.

> It's that link with the university . . . that link with people who are really involved in studying and asking the difficult questions and doing research and writing papers that begins to change a fabric and alter a culture, so that everybody is always thinking about what they can do and what they can do better.

At Buckingham, Browne, and Nichols, interns—or mentees—are assistant teachers in classrooms of "master teachers," who also teach online courses. Mary explained that these relationships support the growth and learning of both master and intern teachers:

> The questions that [the interns] ask and the papers they're writing and the studies they're doing, they infuse an intellectual piece into the entire lower school, and when interns come into the upper school, they do the same kind of thing for classrooms and for master teachers and for departments.

These mentoring relationships produce higher levels of energy and creativity, in Mary's view. The mentoring/intern program helps to "infuse an intellectual piece into the entire lower school" and encourages new ideas and ongoing questions. Mary believes that the mentor learns and grows from the relationship and is "kept alive by the questions" of the mentee.

While both the lower and upper schools have mentoring programs, Mary said that there is a "difficulty" with the upper-school program:

> In an upper school such as this, it's so demanding and it's so competitive as an institution that you need to hire master teachers, people with masters or doctorates teaching in the classroom. . . . We would be less likely to turn out a whole class, a whole semester's class over to an intern. So it means that a teacher has to skillfully use that intern. That's a bit more of a challenge than it would be in the lower school, where they automatically become the number two teacher in the classroom.

At the Trotter School in Boston, Joe Shea, like other principals in this study, has developed very strong school-university collaborations. He invites teachers who are graduate students into the school to be mentored by experienced teachers, and mentors receive a 10% salary increase. At Trotter, mentors are also "lead teachers" who have been trained at Lesley College to guide, observe, and coach other teachers who will eventually become mentor teachers. Joe sees this program as building "capacity." In Joe's words, it is important to "train your core. And then . . . it builds from there."

In addition to this one-to-one mentoring, one mentor invites other teachers who are not mentors to share their expertise with the interns and new teachers. This has evolved into a tradition for other teachers to follow.

A CASE STUDY: AN EXEMPLARY MENTORING PROGRAM

While previous chapters presented an illustrated case study from Dr. Sarah Levine, this chapter presents the case study of Joe Marchese, principal of Westtown High School in Pennsylvania. I chose his case for this chapter because his mentoring program is truly a model of mentoring for transformational learning. Westtown High School has a well-established mentoring program, which was eight years old at the time of our interview. According to Joe Marchese, though, the program has "really been fine-tuned" during the last several years. There are several types of mentoring in this program:

- Pairing experienced teachers with teachers new to the school (regardless of their years of experience teaching)
- Working with interns (faculty who have recently graduated from college or completed a master's program)
- Pairing more experienced and younger teachers for support with issues regarding residential life

In Joe's eyes, his mentoring program is "one of the best," and both new and seasoned teachers learn from these valued relationships.

The mentoring program involves several opportunities for collaborative work, including an orientation week of workshops and retreats for participants. For example, during orientation week in late summer, before the start of the academic year, the faculty engage in a "full week of conversation." During these meetings,

> We talk about a variety of different things. We give people [reading and school] materials ahead of time, so they can look at them. Because we know that . . . once faculty meetings start and once the kids come back, this is such a fast-paced school, that . . . people need to hit the ground running.

During this week teachers engage in "different workshops and discussion groups with many different individuals . . . both on the academic side and on the residential side" of Westtown.

Two senior faculty members serve as directors of the mentoring program, and Joe acts as a support to them. One director interviews prospective faculty at the school so that they can anticipate possible mentor pairings, and experienced faculty mentors at Westtown are selected from a pool of volunteers and by administrative recommendation. Interviewing new faculty gives the directors

> [A] sense right from the beginning about what people are being considered for jobs. And this way, when they go to make the [mentor-mentee] pairings, they've got firsthand experience as opposed to just hearing from me about what this individual is like. So, they come up with a list of pairings.

The mentors at Westtown receive stipends. Their responsibilities include the following:

- Checking in with mentees continually
- Troubleshooting with their mentees
- Advocating for mentees

In Joe's view, mentoring relationships provide a context in which it is okay "to feel vulnerable and not be expected to know everything." He further explained that he wants teachers "to be able to ask questions." Joe also engages in conversation with experienced faculty who are mentors. He explained,

> I also have discussions with them, but I want [the mentors] to do more with [the mentees], to visit their classes more than I will visit their classes, to really make sure that they're okay. And make sure that they have an ongoing sense of support. And that's worked well.

In addition to providing supports for new teacher learning, mentoring also gives experienced teachers a chance to reflect on their practice. When mentees begin asking questions about why a teacher has made a certain decision, suddenly "things you've taken for granted, you need to be able to articulate."

Both experienced and new teachers in these mentoring relationships grow to demonstrate new competency and to act in new ways, Joe reported. For example, he described how mentoring new teachers in the classroom can help experienced teachers grow. In his view, it can transform a teacher from being skeptical into being a "very sensitive" mentor.

He shared an example of how one senior teacher "blossomed" from having intern teachers in his class. Joe believes that this teacher, who was "not particularly good with details," did a "very good job in fostering the growth" of another teacher. Joe also explained that the senior teacher's "observation skills" improved through the process.

CHAPTER SUMMARY

Inviting teachers to serve as mentors is one of the four practices the principals in the study employ to support teacher learning. Almost all of these principals believe that mentoring serves as a context that supports the development of both the mentor and mentee.

As these principals illustrated, mentoring enables teachers to share expertise, encourages both partners to consider alternative perspectives, helps adults to manage change, and builds interpersonal relationships. In addition, the mentoring relationship serves to create "holding environments" (Kegan, 1982) for growth.

REFLECTIVE QUESTIONS

Please take a moment to respond to these questions before turning to the next chapter.

1. How do the mentoring practices you and your teachers employ serve to create a "holding environment" at your school?

2. How do you think teachers, as mentors or mentees, with different ways of knowing experience mentoring? What kinds of supports and challenges exist in your school context? You may find it helpful to consider the following contemporary depictions of mentoring relationships: (a) *Good Will Hunting*, (b) *Stand and Deliver*, (c) *A Few Good Men*, (d) *Up Close and Personal*, (e) *Men in Black*, (f) *Goodfellas*, (g) *Educating Rita*, and (h) *A Doll's House*.

3. How do you define the role of a mentor? (You may find it helpful to recall some of your own mentors, or some of the ways that you mentor others.)

4. How do you think that the holding environment could be reshaped, if it should, to accommodate teachers in their roles as mentors or mentees at your school?

5. What kinds of mentoring do you participate in at your school?

6. What do you see as the benefits and challenges for particular teachers in assuming roles as mentors and mentees?

7. In what ways, if any, does this chapter and/or constructive developmental theory help you to better understand how teachers with different ways of knowing might experience mentoring within your school and within their classrooms?

8. In what ways, if any, does the case presented at the end of this chapter resonate with you and your experience?

9. In what ways are teachers supported and challenged in your school as they engage in mentoring relationships?

10. After reading this chapter, what do you think are some additional supports and challenges you and/or others in your school might provide?

9

*Bringing It
All Together*

*A Case of Learning–Oriented
Leadership in Action*

I n this chapter, I present an in-depth case of how one principal, Dr. Sarah
Levine, and her school approached their self-study evaluation as an
opportunity for learning. By exploring their experiences, I highlight how
the four pillars of my model can work together to create a context
supportive of teacher learning. As I will discuss more fully in the final
chapter, principals can implement any one or more of these practices to
suit their unique school contexts. In this instance, the self-study provided
an opportunity for working together to broaden perspectives, build community, and help adults manage change and foster diversity. The self-
study also enabled community members to share leadership, power, and
decision-making authority. This case illustrates how principals can tailor
forms of support and challenge to individual needs and how the self-study
evaluation process can be a context for growth.

A SELF-STUDY EVALUATION

During the last year of my first research project with Sarah, she combined
all four of the pillars in a schoolwide project to develop a self-evaluation

document as part of a national evaluation (though I did not refer to these practices as such at that time). In this yearlong process, teachers and staff worked in teams to put their ideas into writing in the document. Parents and trustees also contributed to the document, and the national evaluation committee eventually added the children's assessment to the self-study document.

Establishing Collective Definitions—The First Workshops

At the outset of the self-evaluation, Sarah explained that she saw the process as a collaborative effort and that recommendations for changes in practice and philosophies would be welcome from the school community. To facilitate reflection on issues of student and faculty diversity, Sarah hired two workshop facilitators. One consultant led a workshop for the board of trustees, and the other directed two workshops for teachers, administrators, and staff. Before each workshop, participants wrote statements expressing their thinking on diversity and difference.

The board of trustees and the faculty and staff participated in identical workshops. At the meeting for faculty, administrators, and staff, the participants reflected privately and then shared their thinking in order to develop common definitions of "diversity" and "multiculturalism." During this workshop, most participants contributed to the discussion. Several teachers wanted to learn more about issues of diversity, especially since they found them to be "touchy issues" in their classrooms. Some teachers described how they incorporated diversity and multiculturalism into their curricula and teaching styles and respected differences in their classrooms. For example, one class learned about cultural differences by sending computer messages to students in other countries. In addition, some teachers talked about the need to heighten parents' consciousness about issues of diversity. The consultants spoke to the group about how diversity influences educational practice.

This discussion in the first workshop made it clear that the community wanted to value diversity even more. As a result, the participants planned a second workshop in which they explored ways to promote diversity in the school. They pursued "real problem solving" and opportunities for learning from each other and broadening their individual perspectives.

Appointing a Leader

Like so many of the principals in this study, Sarah believes that teaming to reflect upon the school's philosophy, programs, and curricula gives leadership roles to all members of the community. She also appointed a specific leader to orchestrate the entire self-study effort, including "motivating participants and writing and reviewing the document produced by the school community." She chose John, a 10-year veteran teacher at the school, who had previously held a smaller role in self-evaluations in other schools and expressed an interest in writing.

This was John's first experience in taking a leadership role of this type, and he knew there would be many challenges and responsibilities. Sarah worked closely with John to create an opportunity for his development, supporting him during difficulties and challenging him to take risks. The two met regularly to discuss the study's process and progress and considered alternative ways of proceeding. They solved problems together and learned from each other as they attended to various issues. Like Sarah, John thought that reflection, challenging assumptions, and collaborating allowed voices in the community to be heard. He told teachers many times,

> It's really a chance to put your money where your mouth is. . . . This is the time to get your ideas and criticisms put down in writing. Because people are so concerned about this document—the parents, the board, who are now already asking to see it—it's going to be looked at very carefully. So if you've got an idea, it's worth your time and effort now, because [the self-evaluation] comes up only every 10 years. Now's the time to get it in writing.

Teams in Action

As they organized the self-study effort, Sarah and John decided that the faculty, staff, and administrators would also team to focus on different aspects of the school. For example, one team would reflect on how the school practiced its current philosophy and would revise the school's philosophy statement. Sarah and John decided against designating team leaders and instead allowed each team to decide on leadership. John permitted teams to have a leader or not to have one, and two teams decided they would be "leaderless." The majority of teams elected a leader, and of these, only two teams experienced difficulties working together. He assured them he would mediate any problems, but, he recalled, "Nobody asked me to do that. There were some groups that did have trouble working together, but they worked it out."

A Faculty Meeting Focused on Community

Both Sarah and John thought it was important to invite community members to consider how the school was or was not a community. They decided to create an opportunity early in the academic year for community members to share their perspectives at a faculty meeting. Sarah and John asked faculty, administrators, and staff to work, first, in teams of four or five people and later to present their thinking to the entire community.

John facilitated this meeting and later conducted a similar workshop with the board of trustees.

During each workshop, John gave each participant a small piece of cloth and invited them to write their reflections about the school as a community on the back of the patches. On the front, they were to draw their visions of the community. After the meeting, faculty, staff, and administrators pieced together a quilt with the completed patches. In Sarah's view, the exercise was an important community-building activity that raised the consciousness of all participants.

The Inservice Day

In the spring of the academic year, prior to the formal national assessment, Sarah and John designated a whole day for teachers, administrators, and staff to engage in inquiry with their teams and the entire school community. All classes were canceled, and all community members were released from other responsibilities in order to focus on the self-study.

The result of this inservice day was a collaboratively written draft document that included a revised mission statement and educational philosophy. It also entailed detailed descriptions of the school's programs, decision-making processes, purposes, and curriculum. Different teams focused on different parts of the document, but they worked collaboratively to challenge each other. For example, one team worked on the role of the library in the school, another focused on how the school acted upon its value for diversity, and yet another considered the role of ethics.

The "diversity issue" team, which did not elect a leader, reflected on the school's diversity. They considered how diversity was mirrored in the current curriculum, activities, and attitudes. Team members asked questions about the document produced earlier in the school year that had elaborated on the school's value for diversity. Team members discussed the school's core value for "celebrating differences" and reflected on how they, as a school community, enacted this in their teaching. They pondered questions such as "Do we really want to do this now?" and "Do we really believe this statement?" They discussed the ways in which their espoused multicultural and antibias curricula were actually implemented in different grades. Team members with specific knowledge about some of the school's practices relating to diversity informed other members, and people appeared sincerely interested in learning from each other. For example, they discussed how the "International Week" program mirrored values for respecting other cultural traditions.

After two hours of discussion, the team moved to the computer room to piece together the section. John was a member of this team. He was impressed by the "energy" of his teammates and their abilities to reflect on complicated issues. The collaborative writing process served as yet another opportunity for continued reflection. Members of the "diversity issue" team hovered around the computer and talked about how to write the piece. One person typed as they all discussed what they would say. After some discussion, the team decided to "invent" its own new model.

Another team worked on school goals and the forms of assessment used for evaluation. The current model focused on setting goals with Sarah at the start of the academic year. The team concluded that teachers would be more supported by meeting with colleagues two or three times a year to reflect on and receive feedback about each teacher's progress. After thinking through ways to implement this improvement, the team wrote an assessment of the current system and their proposal for change. They shared this document with Sarah, the upper- and lower-division directors, and the school community so that everyone would be better able to support one another in achieving individual goals.

Deciding on Goals for the Next 10 Years:
An Afternoon of Collegial Inquiry

During the afternoon session of the inservice day, Sarah invited all participants to examine the community goals for the next 10 years. Everyone wrote down his or her thoughts before the group discussion took place. Sarah witnessed this process as opening up lines of communication and felt that the community shared a common "language."

After lunch, everyone convened in a large meeting hall to share results from the team meetings. Participants talked informally about the morning's work, Sarah shared the agenda for the afternoon, and John led a discussion about progress. Individuals voiced concerns, asked questions, and shared the details of their own work. Sarah participated in the conversation, listening intently and asking questions. Then she invited people to reflect privately for a few minutes, writing down the 5 to 10 items that "we might like to spend the next 5 to 10 years working on." Next, Sarah invited people to share their thinking. John positioned himself near a blackboard and wrote down their ideas as Sarah called on them. Soon people began building upon one another's comments.

During the afternoon meeting, almost everyone contributed to the conversation, asking and responding to questions such as "How does a norm or a tradition get introduced into and ultimately embedded in a school's culture?" Sarah offered her ideas, which were added to the ever-lengthening list on the blackboard. New opinions led people to reconsider their own perspectives and to explicitly question various school goals.

Soon the blackboard was filled with ideas. Sarah then asked everyone to select the two items most important to them. After repeating this process, they agreed on a final list that represented everyone's interests. The ultimate list of goals for achievement of the school's mission was settled upon collaboratively. These goals included "serving a broader range of kids," "finding alternative assessment methods," and "addressing multiple intelligences." Some of Sarah's items were found on the final listing, but many were not.

At the end of the meeting, Sarah publicly congratulated everyone on the good work they had done in reflecting together, challenging each other's thinking, and contributing to the self-study document. She distributed a list of humorous parodies concerning this intensive self-study effort and asked various people to read a line until the entire list was shared. In the final self-study document, the good work of teams was acknowledged, and team members' names appeared at the end of the sections they had produced.

After a brief recess, the school community reconvened for dinner with the board of trustees, at which they talked about their work and the results achieved in the self-study.

Putting the Finishing Touches on the Draft

Later in the year, each team shared its drafted section of the document with Sarah and John and a team of "final readers." Sarah provided feedback to the teams by asking questions and/or suggesting alternative ideas for consideration, especially regarding how the specific pieces might be better tied to the school's vision. She then gave the draft to John, or to the team itself, for final review.

Community Members' Perspectives on the Self-Study Evaluation

Several community members told me that the self-evaluation process created an opportunity to reflect, share decision making, and assess their own practices. One administrator was impressed by the faculty's interest in reflecting upon schoolwide issues. She noted that they continued to talk with her and one another throughout the year about how the self-study could be optimized. In her view, the community was "invested" in both the issues addressed and the decisions made as part of the process.

One teacher who had been actively involved in the self-study said that it was important for teachers to have a voice in the information put into the self-study document. However, she sometimes thought that her own agenda differed from Sarah's. She was also less concerned with current thinking about assessment and more concerned with improving her own teaching. Another teacher commented that the self-evaluation gave her and others an opportunity to "speak their minds" about important policies. Yet another said that the collaborative work helped build a sense of community. In her view, the school was engaging in a process that would lead to a document that they "all believed in together."

In reflecting on his leadership role in the self-study, John said that he enjoyed the challenge but sometimes found it difficult to manage the self-study work along with his own teaching. Several people praised John's leadership and his ability to "motivate the community." Several teachers also praised Sarah's ability to pick a good leader.

Community as a Context for Growth

In Sarah's view, a community must value difference to be a *real* community. Sarah encouraged community members to "take stands" on behalf of their beliefs and values. Although it was sometimes difficult to hear, she wanted disagreement brought from "underground."

Sarah saw diverse perspectives as a way to help the school community deal with conflict more effectively. She appeared interested in helping community members engage with both the "light" and the "dark" sides of community life, especially those affecting their work or that had not represented their own voices.

Encouraging and listening to differing opinions embraces diversity. Other ways of valuing diversity include letting others' perspectives inform one's own thinking, allowing an influence where it has not previously been permitted, and developing a shared opinion or an agreement to disagree during discussion.

Helping people to embrace diversity so that it becomes a natural part of their activities may be a developmental challenge. A person's ability to "hold" diverse perspectives may be related to the way in which he or she organizes experience and makes sense of it. At the same time, I acknowledge that individuals may have a difficult time embracing diversity for many other reasons. Sarah used practices of teaming, inviting adults to assume leadership roles, and engaging in collegial inquiry to try to build a community in which both agreement and disagreement were seen as opportunities for learning and development.

A Developmental Perspective

The community discussions in this self-evaluation project held the potential to support participants' transformational learning. Participants in these conversations had the opportunity to consider alternative ways of viewing situations and to let these different viewpoints inform their own ways of understanding them.

Team and community members appeared eager to share their viewpoints and perspectives. The community actively questioned each other's ideas so that they could better understand the perspectives. Diverse opinions seemed to be considered seriously in ongoing conversations. This sharing of diverse perspectives often led to new practices, new policies, or a change in the curriculum or philosophy.

Sarah's goal in these reflective conversations was to share leadership and responsibility of the self-evaluation with the school community. She believed that involving as many members of the community as possible would improve the outcome of a decision for the entire school. Teaming, inviting adults into leadership roles, collegial inquiry, and informal mentoring seemed to create a kind of synergy.

Sarah appeared to be interested in helping people become increasingly able to see themselves as authorities. The shared decision-making processes created a context for people to act on their ideas, set goals, and support each other's transformations. Everyone encouraged each other to look internally as they reflected upon problems, issues, and policies. By encouraging community members to explore perspectives and assumptions and consider alternatives, the context held potential to support the growth of all participants.

When the school community voted on the final preferred list of goals, Sarah did not veto or override any of the contributions. Instead, she congratulated the community and thanked them for their efforts in sharing the responsibility with her. By accepting the community's list, Sarah demonstrated her commitment to collaboration even though it meant letting go of goals she considered important. Clearly, good leadership involves more than creating, building, and empowering others. It also requires letting go. In this way, Sarah illustrated how the self-evaluation study served as a context for her growth as well.

CHAPTER SUMMARY

This self-study provides a case of collegial inquiry, teaming, leadership roles, and informal mentoring to support teacher learning and to move the school forward.

Many of the other principals in the sample explained that their self-study evaluations include several, if not all, of these practices, which also give teachers the opportunity to develop their ideas and grow. Inviting adults into this process is one way in which they share ownership of ideas, build community, and promote individual learning and school growth.

Sarah combined these four practices based on the type of issue or activity they were approaching and the unique characteristics of the individuals who comprised her school community. This combination of approaches worked for well for Sarah and her school. When applying these four practices or combinations of them, they can be adapted and applied to other contexts in light of each leader's style, each school's context, and teachers' preferences, needs, and developmental diversity. Ultimately, these practices can make a powerful impact on a school environment and provide rich soil for growth.

REFLECTIVE QUESTIONS

Please take a moment to write about these questions before turning to the next chapter, where I discuss the principals' efforts to renew themselves.

1. How does your self-evaluation process serve as a "holding environment" for growth and learning for you and others at your school?

2. What kinds of practices do you and your teachers engage with in working on this process? For example, do you use teaming, collegial inquiry, or leadership roles? If so, how do you think these practices work to support teachers' learning? What types of mentoring are used in your self-study process?

3. How do you think the practices you've listed in Question 2 support teachers with different ways of knowing? What kinds of supports and challenges exist in the context of your school's self-evaluation process?

4. How do you think that the "holding environment" could be reshaped, if it should, to assist particular teachers as they engage in the self-study process? How might you go about taking small steps toward reshaping it?

5. What kinds of leadership roles do teachers have in your school's self-evaluation process? What kinds of teams are in place? How are they working?

6. What have you noticed in terms of benefits and challenges for particular teachers as they engage in your school's self-evaluation?

7. In what ways, if any, does this chapter and or constructive-developmental theory help you to understand how teachers with different ways of knowing might experience the practices in your school's self-evaluation process?

8. How does Sarah's school's self-evaluation process resonate with your own?

9. In what ways are your teachers supported and challenged in the self-evaluation process?

10. After reading this chapter, what are three ideas that you'd like to build into your school's self-evaluation process? Why?

11. What kinds of additional supports and challenges would you like to offer your teachers as they engage in your school's self-evaluation process?

10

Leadership for Learning's Wellspring:

Self-Renewal Through Reflective Practice

I n this chapter, I discuss a continuum of self-renewal practices used by the principals in the sample, despite the context-specific challenges they face in their leadership.

In prior chapters, I discussed how principals practice collegial inquiry to support teacher learning, yet a powerful lesson from this study concerns the importance of reflective practice for principals to support their *own* development. Interestingly, when asked how they renew themselves while managing their complex responsibilities, all but one spontaneously discussed a craving to regularly reflect with colleagues. They believed this kind of dialogue would help them become more effective leaders, yet only three of the principals were benefiting from reflective practice communities.

This chapter highlights how these school leaders renew themselves and emphasizes their thinking that they, like their teachers and all of us, can grow from reflective practice with others.

PRINCIPAL RENEWAL: REJUVENATION THROUGH REFLECTIVE PRACTICE

Research shows that supporting both new and experienced principals is crucial to principals, their teachers, and our schools.

Theoretical Principles of Supporting Principals' Renewal

Houston (1998) offers three reasons for the shortage of principals: (1) abuse and accountability, (2) excessive blame and a need for greater balance, and (3) issues of confusion and compensation. While accountability is applauded in today's schools, Houston (1998), among others (Kelley & Peterson, 2002; Sykes, with King & Patrick, 2002), maintains that principals are expected to fix schools and communities without the necessary resources. Houston (1998) also attributes the shortage of principals to blame and balance:

> Americans are increasingly aware of the need to have a balanced life—you need a sound mind and a sound body to function in a hectic and complex world. . . . School administrators often do not have the time to [maintain balance]. (p. 44)

Excessive blame without time and energy to sustain a balanced life easily breeds stress for both aspiring and seated principals. Principals are increasingly resigning due to the stress and complexity of their work, as well as the inadequate training they report (Klempen & Richetti, 2001). Furthermore, Houston (1998) argues that many qualified candidates may resist principalship because they are uncertain about expectations for their roles. They are aware of the burden placed on school leaders to inculcate children with a knowledge base that we, as a nation, cannot agree upon. To remedy these problems and better support principals in their extremely demanding work, researchers suggest that principals both receive and seek support (Houston, 1998; Kelley & Peterson, 2002; Sykes et al., 2002).

I suggest that data (Drago-Severson, 1996; Kelley & Peterson, 2002) related to the shortage of principals and the stress of their multifaceted work indicate the need to better support principals and their self-renewal. Given the demands of leadership in a nation with increasingly diverse school populations, researchers, policymakers, and principals *themselves* are searching for more effective ways to train and support school leaders (Ackerman & Maslin-Ostrowski, 2002; Kegan & Lahey, 2001; Kelley & Peterson, 2002; Tucker & Codding, 2002; Wagner, 2001). Due to the lack of support and rapid, dramatic changes in the profession, some states now offer training and mentoring programs for new principals, while others aim to teach cognitive skills and decision making (Klempen & Richetti, 2001; Sykes et al., 2002). Helping principals manage their multiple roles as instructional, managerial, and visionary leaders is recognized as a vital measure in their renewal and development (Ackerman et al., 1996; Donaldson, 2001; Tucker & Codding, 2002). *How* do we better support principals in meeting challenges and caring for themselves while caring for the learning and development of others?

Enabling school leaders to renew themselves holds great promise. One important way by which this can be accomplished is to provide them with opportunities to make sense of their own and others' experiences in reflective practice groups, which also foster new ways of thinking and acting.

Examples of the Need for Replenishing and Self-Renewal

> With the pressures of this job . . . the trick [is] to let go of things. And that's not very easy 'cause I'm an intense person, and I bring a high level of energy to this [work]. (Sr. Judith Brady, St. Barnabas High School)

All of the principals said they often need replenishing, but when asked about their self-care efforts, several principals inquired, "Can you give me a prompt as to what other principals said?" As one principal explained,

> For me, an average day really is like six to six. If I get home at six, I'm like, "This is a short day." If I get home at six, once I get home . . . I'm so tired that I'm completely useless for anything else.

Nearly all of them said that while their work is satisfying, it is also exhausting and "lonely at the top." Almost every principal feels challenged by the consuming and inflexible nature of the job, and some of these principals emphasized that working intensely for many years without replenishment can leave them burned out. When asked about how they care for themselves, many explained the difficulty in separating their personal and professional lives due to time, fatigue, or just that these aspects of their lives are "intertwined."

Strategies for Self-Care

Across school type, principals named a range of ways in which they care for themselves in order to renew. More than half said that they value "time to totally reflect and come back to myself." The list below details some of these strategies (in order of most-commonly to least-often referenced sources of support).

1. Spending time with family and friends

2. Reading independently and/or participating in book groups

3. Conversing with school board members, trustees, or school council members

4. Making time for reflection and retreats

5. Attending, speaking at, and meeting with colleagues at conferences

6. Continuing learning and renewal through formal programs and fellowships

7. Prioritizing some portion of the summer to get away from school

8. Mentoring: sharing lessons with current and aspiring principals

9. Sabbaticals

10. Participating as board member for professional organizations

11. Writing to renew oneself

12. Appreciating art and music

13. Participating in reflective-practice groups with fellow principals

Next, I present several examples to illustrate how these principals understand their own efforts to care for, support, and renew themselves.

Family and Friends: Balancing Commitments

I'm seeing more strongly the importance of having that balance because it'll make me better in what I do in my work. (Joe Marchese)

Given their long hours, one prevalent theme that emerged was the need for "balancing" work with family, which is one form of renewal. Nearly all of the principals depend upon very tolerant and supportive families—especially partners. Most of the principals' supports have both a personal and professional component, such that a rich personal life rejuvenates their professional lives. As one principal explained,

One way in which I replenish myself is to make sure that I'm much more in-tune to the signals that my [spouse and children] are giving to me about spending time with them, and doing that guilt-free. That's a very tough thing to do.

By investing time away from their work with family, their families see them "without the stress level that they're accustomed to seeing," which provides them with "even more of an affirmation of [the] importance of taking the time to balance." Creating a balance is especially key for principals who are starting families.

Jerry Zank and others highly value "associations with colleagues" and said that these are helpful sources of their own renewal. Jerry has a long-time colleague and friend with whom he feels that he can "be very open." Sharing experiences and honestly discussing situations with his colleagues brings him "new energy."

According to Mary Newman of Buckingham, Browne, and Nichols School in Cambridge, renewal with family and friends strengthens her work:

> I also nourish myself through . . . intimate relationships with family and with friends, so it's not just art and music, but I would say, principally, family and friends and travel [with them]. . . . I try very hard and always have to keep up a very rich personal life. And if I don't, I don't have as much to bring to my work. Both the work and the home are really of primary importance to me.

Reading Independently and in Book Clubs

Nearly all of the principals explained that reading independently provides a respite and keeps them up-to-date with learning about new ideas. Kim Marshall, for example, like many principals, explained that "all the way through my development, I've found that my reading [has] changed me, profoundly." Sr. Judith Brady also values readings that are "inspirational," and she sees this as part of her job as well as a private source of renewal. "I need that personally," she shared, because "I get tired and worn down."

Book clubs were also named as an important source of self-renewal for almost one-third of the sample. Interestingly, these principals participate in book clubs with colleagues of the same gender. They participate in book clubs not only because of the intellectual benefits but also because they find the social interactions to be a source of self-renewal. For example, Dr. Dan White explained how his book club was transformative:

> [Book club members] spent 15 minutes on *Tuesdays With Morrie,* [and] we spent the rest of our time talking about our relationships with our fathers. It was just unlike any other experience of my life. And for three of us, including me, our fathers had just died within the last year, and Jimmy's dad wasn't dead, but he had been kind of alienated from him, and so, oh, it was just this powerful thing. Well, that's the personal growth.

Making Time for Reflection and Retreats

While wishing for more time, almost all of the principals explained that time for both private and collaborative reflection is important. Some make private reflection a part of their daily rituals, and others secure spaces for reflection in other ways. In addition to daily reflection and prayer, retreats are the most popular form of reflection among the Catholic school principals.

John Clarke explained that his daily ritual entails a "habit" of visiting Cardinal Newman's Chapel for meditation and "deliberation." He takes a "spiritual angle" to "center myself back into who I am" and to draw "strength for" his work as a principal. In addition, like other Catholic school principals, he attends semi-annual retreats, considering them "a time for reflection and personal renewal."

Retreats enable Sr. Judith Brady "to get completely away because it's the only way that I can clear my mind of the responsibilities and things here." Retreats also create space for relating to God, she explained, knowing that she is "not alone doing these things. I may feel inadequate, but somehow God can operate through me. I'm certainly looking for God's help."

Mary Newman, like others, emphasized that all school principals need to "be able to look at an institution from some distance and not be buried in the sort of everydayness of it." This not only helps her to reinvigorate but also gives her an "aerial" view of the larger picture and the school's broad objectives.

Time Away From School for Oneself: Recharging "Batteries"

I absolutely agree that teachers and principals need the summer. They need long periods of time because . . . you spend the first two or three or four days unwinding, before you remember who you really are and what your real priorities are and then you'd better have some time in that state, to . . . get your batteries back up. (Dr. Larry Myatt)

Across school type, principals emphasized the need for "getting away" during the summer or for school holidays, or even for a long weekend, which provides an extended time to recharge and reinvigorate themselves.

Like most of the others, Gary LeFave of Matignon High School, in Cambridge, attends to his own personal and professional development through taking courses and serving on various committees and boards. He also treasures his time at the house he is building in New Hampshire. For Gary, this is crucial because it provides a place "where you can reflect on what you do." Many of the other principals echoed this sentiment.

Attending Conferences: Delivering
Talks and Speaking With Colleagues

Nearly all of the principals value attending conferences during which they have opportunities to talk with other school leaders. Sharing stories and thinking through issues in a safe context are important to their growth and renewal, and many of these principals find that safe space at professional conferences. Several principals also reported that their renewal stems from delivering speeches on topics that matter deeply to them.

Jack Thompson described how his own professional development needs and preferences have changed over time. At first, he often attended conferences and workshops to learn new ideas, but he has come to believe that it is more useful for him to exchange ideas with other heads-of-school as well as with staff in his own school. Talking with other principals is both a social and an intellectual activity, and he values the opportunities and privacy that conferences present. For Jack, these types of conversations are "really professional development. Sometimes you can contribute, sometimes you can learn."

In addition to meeting with fellow principals at conferences, many claimed that their involvement in local associations supports their renewal process. For example, Sister Joan Magnetti nurtures herself through involvement in the Sacred Heart Society and the National Association of Independent School Heads Association in the local area. Sr. Magnetti also mentioned a "wonderful model," in which she participated while acting as head at another school, where principals met regularly to share experiences:

> We got together maybe four times a year as heads. . . . We used to get together for lunch faithfully, every six weeks. And we'd go to a different school, just go through the lunch line with the kids and then we'd come together and we'd talk. . . . It was such a great [experience] . . . it was so nurturing.

Engaging in reflective activities was, in her view, "just wonderful because people come from all different points."

Conversations With School Board Members, Trustees, or Council Members

Across school type, nearly half of the principals find conversations with members of their school boards, especially school board presidents, to be a source of support and of self-renewal. For example, Dan White commented that his relationships with members of the trustee group are not only "people who I can talk with [and] not just to sort of commiserate about the school, but there's opportunity for . . . personal growth." Similarly, Jack Thompson explained that he and his board president exchange ideas about what each one could do to make the other's life easier, which he finds very effective and supportive.

Learning and Renewal Through Formal Programs and Fellowships

Many principals in this study seek more formal learning experiences to support their renewal. Some enroll in graduate courses or doctoral programs, and still others enjoy fellowship work.

For example, when I met Muriel Leonard, not only was she a relatively new principal at the McCormick Middle School (after serving as a principal for 18 years in other schools), she was also in a doctoral program. Muriel discussed how the Institute for Learning allows her to work with other principals in a collegial fashion, which she named as being a support to her own renewal.

Like Muriel, John Clarke of Cardinal Newman High School enjoys collaborating with colleagues at the university where he recently earned a degree in educational leadership. As hard as it was to attend night school while working as a teacher and administrator, he feels that it was worth it. He explained,

> And as difficult as it was, it was so helpful to be with other educators, to talk, to learn together, to read together, to study together, to sometimes commiserate together. I found . . . it very helpful to be studying and working at the same time.

Taking Sabbaticals

Like other principals in independent and Catholic schools in this study, Joe Marchese of Westtown High School renews himself by taking sabbaticals to reflect on his work and to set new goals for himself and the school. Others expressed a desire to take sabbaticals sometime in the future for similar purposes.

To support his own development during his sabbatical, Joe engages in "a lot of reflective writing." During his sabbatical, he read Roland Barth's (1990) book, which recommends that educators journal their personal visions of education. Inspired by Barth, Joe traveled to Vermont and took "the opportunity to write [his] own vision and to figure out what I stood for." This writing rejuvenated Joe—so much so that upon returning to school, he has focused on learning more about reflective writing and may start a group to engage in that process.

Having not taken a sabbatical in 20 years, Barbara Chase voiced that she would like to spend time with children in the "developing world" or a low-income area and do something very different from her current work. "Learning from them," Barbara explained, "would be a really helpful and great way for me to learn about something that's really important."

Participating as a Board Member in Professional Organizations

Like several other principals in this sample, Sr. Barbara Rogers supports her professional growth and self-renewal through involvement as a board member in school and nonschool association work. Sr. Rogers has been the regional director of Bank of Boston, which maintains her connection to business and finance. Like several other principals, Sr. Rogers is also part of a "discussion group of business people downtown that meets periodically." She explained, "I love that kind of exposure to a different world. I find that . . . again, restorative and all of those things, but mostly great fun."

Writing to Renew Oneself

Many principals discussed how writing serves as a method for self-renewal. For some, writing in private journals is a source of solace, whereas for others, writing for a public audience provides rejuvenation. For example, Dan White described writing a book as one of the important ways in which he continues "feeding" himself. Other principals explained how writing articles and books serves as a source of inspiration, while several find comfort in epistolary writing (e.g., writing to friends, colleagues, and staff).

Kathleen Perry discussed how writing with other administrators for presentations to other schools about various Lake Worth programs provides her an opportunity to write about "sharing ideas." Kathleen also revives herself by writing privately. By reflecting through writing, she can "examine what we do on a day-to-day basis and look at what our practices are." Writing is a way to "grow," she explained, because she is to be able to "see where you are, how you got where you are, and then to pull together your ideas." Writing requires a "real examination" of oneself and what is important.

Mentoring: Sharing Lessons With Current and Aspiring Principals

Several principals described how sharing their own learning with current or aspiring principals is a source of replenishment. For example, Kim Marshall began as a principal with "an ultra look and learn" stance, and feels that it "took a while" to turn around the school climate. Emphasizing that he learned from his mistakes, he described a summer course he offers to new and aspiring principals—to help them avoid the same hard lessons through sharing his own experiences. This is also a way he renews himself. He explained,

I'm trying . . . to give them a road map for how, as I put it, how they can get to the heart of the matter sooner than I did. You know, how they can skip over some of the stupid stuff that I did, and how they can kind of get right down . . . into the process of improving learning.

Kim wants to share his "wisdom," learned as a school leader, and he finds satisfaction in working "hard on passing it along."

Appreciating Art and Music

Many principals also voiced how viewing art or listening to music helps with self-renewal. For instance, Sr. Judith Brady explained that she enjoys "simple beauty." She appreciates and values it and explained that it is "very important to me" as a source of self-renewal. "Living by [herself]," she likes to view beauty in her home, and she considers "a bowl of fruit—one pear, one apple, one lemon—with different colors and textures"—to be "something beautiful" that provides a source of comfort and rejuvenation.

Participating in Reflective Practice Groups With Fellow Principals

Three principals discussed how reflective practice groups composed of principals are an invaluable source of renewal and support. These groups meet regularly for several hours each month (or week) throughout the year. In some cases, principals engage in dialogue as critical friends in response to a protocol of questions, enabling the principals to share experiences, validate each other's experiences, and expand possibilities for more effectively understanding and managing complex situations.

Joe Shea participates in a reflective-practice group with fellow principals that centers on engaging in collegial inquiry about practice. Joe explained how principals in these groups share lessons from their practice and ask questions of one another, which provides a context for collaborative problem solving. For example, one of Joe's reflective practice groups involved training in mediation, which helped him to negotiate new teaching contracts with the union. These groups enable Joe to refresh himself and support his own development by learning from colleagues. While attending such reflective practice groups often requires leaving the school, he believes that it is worth it because the learning is "fabulous," and it strengthens his leadership.

Dr. Larry Myatt also spoke powerfully about the benefits of reflecting on practice in groups, describing how they have enriched, revived, and challenged his professional life. Recently, he was invited to join a reflective-practice group, "The Leadership Project," at a local university. Since joining, he explained that he aims to bring this type of reflective-practice group to other Boston schools:

> [Reflecting with others in this project is] a nice culture and a nice pedagogy [for] the way we work. And I benefited from it here, [and] hopefully when I go other places I might bring it with me. I wasn't sure I had the time or energy to do the leadership project, but it's been fabulous.

In this group, Larry explained, principals bring their own practice and their own questions in order to brainstorm better ideas. The key to these groups, according to Larry, is a willingness to reflect, which he sees as central to supporting his own growth. He explained how his groups work:

> What we tried to do is work differently, which is to really use the power of our own integrity of work and our own questions and be more reflective and make better use of other people's ideas, . . . really looking at them and deconstructing them and casting assertions about the work and really staying with it.

A Craving for Engaging in Principal Reflective-Practice Groups

One important theme that emerged from my studies is that principals who were not participating in reflective-practice groups explained that they yearn to join such groups. Kim Marshall's sentiments are emblematic of what others desire: "I would love to be in a principals' group" because "I am fairly isolated as a principal."

Like Kim and so many others in this study, Jerry Zank longs for a reflective-practice group with colleagues. Also, like others, Jerry tends to support his own growth in isolation. As such, he has had difficulty building a community of principals given the demands of the work and the lack of time for reflection, despite believing it would support him.

Like so many of the principals in this study, Jerry takes responsibility for not making time for his own self-renewal. In response to my question about how he supports and renews himself, he shared,

> I'd love to find something more programmatic, 'cause I feel [my practice of self-renewal is] always in isolation. . . . There's a hunger that I have for these collegial contacts that are not just chitchat or over a Scotch. But something that's a little bit more in depth. And I don't have that. I don't know very many people that do.

Engaging in ongoing reflective practice with peers, they said, would support their efforts to become more effective leaders. This critical lesson suggests that even exemplary school leaders lack and *need* structures for this type of ongoing support.

CHAPTER SUMMARY

This chapter illuminates the range of ways in which the principals, across school types and resource levels, renew themselves. Nurturing themselves, they explained, reduces isolation and enables them to better support teacher learning and engage in their multifaceted work. Just as it is important to provide contexts for teachers to engage in collegial inquiry, so too is it important for principals.

Reflective-practice groups can also assist principals in self-renewal and heightening awareness of their assumptions so that they can examine their influence on performance. This type of model for school principals' renewal could be effectively incorporated into university principal centers and school-university partnerships across the nation to more effectively support principals in their complex, important, and meaningful work.

REFLECTIVE QUESTIONS

Please take a moment to consider these questions. In the last chapter, I discuss implications of the lessons I have covered in this book.

1. What are two or three practices you engage in to renew yourself? How are they working?

2. In what ways would you like to support your renewal? How might this process help you personally and professionally?

3. How do any of the practices you named above serve as a "holding environment" for your self-renewal, growth, and/or learning?

4. What supports at your school could better support your renewal? How, ideally, would you restructure these? How could you take small steps toward reshaping these?

5. In what ways, if any, does this chapter help you in thinking about the process of self-renewal? What, if anything, resonates with your own experiences? What ideas would you like to incorporate into your own self-renewal and self-care processes?

11

Leading in the 21st Century

New Opportunities for Learning

This last chapter brings me to the implications of the four pillars of the learning-oriented school leadership model: teaming, providing leadership roles, engaging in collegial inquiry, and mentoring for use in different school settings. It is important for readers to understand that there is no panacea for professional development quandaries: Every school must consider its particular characteristics when it decides to adopt a culture that can better support the learning and growth of all its members. This chapter highlights a qualitatively different way of thinking about professional development and leadership supportive of transformational learning. And I hope that this book offers a helpful perspective on how to better support teacher learning.

REVIEW OF CHALLENGES TO A CLIMATE SUPPORTIVE OF TEACHER LEARNING

The principals in the study named important context-specific challenges they face as they dedicate themselves to leading well and supporting adult learning. They work despite these challenges, which include school size, mission, student population, teaching staff, their own past experiences, and school location. By far, they cited adults' "resistance" and "fear of change" and resources—*financial, human,* and *time*—as their most common challenges. In certain school contexts, principals also referred to the challenges of working with younger faculty who may leave after a short time. Almost all of the public school principals also experience the pressure to improve state test scores, sometimes compromising their actions toward supporting teacher learning. In the low-financial-resource Catholic schools, principals cite low resources as their greatest challenge (e.g., teacher turnover due to low salaries).

Some principals develop rich partnerships with community organizations and businesses to secure additional funding or to place more adults in the classrooms, which gives teachers more time to collaborate. Others develop alternative ways to maximize financial and human resources to secure time and promote teacher learning. In sum, principals from low-, medium-, and rich-resource schools work differently to support teacher learning—despite the complex demands of leadership in the 21st century.

IMPLICATIONS OF THE NEW LEARNING-ORIENTED MODEL OF LEADERSHIP

The work discussed in this book has multiple implications for better supporting teachers' transformational learning. Below are the most important implications of this work, as I see them:

- *Attending to teachers' ways of knowing:* Principals need a mindfulness of development and an understanding that teachers with different ways of knowing will experience the exact same learning-oriented practices in qualitative ways.
- *Implementing the new learning-oriented model of leadership:* Principals would be wise to implement the four broad pillars to better support the transformation of teachers' ways of knowing and working in their schools.
- *Adapting challenges and supports to meet teacher needs:* Since adults vary with regard to ways of knowing, teachers will need different supports and challenges to transform their work and meaning making. These supports and challenges should be embedded in implementation of the four practices to reap the most benefit from teachers' participation and growth.
- *Shaping the holding environment:* I advise principals to consider the goodness of fit or developmental match between their individual school cultures and teachers' capacities to meet their expectations. This analysis will help them shape "holding environments" (Kegan, 1982) that support and challenge teachers with different ways of

knowing. A corollary to this is that principals should consider the explicit *and* implicit developmental demands of teacher learning activities and professional development practices so that they are supportive of teachers with various ways of knowing.

- *Providing challenges and supports for principal learning.* Principals, as leaders and principal adult developers, need supports and challenges for their own learning to support their complex work *and* teacher learning.

Attending to Teachers' Ways of Knowing

Throughout this book, I have called attention to the qualitatively different ways in which adults with various ways of knowing will experience the four pillars of the learning-oriented model of school leadership. You might recall that a person's way of knowing shapes how all experiences are taken in, managed, and understood. As I have discussed, Kegan's theory (1982, 1994) helps us to understand how differences in behaviors and thinking are often related to differences in how a person *constructs* experience.

Learning from prior research on adults' meaning making of their learning experiences (Drago-Severson, 1996, in press; Drago-Severson et al., 2001; Kegan, 1994; Kegan et al., 2001), we know that any class of adult learners is likely to be populated by adults with diverse ways of knowing. Developmental awareness helps us to understand the important distinction between leadership practices that aim to *inform* and those that aim to *transform*. Transformative practices consider how different people will *make meaning* of the experience. These practices also support learners in developing the capacity to benefit fully from the practice and grow from participation. Using learnings from constructive-developmental theory (Kegan, 1982, 1994) as a guide, we see that the most consistent way to support adult learning and growth is by way of a philosophy and model that resemble how we support the growth and development of youth. This is especially true in K–12 schools. Of course, there may be other reasons why teachers prefer different types of practices and experience them distinctly, such as age, educational background, and career phase. While I am suggesting a developmental perspective will assist principals in responding better to teachers' preferences, strengths, and needs, I am also advocating that principals continue to attend to other contextual and personal variables to best support teacher learning.

Implementing the New Learning-Oriented Model of Leadership

In this book, I have described how principals in this study employ four mutually reinforcing practices that support teacher learning. Each of these practices is *developmentally robust;* implementation of any one of them can support the growth of teachers with different ways of knowing. In this section, I discuss some of the varied ways in which these practices can be implemented.

The four components of the learning-oriented model of school leadership presented in this book can be refined and adapted to other school contexts in light of a principal's style and a school's contextual features. For example, while a principal will eventually want to invite teacher participation in all four practices, the leader might want to implement one or two at a time with different pilot groups of teachers. Also, teachers with different developmental orientations might prefer specific practices, especially at first. However, even *one* of these practices can provide a rich context for learning and growth. This is especially true because each practice enables teachers to meet regularly, examine their thinking and practices, and consider new ways of thinking and practicing.

I suggest that principals might alternately implement several of the four pillar practices and provide teachers with choices for participation. This option creates a "buffet" for teachers to sample and gives them the opportunity to learn and grow from sharing their experiences in several different pillar programs. This initial individualization of the model honors teachers' preferences and developmental orientations and empowers them through choice. In other words, principals would be wise to implement more than one teacher learning practice because a variety will attend to different career phases, learning needs, and ways of knowing. With time, teachers will likely take ownership of these practices, and the practices can become part of the fabric of the school. Again, these practices should be adapted to school context. As shown in previous chapters, the practices appear differently from school to school.

Adapting Challenges and Supports to Meet Teacher Needs

Because teachers make sense of practices aimed at facilitating learning and growth in qualitatively different ways, they need different forms of both support and challenge. A developmental framework helps us to understand the kinds of supports and challenges that will help adults across ways of knowing to facilitate their growth.

While each of the four practices is developmentally robust, supports and challenges can be implanted in the four practices to enhance their effectiveness for adults with a diversity of meaning-making systems. Table 11.1 details supports and challenges for adults with different ways of knowing that can be threaded through each of the practices.

For instance, as Table 11.1 shows, embedding some structure for dialogue into each practice may help instrumental knowers to participate

Table 11.1 Supports and Challenges for Adults With Different Ways of Knowing That Can Be Embedded in Pillar Practices

Way of Knowing	Supports	Challenge (Growing Edge)
Instrumental knowers	• Clear expectations and guidelines • Step-by-step directions • Facilitators who act as experts and have valued experience • Explicitly stated timetable • Providing examples of the rules, purposes, and goals • Providing explicit prompts (questions) for written exercises • Establishing rules for engaging in conversation or dialogue with colleagues • Explicitly stating reasoning or argument behind perspectives • Establishing concrete outcomes of process	• Learning about multiple perspectives through dialogue • Developing abstract thinking and transferability of ideas, opinions, thus enhancing capacities for perspective broadening • Moving beyond what they see as the "right answers" and toward open-ended discussion that could broaden their perspectives and stretch their thinking • Beginning to hypothesize and starting to test out alternative ideas and the analysis of outcomes
Socializing knowers	• Explicit encouragement to express perspectives and *acknowledgment* of various points of view • Creating a context of acceptance and a sense of belonging • Sharing perspectives in pairs before sharing them with a larger group • Emphasizing that differences of opinion do not jeopardize friendships/relationships • Establishing ground rules for conversations and process before the inquiry begins • Explicitly providing positive affirmation of their perspectives when appropriate • Posing reflective questions that address feelings about issues or changes	• Considering one's own perspective and sharing it before learning about the perspectives of others • Articulating what should be done to support them • Understanding that conflict is okay and can serve to help everyone learn and grow • Voicing assumptions and testing new thinking and behaviors in a supportive context

(Continued)

Table 11.1 (Continued)

Way of Knowing	Supports	Challenge (Growing Edge)
Self-authoring knowers	• Allowing some freedom in designing the inquiry process • Creating opportunities within reflective forums or teams for teachers to demonstrate their own competencies • Creating spaces within the context of collaborative work for teachers to pursue their own self-generated goals • Engaging in dialogue that enables testing of thinking and sharing perspectives before adopting a new idea • Offering feedback that further develops current competencies • Providing opportunities for teachers to critique proposed ideas and to offer feedback to authorities and team members • Inviting these teachers to design learning activities • Creating spaces within reflective conversations for these teachers to pose their own questions and respond to them	• Considering ideas and perspectives that are in opposition to their own • Seeing commonalities in perspectives through dialogue with others • Working with colleagues who have perspectives on issues or situations that are in opposition to their own • Encouraging teachers not be wedded to any one particular way of completing a task (i.e., their way) • Welcoming alternative standards for and approaches to problem-solving processes that are in opposition to their own preferred way

and feel supported in their learning. However, practices also need to allow freedom in their design, because too many specific and concrete guidelines may lead socializing and self-authoring teachers to feel restricted or frustrated. The lesson is that a variety of supports for teachers within one practice will attend to varying developmental needs and lead to a practice's increased success.

To stimulate private reflection and collective dialogue, including protocol questions that call for different types of responses will support teachers with different ways of knowing. Some questions might invite teachers to describe concrete action steps; others might invite teachers to articulate opinions; others might invite teachers to propose a process for group discussion. Socializing and self-authoring knowers will likely respond to questions in more abstract ways than instrumental knowers. Before asking teachers to share their written responses with a larger group, principals (or others leading discussions) should invite them to dialogue in pairs because this will validate most teachers, especially those with a socializing way of knowing. This strategy will assist socializing knowers in taking risks and developing a sense of belonging with individual colleagues and eventually with the larger group or team. Furthermore, flexibility in the design and implementation of these practices will support and challenge self-authoring knowers to address their own goals and exhibit their competencies.

Shaping the Holding Environment

When shaping school contexts and practices supportive of teachers' transformational learning, it is essential to seriously consider the goodness of fit between the person and his or her school context. Because learning is a developmental process and teachers need support and challenge, how teachers with different ways of knowing may experience the expectations of school culture and the developmental demands of learning activities needs to be attended to in terms of the goodness of fit.

Recall that a safe context for growth, or "holding environment" (Kegan, 1982, 1994), serves three functions. First, the context must "hold," or affirm, different ways of knowing and welcome people *as they are*. Second, it should appropriately challenge them by offering opportunities to transform their ways of knowing. Last, it must provide continuity, which means making room to recognize an individual's new self. Kegan (1994) highlights the "intellectual mission for adult education" found in adult education literature, which frequently aims to help adults become "self-directed learner[s]" (p. 274). Requesting that adults direct their own learning can place "internal demands upon participants" (p. 274). Kegan urges educators to reconsider this orientation because it can place excessive and unsupported demands on how adults make sense of their experience.

Constructive-developmental theory (Kegan, 1982, 1994) helps us understand the unintentional demands that school cultures may make on teachers. By considering the structure and process of each way of knowing, this theory can inform how school cultures may ask teachers to perform in ways that exceed their developmental capacities.

Kegan and Lahey (1984) maintain that people respond to a leader's actions—and by extension, I suggest, their expectations—differently, depending on how they construct reality. For example, consider the inherent developmental demands in the following depictions of principals' well-intentioned efforts to promote teachers' learning. What developmental capacities might teachers need to meet the demands in these descriptions? What types of supports and challenges would different teachers need to grow toward meeting these expectations?

1. "We value professional development here at school, and I want teachers to value learning and growing as well. I tell teachers that all the time, if you try something even for a week or two and it's not working, by all means, stop it. Don't do it all year because you made a commitment to do it. I think that's what happens in schools, occasionally. . . . [What's important is] whether it's working for you personally. Whether it's working for your class. How do you know that's making you a better teacher and a better person? That is really where [teachers really] want to try to go."

2. "In a good strong faculty, I think something that you will find is the ability to take on different perspectives. . . . That's important, because when you put a team together, or when you're looking for input, you try to get all the perspectives. . . . All the perspectives [need to be] acknowledged and people feel free to express them because they're all important to the decision making."

3. "[I don't want teachers to be] looking to me for answers all the time. They need to provide their own answers and do their own thinking."

The above excerpts call for self-authoring capacities. These principals' expectations inadvertently place demands upon teachers' ways of knowing and likely do not meet the ways of knowing of a diverse faculty. It is necessary to better understand how teachers with different ways of knowing may experience these expectations and offer an environment that will enable them to grow from practices aimed at supporting their learning, growth, and development.

For example, many principals want teachers to take responsibility for their own learning. As the above quotations show, principals often want to empower teachers. Giving them freedom and responsibility for their learning can unintentionally leave them unsupported and unsuccessful in professional development efforts. The principal in the first quotation, like others, wants teachers to identify with the school culture of teacher learning because they are intrinsically committed to development. This idea might require some degree of self-authorship. Teachers would need to be able to evaluate their teaching according to a set of internally developed ideals. Likewise, they would be called on to categorize their priorities.

Teachers with a socializing way of knowing, however, could internalize their schools' value for professional development. In this case, teachers would evaluate their own learning according to the school culture's value rather than their own values for learning. Socializing knowers do not yet have the capacity to generate their own set of internal values. Instead, they look to authorities for values, expectations, and indications of success, and they make them their own. However, the appropriate supports and challenges will help socializing knowers develop their own internal values and make assessments based on them.

The second quotation highlights a common theme expressed by principals across the sample: Welcoming different perspectives can lead to stronger decisions. Rather than being threatened by opposition, this principal, like many others, believes diverse perspectives enrich the community. Accepting this invitation to share one's point of view and take a stand will be experienced differently depending on a person's way of knowing. When invited to voice their perspectives, particularly in public, some people may resist or feel uncomfortable. Viewing this resistance developmentally and providing additional supports to teachers will enable them to transform their ways of knowing and grow toward greater participation. Importantly, reluctance or resistance may be due to other contextual factors, such as a perceived inability to make a difference, or lack of interest. However, when viewed through a developmental lens, voicing opinions and standing up for beliefs typically call for a self-authoring way of knowing. This enables us to understand how some learning activities and professional development practices can feel satisfying to teachers with one way of knowing and be experienced as overchallenging to those with another way of knowing.

The third quotation encourages teachers to make their own decisions and illuminates another common theme expressed by principals in the sample: Encouraging teachers to make decisions empowers them. However, teachers who are socializing knowers may feel threatened when they are expected to make decisions themselves, because they need acceptance from authorities and depend on them for direction. Socializing knowers might feel overwhelmed by the invitation to make decisions *on their own* about proposed ideas or problems. In other words, socializing knowers need the approval of others to make the self cohere. If an opinion they voice is contrary to the views or decisions of valued others or authorities, they, literally, feel torn apart. Socializing knowers will orient toward decisions that they believe are aligned with the needs and interests of important others, rather than satisfying their own needs and interests.

Encouraging socializing knowers to look internally and share what they think they should do will support their growth and learning. Although teachers with this way of knowing have the capacity to look internally, it is critical that authority figures explicitly acknowledge their perspectives and decisions. In addition, valued others can support these teachers by encouraging them to see themselves as capable of generating good decisions.

In Table 11.1 I offer additional guidance on how to shape school cultures and practices supportive of teacher learning and development to provide a "holding environment" (Kegan, 1982) supportive of teachers' growth.

Working in a context where each person is encouraged to share and take risks facilitates learning and creates a holding environment for adult development. A developmental perspective on teacher learning highlights the following critical features of a robust environment for teacher growth:

- A one-size-fits-all model for teacher learning may not meet all teachers' developmental needs and abilities.
- We must first meet teachers where they are, and then offer developmentally appropriate supports and challenges to facilitate growth and learning.
- Developmentally oriented practices will contribute to the success of learning contexts for teachers at different developmental and career phases.
- Opportunities for teachers to ask questions of each other can raise awareness of assumptions and create a space for them to question their assumptions.

The practices I describe in this book are robust in two ways. One, they are practices that will support and challenge teachers with different ways of knowing. They thus provide a goodness of fit between teachers' developmental orientations and the practices themselves. And second, different supports and challenges can be embedded or woven into the practices to accommodate teachers with different ways of knowing. In Table 11.2 I summarize the ways in which the four practices support adult growth and in which developmental principles inform those practices.

Providing Challenges and Supports for Principal Learning

Principals, as leaders and adult developers, need supports and challenges that will sustain and renew them and facilitate their own learning and growth. Developing structures and practices that will support principals as they meet the highly complex demands of leadership in the 21st century will enable them to better support teacher learning. This is especially

Table 11.2   Developmental Opportunities—Supports and Challenges in All
Four Pillar Practices: Teaming, Providing Leadership Roles,
Collegial Inquiry, and Mentoring

Developmental Opportunities in All Four Pillar Practices
• Articulating thinking through writing, acting, or speaking • Uncovering assumptions and beliefs that guide thinking and behaviors • Assuming more work-related responsibility • Supporting a teacher as he or she integrates multiple perspectives • Challenging and supporting one's own and another person's thinking and internal assumptions that inform actions • Identifying and questioning internal assumptions in a supportive context • Supporting and challenging enhanced risk taking • Challenging individual and organizational norms, values, and envisioning alternatives • Recognizing internal "truths" and sharing them publicly • Increasing perspective-taking abilities • Becoming more aware of one's own or another person's motivations, actions, thinking, or justifications • Identifying and increasing awareness of convictions (ethical, practical, personal convictions, or questions) • Becoming aware of and having opportunities to discuss personal ambiguities, contradictions, faulty reasoning, and lack of clarity in thinking, ideas, and values • Opportunities for envisioning alternative way of thinking and behaving • Opportunities to act on new thinking—to test new ideas • Opportunities to learn about and consider incorporating alternative points of view • Potential to support movement of thinking from being identified with it to taking a broader perspective on it • Potential for greater self-authorship and self-ownership • Potential for supporting transformational learning

important because principals are leaving their posts due to work-related
stress and because fewer people are pursuing principalship as a career.

I have described a continuum of ways in which the principals in this
study renew themselves, and I have highlighted their desire to engage in
reflective practice with colleagues. Significantly, eight of the principals in
this study have left their positions since the conclusion of this research, for
various reasons. All but one of the principals in this study told me how
much they valued our conversations for giving them space to reflect on their
practice and thinking, and all of these principals invited me to visit again.

In Chapter 10, I discussed principals' practices for self-renewal and
illuminated a particularly powerful need for ongoing communities for

reflecting on practice. This, as they explained, would not only decrease their isolation but would also support their *own* development while they support the development of others in their schools. Just as it is important to create structures for teacher reflection, so too is it important for principals to benefit enormously from these communities of inquiry. While it is beyond the scope of this book to discuss, principals, too, have different ways of knowing, and they may benefit from considering this when applying the four practices of this model of learning-oriented school leadership. Reflecting with colleagues on the experience of being a principal in today's complex world is an opportunity to support principal development as well.

Schools must become much better contexts for principals' development so they can better support the development of both adults and children. Providing contexts for principals to reflect on their practice is important for them and for our schools.

FREQUENTLY ASKED QUESTIONS

The following are answers to questions that many principals, teachers, and other school leaders have asked me about implementing the learning-oriented model of leadership. However, I hope that readers will not be completely satisfied with the answers. I hope that you will discuss these and other questions to better employ ideas and learnings in your practice that are addressed in this book.

1. How will I, as a principal, be able to assess the meaning making of all teachers in my large school?

First, infusing the four pillar practices with different types of developmentally appropriate supports and challenges will cover your bases to support teacher learning. Second, in an ideal world, you would want to assess each adult's meaning making. This is not usually feasible, so it can be helpful to apply the broader principles from Chapter 2 to cultivate a holding environment that carefully attends to the ways in which teachers make meaning in developmentally different ways. Employing a developmental perspective does not mean that you will need to assess each teacher's developmental level. The descriptions of the different types of knowers as described in Chapter 2 and throughout this book will enable you to better support teacher learning.

2. While I'm happy to adopt a developmental perspective, how can I help others in my district or building to get onboard with these ideas?

*One very important strategy for effectively supporting adult growth and learning is to teach others about the value of a developmental perspective. Doing so provides a **language** for understanding and considering how to best support adult development. Please share this book with them, especially Chapter 2. Providing* *others with examples of the different ways of knowing and the basic principles of a constructive-developmental framework will, I think, resonate with their experiences. Feel free to use the examples provided in this book. The principals in this study found both the broader ideas and the language for considering what development means and how to support it to be extremely helpful.*

3. I have a district of 2,000-plus teachers. How can I scale this up to meet the needs of all of the adults?

*Remember that it is important to take this one step at a time. I would start by engaging with small groups of principals within your district and implementing some of the ideas shared in my responses to Questions 1 and 2 above. Also, prioritizing spaces for principals to converse about implementation of the four pillar practices will support them and facilitate implementation across your district. As a next step, you might want to consider inviting principals to participate in piloting the four practices, or a few of them, in cross-functional teams within schools. Doing so will enable them—and you—to build capacity, support growth, and tailor these practices to meet the needs of **your** district.*

STEPPING FORWARD: NEW BEGINNINGS FOR LEADERS OF TRANSFORMATIONAL LEARNING

In the growth and development of any school, it is the growth and development of people that make the difference. There are important individual characteristics to consider, such as age, gender, educational background, ethnicity, and career phase, when thinking about how to best support adult learning. Still, it is also important to be mindful of developmental differences. Merely acquiring information or learning new instructional skills, while important, can never satisfy teacher growth. Support for adult learning and growth must include efforts to improve their capacities for managing the complexities of work and life.

The four pillars I discuss in this book illuminate a qualitatively different way of thinking about attending to teachers' transformational learning; they compose a new learning-oriented leadership model. I have drawn from current research, employed an adult constructive-developmental framework, and carefully examined how the principals in the study understood their practices. This book offers specific practices to help principals, teachers, and other school leaders create contexts that support teachers' transformational learning.

Each practice needs to be modified and shaped to meet the needs and conditions of particular school contexts. Principals may choose to implement combinations of these practices at first and then implement additional practices as they weave them into the fabric of their schools. However, my hope is that presenting a variety of practices at different stages will provide a map for other principals and teachers.

I also hope that this work illuminates how various learning theories, in particular constructive-developmental theory (Kegan, 1982, 1994), can be used to better understand adult growth and learning. Constructive-developmental theory facilitates understanding *how* adults behave, think, and solve problems *in different ways* while involved in practices aimed at supporting learning and development. This is especially important because the demands of the 21st century require more than acquisition of new skills; more complex ways of knowing are necessary. Since a person's meaning system shapes his or her worldview and guides interactions, an understanding of constructive-developmental theory will enhance efforts to support teacher learning.

Principals who attend to the differences and similarities in teachers' ways of knowing will be better equipped to support a variety of preferences, styles, and developmental orientations in their faculties. My hope is that this work will inform school practice and possibilities for supporting teachers' transformational learning. I also hope it will fulfill its promise to make all schools into places where adults as well as children can grow.

Epilogue

ig trees hold within them a potential to yield some of the most savory fruit I can imagine, but these trees can also be quite needy. Trees should be strong and hearty, I remember thinking as a child, not as fragile as a garden plant or a flower.

As far back as I can remember, one certain fig tree quietly accompanied the playing time my six siblings and I so enjoyed in the backyard of our childhood home in the Bronx, New York. Each summer, the gentle fig tree offered its seasonal fruits to me and my family. The tree grew along with us throughout the many years of changing seasons. In no small way, this fig tree was an important member of the family. We all considered it, watched over it, protected it, and took our turns at caring for it. Our parents instilled this value in us, a value for the successful growth and development of a tree that thrives today and bears fruit each summer just as it did so many summers ago.

My parents acquired our family's fig tree in 1961. It was passed along to them from my father's aunt, my great-aunt Rose, after she had cared for it for some 70 of her almost 90 years. The family tree that we adopted was actually a cousin to yet another fig tree that grew along with my own father's childhood family, also in New York. My father could be overheard at family gatherings telling stories to his grandchildren of his own childhood times in a place where a wonderful fig tree grew up alongside him and his seven siblings. He also told of helping his own parents care for the "cousin tree." When my father's siblings grew to adulthood and their own next-generation families, they all could be counted on to be nurturers of fig trees.

While each season and month and holiday time of my childhood seemed to have its own celebrations and preparations, the autumn of each year found all of us thinking about and discussing over dinner the fig tree in our backyard. Soon after the first frost, my parents would gather together winter overcoats that had outworn their usefulness for us, blankets that had once kept us warm but no longer served, several large green plastic trash bags, and a supply of twine, all collected over time in a storage corner of our basement. My siblings and I would run and play about our parents as they reorganized the collected coverings outdoors near the family fig tree. It was time to wrap the fig tree so that it would be protected from the cold and frost and snow and wind of wintertime.

My parents would rake leaves onto the base of the fig tree before trimming from it any decaying branches and unwanted foliage. They would use longer strips of cloth to embrace the near-horizontal branches, pulling them up close to the central trunk of the tree. It was usually my mother who collected the outer limbs by encircling the tree with her arms, as if she were hugging a small child, while my father tied snug knots in the cloth strips. At these times, I noticed that the fig tree was finally looking more like a narrow tree reaching up toward the sky than the broad bush it resembled throughout the warm summer months. The tree was then wrapped with several layers of clothing and blankets handed down to it from each of us. The entire bundle was tied together with the twine and covered with a final skin of plastic. So much work for a fig tree, I thought to myself, though I remember wanting to help with the wrapping and care.

Early on, I watched this careful process performed almost as ritual by my parents, and later on with the help of older brothers. Something about it seemed good and comfortable and fun; although I could not fully understand why it was so important to take such great care of a tree that didn't even look like one. There were many other trees in the yard, I thought. Why do we only wrap the fig tree? Wouldn't it also be good to wrap the elm or the dogwood? As the years passed, and we all grew taller, the responsibility and joy of wrapping the fig tree increasingly became a shared activity for everyone in our family. My youngest brother, Paul, and I were all too soon old enough to join in. Surely, we all believed, such important care would be rewarded.

Each year as spring grew near, our dinner conversations seemed to include discussion of the fig tree along with our talk of school and friends and family developments. Although we always knew it would come eventually, everyone at our table grew excited when Dad would announce that it was time to unwrap the fig tree. He set the date, and as much as we wondered why one day might be better than another, we nonetheless looked forward to the event with the same eagerness with which we anticipated that first warm and sunny day that confirmed in us that winter was over and summer was not far away.

In 1992, my parents decided it was time to move from their home of 31 years to a newer, remodeled house that happened to be immediately next door. Although much needed to be done to ensure the success of such a move, Mom and Dad seemed to welcome the change. My father, however, was worried about the fig tree. He wondered aloud about whether it could survive the move. The sensitive sapling had to be transplanted to new and different soil only 30 yards or so from the seat where it had watched all of us over many years.

"Why are you so worried, Dad?" I asked the man who was adopted by fig trees, before he adopted them.

"Well," he began, "when the fig tree is transplanted, the gardeners we hire to do the job will have to dig up its roots, and they are deep. Some of the roots will probably be destroyed and some will be damaged. We're going to have to pay very careful and special attention to it after it's planted in its new soil." Just as my pediatrician father knew that a child surviving the trauma of an operation must also make it through the post-trauma period for full recovery to be certain, so too did my father the gardener appreciate the fig tree's important posttransplant time.

Before allowing the gardeners to begin their digging and transplanting work on the fig tree, Dad carefully cut off a single branch of the tree. The cut branch was brought indoors, placed in water, and given plenty of light. The single branch would itself soon sprout growth, so that a part of the family fig tree might again bear fruit on yet another day in the sad case that the transplant would not be successful. Despite such good planning, safety precautions, and even a backup plan in case the fig tree didn't make it, my father continued to worry that the tree we loved and nurtured over so many years might experience more shock than it could handle. We found ourselves attending to the transplanted fig tree, waiting for a sign that it would indeed grow and bear fruit in the new soil and location.

The transplanted tree appeared to be doing fine, but some of the soil about its roots was washing away with each rainfall. In response to a request from my father, my husband and I built a more protective foundation for the tree. A long wooden board was added to one side of ground at the tree's base. The exterior wall of my parents' new home made a second border. We used smaller bricks, mounted on top of one another, to make a third protective side for the soil that was responsible for supporting and nourishing the tree. With the soil more evenly distributed about the fig tree's roots and base, the three-sided support prevented any more soil erosion.

Although that winter following my parents' move seemed particularly long and snowy and cold, we all wondered about what we would find in the spring when the fig tree was freed yet one more time of its clothing and blankets, twine and plastic. We all waited anxiously to see whether or not the treasured tree would make it in the new location. The fig tree was unwrapped that spring and watched over and nourished in succeeding weeks.

Leaves sprouted, and buds appeared. Small green pea-sized growths soon could be found among the leaves; but you had to search for them. The tiny green growths transformed over the summer months into dark brown, luscious figs nearly the size of plums. Our family fig tree survived the stresses, trauma, and shock of being transplanted. It bore enough figs that first summer so that everyone in our family was able to eat at least a few of the treasured gifts, usually at the end of a dinner meal. The summers that followed since the move and transplant of the fig tree have been warm and restorative, good enough to support the fig tree in making its special fruits.

❖ ❖ ❖ ❖ ❖ ❖

This tale of a father, a mother, and a family preserving, protecting, and saving a fig tree has come to mean much more to me, of course, than the mere telling of a childhood remembrance. The episode involving the fig tree of our family also reminds me of some things important about good leadership, learning-oriented leadership-in-practice. Whether one commits to the growth of a tree or a flower or a human being, the promise can only be fulfilled with time and genuine concern, attention, and the right kind of support and challenge. Committing to the practice of leadership for adult learning and development has become, for me, like committing to the growth and development of the fig tree of my childhood; it will always call for labor and paid attention. It can also become, over time and with reflection, a labor of love and *heart* that yields results as wonderful as the miracle of learning.

In pursuing the questions that guided my inquiry into school leadership and teacher learning, I was privileged to learn from the thinking, philosophies, challenges, and practices of school leaders and their work of supporting adult learning and development. As a child, I may not have fully understood or appreciated the care my parents invested into raising the family fig tree; as an adult, I now better understand. Care, attention, nurturing, and support were offered to and needed by the fig tree to sustain its growth and development. There is also something important about having the right kind of soil and protection for growth and development.

Learning-oriented leadership on behalf of supporting adult development calls for special attention to creating a holding environment for growth and protection from harm during developmental moves. The principals in this study know of and care about and dedicate themselves to these things.

While my fig tree story may hold many morals and teachings, one in particular deserves mention. When the fig tree was uprooted and transplanted in 1992, special preparations, plans, and attention needed to be given to support and encourage the tree as it moved through its changes. In the same way, people come into and leave school contexts. We transplant our ways of knowing as we grow and develop. All such movements and changes require support and that attention be paid to ensure continued success. As shown throughout this work, these leaders provide nurturing and support for growth. The school leader protects and encourages the passage through stages of growth experienced by teaching and administrative adults, or does not.

School leaders also need support, encouragement, and protection in order to grow. They, too, need a holding environment for self-development. The soil for growth present in the garden we call school can have the nutrients needed to support and challenge school leaders so that they can thrive in their evolving school environment. The practices discussed in these pages illuminate how a learning-oriented school leadership can better support adults' transformational learning and development and build stronger schools. This kind of informed leadership suggests a new way to think about supporting adults, and a new way to think about leadership practices exercised in support of adult development.

Glossary

Assumptions: are the taken-for-granted beliefs that guide our thoughts, actions, and convictions in the learning process. We hold our assumptions as big Truths and rarely question them unless provided with opportunities to consider them. Examining assumptions is essential for the development of lasting change and the successful implementation of new practices.

Collegial inquiry: is a shared dialogue in a reflective context that involves reflecting on one's assumptions, convictions, and values as part of the learning process. See Chapter 7.

Constructive-developmental theory (Kegan, 1982, 1994, 2000): is based on two key ideas: (1) people *actively make sense of* their realities, and (2) people can *change or develop* their meaning making with appropriate supports and challenges. See also "Way of knowing." See Chapter 2 for further explication of this theory.

Development: is defined, according to Kegan's theory (1982, 1994), as a process of increasing differentiation and internalization. When development occurs, a person has a broader perspective on himself/herself and others and is better able to better manage the complexities of work and life.

Developmental demands: are the implicit or explicit expectations inherent to work and life that may be beyond the developmental capacities of those expected to perform them.

Developmental level: See "Way of knowing."

Financial resource levels: were determined in this study by using school Web site information, budgets, publication materials, public school system financial reports (e.g., Boston Public Schools Fiscal Year Budget, 1999), and self-report. See Chapter 1 for more detail.

Goodness of fit (developmental match): concerns the match between a practice, expectation, or environment and a person's developmental capacities that are determined by his/her way of knowing. See Chapters 1 and 11.

Growth: increases in developmental capacities (i.e., cognitive, interpersonal, and intrapersonal) for better managing the complexities of daily life and work. These increases enable people to take broader perspectives on themselves and others—and on their work and life. Growth constitutes or is marked by a qualitative shift in *how* individuals organize, understand, and actively make sense of their experiences. Also see "Transformational learning."

Holding environment: is a context that provides both supports and challenges in order to support growth. It serves three functions: (1) meeting individuals at their developmental levels, (2) challenging learners to grow beyond their current levels, and (3) providing continuity and stability. See Chapter 2.

Human resource levels: in this study refers to how many adults worked at each school and were learned about through Web sites, school documents, and principal reports.

Informational learning: focuses on increasing the amount of knowledge and/or skills a person possesses, augmenting *what* a person knows. See Chapter 2.

Instrumental way of knowing: is a system of meaning making. Instrumental knowers understand the world in highly concrete terms. While they are able to control impulses, they do not have the capacity to have perspectives on other people's needs, desires, and interests. See Chapter 2.

Learning-oriented model for school leadership: presents the principal as adult developer and educator and employs adult learning principles and constructive-developmental theory to inform leadership practices that support transformational learning. See Chapter 1.

Meaning making: is the sense we make of our lived experience, with respect to cognitive, emotional, and interpersonal aspects of life.

Mentoring: is a pillar practice of the learning-oriented model, and it takes many forms, including (1) pairing experienced teachers with new teachers, (2) pairing teachers who have deep knowledge of the school mission with other teachers, and (3) pairing experienced teachers with graduate student interns from local universities. See Chapter 8.

Object (according to Kegan's theory, 1982): is what a person can take a perspective on, manage, and act on because the person is not embedded in it or identified with it.

Providing leadership roles: is a pillar practice of the learning-oriented school leadership model, and it is an opportunity for teachers to share power and decision-making authority. I use the term "providing leadership roles" rather than "distributive leadership" because of the intention behind these roles, which is to offer supports and challenges to the person in a leadership role so that he/she can grow from them. See Chapter 6.

Self-authoring way of knowing: is a system of meaning making. Self-authoring knowers have the capacity to take responsibility for internal authority. Adults with this way of knowing are able to generate (and identify with) their own abstract values, principles, and longer-term purposes and can prioritize and integrate competing values. Self-authoring knowers evaluate the expectations and demands of others and compare them to their own internally generated systems of values, standards, and ideology. See Chapter 2.

Socializing way of knowing: is a system of meaning making. Socializing knowers have an enhanced capacity for reflection and abstract thought. Individuals with this way of knowing orient to their own internal psychological states and cannot take a perspective on the shared mutuality. Socializing knowers feel responsible for other people's feelings and hold others responsible for their own feelings. However, they are not yet able to have a perspective on their relationships because they are identified with them, so much so that reality is co-constructed. Approval and acceptance from authorities and valued others is ultimate for them. Other people, and often societal expectations, are experienced not simply as resources to be used by the self but also as the origin of internal confirmation, orientation, or authority. See Chapter 2.

Subject (according to Kegan, 1982): is what a person cannot take a perspective on because he/she is embedded in it and identified with it. It is so much a part of the very fabric of the self that he/she cannot look at it or see it.

Teaming: is a pillar practice of the learning-oriented model of school leadership, and it provides a context that enables teachers to (a) question their own and others' educational philosophies, (b) reflect on the meaning of their school's mission, and (c) engage in collaborative decision making. See Chapter 5.

Transformational learning: is learning that helps adults better manage the complexities of work and life. In contrast to *informational learning*, which focuses on increasing the amount of knowledge and skills a person possesses, transformational learning constitutes a qualitative shift in *how* individuals organize, understand, and actively make sense of their experiences. When transformational learning occurs, individuals develop increased capacities (i.e., cognitive, interpersonal, and intrapersonal) for better managing the complexities of daily life and work. This increase in capacities enables people to take broader perspectives on themselves and others and on their work and life. See Chapter 2.

Way of knowing: refers to the meaning-making system through which all experience is filtered and understood and is also known as a "developmental level," an "order of consciousness," or a "stage" (Kegan, 1994). It dictates how learning experiences (and all experience) will be taken in, managed, understood, and used. See Chapter 2.

References

PREFACE

Ackerman, R. H., & Maslin-Ostrowski, P. (2002). *The wounded leader: How real leadership emerges in times of crisis.* San Francisco: Jossey-Bass.

Barth, R. (1990). *Improving schools from within: Teachers, parents, and principals can make the difference.* San Francisco: Jossey-Bass.

Blase, J., & Blase, J. (2001). *Empowering teachers: What successful principals do.* Thousand Oaks, CA: Corwin.

Bolman, L. G., & Deal, T. (1995). *Leading with soul: An uncommon journey of spirit.* San Francisco: Jossey-Bass.

Boscardin, M., & Jacobson, S. (1999). The structure and funding of inclusive shcools. *Journal of Education Finance, 24*(4), 483–502.

Brookfield, S. (1987). *Developing critical thinkers: Challenging adults to explore alternative ways of thinking and acting.* San Francisco: Jossey-Bass.

Brookfield, S. (1995). *Becoming a critically reflective teacher.* San Francisco: Jossey-Bass.

Cochran-Smith, M., & Lytle, S. (2001). Beyond certainty: Taking an inquiry stance on practice. In A. Lieberman & L. Miller (Eds.), *Teachers caught in the action: Professional development that matters* (pp. 45–58). New York: Teachers College Press.

Cranton, P. (1996). *Professional development as transformational learning: New perspectives for teachers of adult.* San Francisco: Jossey-Bass.

Daloz, L. (1986). *Effective teaching and mentoring: Realizing the transformational power of adult learning experiences.* San Francisco: Jossey-Bass.

Daloz, L. (1999). *Mentor: Guiding the journey of adult learners.* San Francisco: Jossey-Bass.

Danielson, C. (1996). *Enhancing professional practice: A framework for teaching.* Alexandria, VA: Association for Supervision and Curriculum Development.

Darling-Hammond, L. (2003). Enhancing teaching. In W. Owens & L. S. Kaplan (Eds.), *Best practices, best thinking and emerging issues in school leadership* (pp. 75–87). Thousand Oaks, CA: Corwin.

Darling-Hammond, L., & Sykes, G. (Eds.). (1999). *Teaching as the learning profession: Handbook of policy and practice.* San Francisco: Jossey-Bass.

Donaldson, G. (2001). *Cultivating leadership in schools: Connecting people, purposes, and practice.* New York: Teachers College Press.

Drago-Severson, E. (1994). *What does "staff development" develop? How the staff development literature conceives adult growth.* Unpublished qualifying paper, Harvard University, Cambridge, MA.

Drago-Severson, E. (1996). *Head-of-school as principal adult developer: An account of one leader's efforts to support transformational learning among the adults in her school.* Unpublished doctoral dissertation, Harvard Graduate School of Education, Cambridge, MA.

Drago-Severson, E. (2001, August). "We're trying to get ahead": A developmental view of changes in adult learners' conceptions of their motivations for learning, expectations of teachers, and relationship to work. In R. Kegan, M. Broderick, E. Drago-Severson, D. Helsing, N. Popp, & K. Portnow (Eds.), *Toward a "new pluralism" in the ABE/ESOL classroom: Teaching to multiple "cultures of mind"* (pp. 477–614, NCSALL Monograph #19). Boston: World Education.

Elmore, R. F. (2002). The limits of change. *Harvard Education Letter,* January/February, 1–4.

Evans, R. (1996). *The human side of change: Reform, resistance, and the real-life problems of innovation.* San Francisco: Jossey-Bass.

Fullan, M. (2003). Implementing change at the building level. In W. Owens & L. S. Kaplan (Eds.), *Best practices, best thinking and emerging issues in school leadership* (pp. 31–36). Thousand Oaks, CA: Corwin.

Fullan, M., & Hargreaves, A. (1992). Teacher development and educational change. In M. Fullan & A. Hargreaves (Eds.), *Teacher development and educational change* (pp. 1–9). Washington, DC: Falmer.

Glickman, C. G. (1990). *Supervision of instruction: A developmental approach.* 2d ed. Boston: Allyn & Bacon.

Guskey, T. R. (1999). *Evaluating professional development.* Thousand Oaks, CA: Corwin.

Hargreaves, A. (1994). *Changing teachers, changing times: Teachers' work and culture in the postmodern age.* London: Cassell; New York: Teachers College Press.

Hawley, W. D., & Valli, L. (1999). The essentials of effective professional development: A new consensus. In L. Darling-Hammond & G. Sykes (Eds.), *Teaching as the learning profession: Handbook of policy and practice* (pp. 127–150). San Francisco: Jossey Bass.

Howe, H. II. (1993). *Thinking about our kids: An agenda for American education.* New York: Free Press.

Johnson, S. M. (1990). *Teachers at work: Achieving success in our schools.* New York: Basic Books.

Johnson, S. M. (1996). *Leading to change: The challenge of the new superintendency.* San Francisco: Jossey-Bass.

Johnson, S. M., Birkeland, S., Kardos, S. M., Kauffman, D., Liu, E., & Peske, H. G. (2001). Retaining the next generation of teachers: The importance of school-based support. *Harvard Education Letter, 17*(4), 8, 6.

Kegan, R. (1982). *The evolving self: Problems and process in human development.* Cambridge, MA: Harvard University Press.

Kegan, R. (1994). *In over our heads: The mental demands of modern life.* Cambridge, MA: Harvard University Press.

Kegan, R. (2000). What "form" transforms? A constructive-developmental approach to transformative learning. In J. Mezirow and Associates (Eds.), *Learning as transformation* (pp. 35–70). San Francisco: Jossey-Bass.

Kegan, R., & Lahey, L. (1984). Adult leadership and adult development. In B. Kellerman (Ed.), *Leadership: Multidisciplinary perspectives* (pp. 199–230). New York: Prentice Hall.

Kegan, R., & Lahey, L. L. (2001). *How the way we talk can change the way we work: Seven languages for transformation.* San Francisco: Jossey-Bass/Wiley.

Kelley, C., & Peterson, K. D. (2002). The work of principals and their preparation: Addressing critical needs for the twenty-first century. In M. S. Tucker & J. B. Codding (Eds.), *The principal's challenge: Leading and managing schools in an era of accountability* (pp. 247–312). San Francisco: Jossey-Bass.

Killion, J. (2000). Exemplary schools model quality staff development. *Results,* December/January, 3.

Klempen, R. A., & Richetti, C. T. (2001). Greening the next generation of principals. *Education Week, 21*(15), 34, 36.

Leithwood, K., & Jantzi, D. (1998, April). *Distributed leadership and student engagement in school.* Paper presented at the annual meeting of the American Educational Research Association, San Diego, CA.

Levine, S. L. (1989). *Promoting adult development in schools: The promise of professional development.* Boston: Allyn & Bacon.

Levine, S. L. (1993). Reflections on school leadership: Perspectives on change. *Independent School, 15,* 25–28.

Lieberman, A., & Miller, L. (1999). *Teachers—Their world and their work: Implications for school improvement.* New York: Teachers College.

Lieberman, A., & Miller, L. (Eds.). (2001). *Teachers caught in the action: Professional development that matters.* New York: Teachers College Press.

Little, J. W. (1990). The persistence of privacy: Autonomy and initiative in teachers' professional relations. *Teachers College Record, 91,* 509–536.

Little, J. W. (2001). Professional development in pursuit of school reform. In A. Lieberman & L. Miller (Eds.), *Teachers caught in the action: Professional development that matters* (pp. 23–44). New York: Teachers College Press.

Mann, L. (2000). Finding time to collaborate. *Education Update, 42*(2), 1, 3, 8.

Meier, D. (2002). *In schools we trust: Creating communities of learning in an era of testing and standardization.* Boston: Beacon.

Mezirow, J. (1991). *Transformative dimensions of adult learning.* San Francisco: Jossey-Bass.

Mezirow, J. (2000). Learning to think like an adult: Core concepts of transformation theory. In J. Mezirow and Associates (Eds.), *Learning as transformation: Critical perspectives on a theory in progress* (pp. 3–33). San Francisco: Jossey-Bass.

Oja, S. N. (1991). Adult development: Insights on staff development. In A. Lieberman & L. Miller (Eds.), *Staff Development for education in the '90s: New demands, new realities, new perspectives* (pp. 37–60). New York: Teachers College Press.

Peterson, K. D., & Deal, T. E. (1998). How leaders influence the culture of schools. *Educational Leadership, 56,* 28–30.

Rallis, S. F., & Goldring, E. B. (2000). *Principals of dynamic schools taking charge of change.* Thousand Oaks, CA: Corwin.

Renyi, J. (1996). *Teachers take charge of their learning: Transforming professional development for student success.* Washington, DC: National Foundation for the Improvement of Education.

Sarason, S. B. (1982). *The culture of schools and the problem of change: Second edition.* Boston: Allyn & Bacon.

Sarason, S. B. (1995). *Revisiting the culture of schools and the problem of change.* New York: Teachers College Press.

Sergiovanni, T. J. (1995). *The principalship: A reflective practice perspective.* Needham Heights, MA: Allyn & Bacon.

Sizer, T. (1992). *Horace's school: Redesigning the American high school.* Boston: Houghton Mifflin.

Sparks, D., & Loucks-Horsley, S. (1990). Models of staff development. In W. R. Houston (Ed.), *Handbook of research on teacher education.* New York: Macmillan.

Stricherz, M. (2001). At 'Motorola U,' school leaders learn corporate lessons. *Education Week, 20*(36), 6.

CHAPTER 1

Argyris, C., & Schön, D. A. (1974). *Theory in practice: Increasing professional effectiveness.* San Francisco: Jossey-Bass.

Barth, R. (1990). *Improving schools from within: Teachers, parents, and principals can make the difference.* San Francisco: Jossey-Bass.

Boston Plan for Excellence and the Boston Public Schools. (1999, December). *Professional development spending in the Boston public schools.* Boston: Boston Public Schools.

Boston Public School Fiscal Year Report. (2001, March 3). Boston: Boston Public Schools.

Brookfield, S. (1987). *Developing critical thinkers: Challenging adults to explore alternative ways of thinking and acting.* San Francisco: Jossey-Bass.

Brookfield, S. D. (1995). *Becoming a critically reflective teacher.* San Francisco: Jossey-Bass.

Coffey, A., & Atkinson, P. (1996). *Making sense of qualitative data: Complementary research strategies.* Thousand Oaks, CA: Sage.

Cranton, P. (1994). *Understanding and promoting transformative learning: A guide for educators of adults.* San Francisco: Jossey-Bass.

Donaldson, G. (2001). *Cultivating leadership in schools: Connecting people, purposes, and practice.* New York: Teachers College Press.

Drago-Severson, E. (1996). *Head-of-school as principal adult developer: An account of one leader's efforts to support transformational learning among the adults in her school.* Unpublished doctoral dissertation, Harvard Graduate School of Education, Cambridge, MA.

Drago-Severson, E. (2002, April). *School leadership in support of teachers' transformational learning: The dramatic differences resources make.* Paper presented at the annual meeting of the American Educational Research Association, New Orleans, LA.

Drago-Severson, E., Helsing, D., Kegan, R., Broderick, M., Popp, N., & Portnow, K. (2001). Three developmentally different types of learners. *Focus on Basics, 5*(B), 7–9.

Drago-Severson, E., Helsing, D., Kegan, R., Broderick, M., Portnow, K., & Popp, N. (2001). Describing the NCSALL adult development research. *Focus on Basics, 5*(B), 3–6.

Drago-Severson, E., & Pinto, K. (2003). *School leadership in support of teachers' transformational learning: Drawing from the well of human resources.* Manuscript submitted for publication.

Drago-Severson, E., & Pinto, K. (in press). From barriers to breakthroughs: Principals' strategies for overcoming challenges to teachers' transformational learning. *The Journal of School Leadership*.

Freidson, E. (1975). *Doctoring together: A study of professional social control*. Chicago: University of Chicago Press.

Fullan, M. (2003). Implementing change at the building level. In W. Owens & L. S. Kaplan (Eds.), *Best practices, best thinking and emerging issues in school leadership* (pp. 31–36). Thousand Oaks, CA: Corwin.

Geertz, C. (1974). "From the native's point of view": On the nature of anthropological understanding. *Bulletin of the American Academy of Arts and Sciences, 28,* 221–237.

Glaser, B. G., & Strauss, A. L. (1967). *The discovery of grounded theory: Strategies for qualitative research*. Hawthorne, NY: Aldine de Gruyter.

Greene, M. (2001). Educational purposes and teacher development. In A. Lieberman & L. Miller (Eds.), *Teachers caught in the action: Professional development that matters* (pp. 3–11). New York: Teachers College Press.

Harbison, A. (with Kegan, R.). (1999). *Best practice programs in professional education: A working paper prepared for programs in professional education*. Unpublished manuscript, Harvard Graduate School of Education, Cambridge, MA.

Howe, H. II. (1993). *Thinking about our kids: An agenda for American education*. New York: Free Press.

Kegan, R. (1982). *The evolving self: Problems and process in human development*. Cambridge, MA: Harvard University Press.

Kegan, R. (1994). *In over our heads: The mental demands of modern life*. Cambridge, MA: Harvard University Press.

Kegan, R. (2000). What "form" transforms?: A constructive-developmental approach to transformative learning. In J. Mezirow and Associates (Eds.), *Learning as transformation* (pp. 35–70). San Francisco: Jossey-Bass.

Kegan, R., Broderick, M., Drago-Severson, E., Helsing, D., Popp, N., & Portnow, K. (2001). *Toward a "new pluralism" in the ABE/ESOL classroom: Teaching to multiple "cultures of mind"* (NCSALL Monograph #19). Boston: World Education.

Kegan, R., & Lahey, L. L. (1984). Adult leadership and adult development: A constructivist view. In B. Kellerman (Ed.), *Leadership* (pp. 199230). Englewood Cliffs, NJ: Prentice-Hall.

Kegan, R., & Lahey, L. L. (2001). *How the way we talk can change the way we work: Seven languages for transformation*. San Francisco: Jossey-Bass/Wiley.

Levine, S. L. (1989). *Promoting adult development in schools: The promise of professional development*. Boston: Allyn & Bacon.

Marshall, C., & Rossman, G. (1989). *Designing qualitative research*. Newbury Park, CA: Sage.

Maxwell, J. A. (1996). *Qualitative research design: An interactive approach*. Thousand Oaks, CA: Sage.

Maxwell, J., & Miller, B. (1998). *Categorization and contextualization as components of qualitative data analysis*. Unpublished manuscript.

Merriam, S. B. (1998). *Qualitative research and case study applications in education*. San Francisco: Jossey-Bass.

Mezirow, J. (1991). *Transformative dimensions of adult learning*. San Francisco: Jossey-Bass.

Mezirow, J. (2000). Learning to think like an adult: Core concepts of transformation theory. In J. Mezirow and Associates (Eds.), *Learning as transformation:
Critical perspectives on a theory in progress* (pp. 3–33). San Francisco: Jossey-Bass.

Miles, M. B., & Huberman, A. M. (1994). *An expanded sourcebook: Qualitative data
analysis.* Thousand Oaks, CA: Sage.

Osterman, K. F., & Kottkamp, R. B. (1993). *Reflective practice for educators: Improving
schooling through professional development.* Thousand Oaks, CA: Corwin.

Schön, D. A. (1983). *The reflective practitioner: How professionals think in action.*
New York: Basic Books.

Seidman, I. E. (1998). *Interviewing as qualitative research: A guide for researchers in
education and the social sciences.* New York: Teachers College Press.

Senge, P. M., Kleiner, A., Roberts, C., Ross, R. B., & Smith, B. J. (1994). *The fifth
discipline fieldbook: Strategies and tools for building a learning organization.*
New York: Doubleday.

Sizer, T. (1992). *Horace's school: Redesigning the American high school.* Boston:
Houghton Mifflin.

Strauss, A., & Corbin, J. (1998). *Basics of qualitative research: Techniques and procedures for developing grounded theory.* Thousand Oaks, CA: Sage.

York-Barr, J., Sommers, W. A., Ghere, G. S., & Montie, J. (2001). *Reflective practice to
improve schools.* Thousand Oaks, CA: Corwin.

CHAPTER 2

Basseches, M. (1984). *Dialectical thinking and adult development.* Norwood, NJ:
Ablex.

Belenky, M., Clinchy, B., Goldberger, N., & Tarule, J. (1986). *Women's ways of
knowing.* New York: Basic Books.

Brookfield, S. (1987). *Developing critical thinkers: Challenging adults to explore alternative ways of thinking and acting.* San Francisco: Jossey-Bass.

Brookfield, S. (1995). *Becoming a critically reflective teacher.* San Francisco: Jossey-
Bass.

Cranton, P. (1994). *Understanding and promoting transformative learning: A guide for
educators of adults.* San Francisco: Jossey-Bass.

Cranton, P. (1996). *Professional development as transformational learning: New perspectives for teachers of adult.* San Francisco: Jossey-Bass.

Daloz, L. (1986). *Effective teaching and mentoring: Realizing the transformational power
of adult learning experiences.* San Francisco: Jossey-Bass.

Daloz, L. (1999). *Mentor: Guiding the journey of adult learners.* San Francisco: Jossey-
Bass.

Drago-Severson, E. (2002, April). *School leadership in support of teachers' transformational learning: The dramatic differences resources make.* Paper presented at the
annual meeting of the American Educational Research Association, New
Orleans, LA.

Drago-Severson, E. (in press). *Becoming adult learners: Effective principles and practices for development.* New York: Teachers College Press.

Drago-Severson, E., Helsing, D., Kegan, R., Broderick, M., Popp, N., & Portnow, K.
(2001). Three developmentally different types of learners. *Focus on Basics,*
5(B), 7–9.

Drago-Severson, E., Helsing, D., Kegan, R., Broderick, M., Portnow, K., & Popp, N. (2001). Describing the NCSALL adult development research. *Focus on Basics, 5*(B), 3–6.

Gardner, H. (1983). *Frames of mind: The theory of multiple intelligences.* New York: Basic Books.

Gilligan, C. (1982). *In a different voice: psychological theory and women's development.* Cambridge, MA: Harvard University Press.

Kegan, R. (1982). *The evolving self: Problems and process in human development.* Cambridge, MA: Harvard University Press.

Kegan, R. (1994). *In over our heads: The mental demands of modern life.* Cambridge, MA: Harvard University Press.

Kegan, R. (2000). What "form" transforms? A constructive-developmental approach to transformative learning. In J. Mezirow and Associates (Eds.), *Learning as transformation* (pp. 35–70). San Francisco: Jossey-Bass.

Kegan, R., Broderick, M., Drago-Severson, E., Helsing, D., Popp, N., & Portnow, K. (2001a). *Executive summary: Toward a "new pluralism" in the ABE/ESOL classroom: Teaching to multiple "cultures of mind"* (NCSALL Monograph #19a). Boston: World Education.

Kegan, R., Broderick, M., Drago-Severson, E., Helsing, D., Popp, N., & Portnow, K. (2001b). *Toward a "new pluralism" in the ABE/ESOL classroom: Teaching to multiple "cultures of mind"* (NCSALL Monograph #19). Boston: World Education.

Kegan, R., & Lahey, L. L. (1984). Adult leadership and adult development: A constructivist view. In B. Kellerman (Ed.), *Leadership* (pp. 199–230). Englewood Cliffs, NJ: Prentice Hall.

King, K. M., & Kitchener, K. S. (1994). *Developing reflective judgment: Understanding and promoting intellectual growth and critical thinking in adolescents and adults.* San Francisco: Jossey-Bass.

Kohlberg, L. (1969). Stage and sequence: The cognitive-developmental approach to socialization. In R. A. Goslin (Ed.), *Handbook of socialization theory and research.* New York: Rand-McNally.

Kohlberg, L. (1984). *Stage and sequence: The cognitive developmental approach to socialization: The psychology of moral development.* San Francisco: Harper & Row.

Lahey, L., Souvaine, E., Kegan, R., Goodman, R., & Felix, S. (1988). *A guide to the subject-object interview: Its administration and interpretation.* Unpublished manuscript.

Levine, S. L. (1989). *Promoting adult development in schools: The promise of professional development.* Boston: Allyn & Bacon.

Mezirow, J. (1991). *Transformative dimensions of adult learning.* San Francisco: Jossey-Bass.

Mezirow, J. (1994). Understanding transformation theory. *Adult Education Quarterly, 44*(4), 222–244.

Mezirow, J. (1996). Contemporary paradigms of learning. *Adult Education Quarterly, 46*(3), 158–172.

Mezirow, J. (2000). Learning to think like an adult: Core concepts of transformation theory. In J. Mezirow and Associates (Eds.), *Learning as transformation: Critical perspectives on a theory in progress* (pp. 3–33). San Francisco: Jossey-Bass.

Osterman, K. F., & Kottkamp, R. B. (1993). *Reflective practice for educators: Improving schooling through professional development.* Thousand Oaks, CA: Corwin.

Perry, W. G., Jr. (1970). *Forms of intellectual and ethical development in the college years.* New York: Holt, Rinehart & Winston.

Piaget, J. (1952). *The origins of intelligence in children.* New York: International Universities Press.

Popp, N. (1998). *Developmental perspectives on working together.* The Developmental Skills Matrix. Louisville, KY: National Institute for Literacy Equipped for the Future Field Development Institute.

Popp, N., & Portnow, K. (2001, August). Our developmental perspective on adulthood. In R. Kegan, M. Broderick, E. Drago-Severson, D. Helsing, N. Popp, & K. Portnow (Eds.), *Toward a "new pluralism" in the ABE/ESOL classroom: Teaching to multiple "cultures of mind"* (pp. 43–76, NCSALL Monograph #19). Boston: World Education.

Sergiovanni, T. J. (2000). Leadership as stewardship: "Who is serving?" In *The Jossey-Bass reader on educational leadership* (pp. 269–286). San Francisco: Jossey-Bass.

Shakeshaft, C., Nowell, I., & Perry, A. (2000). Gender and supervision. In *The Jossey-Bass reader on educational leadership* (pp. 547–566). San Francisco: Jossey-Bass.

Sobol, T. J. (2002). The principal as moral leader. In M. S. Tucker & J. B. Codding (Eds.), *The principal's challenge: Leading and managing schools in an era of accountability* (pp. 77–96). San Francisco: Jossey-Bass.

Winnicott, D. (1965). *The maturation processes and the facilitating environment.* New York: International Universities Press.

York-Barr, J., Sommers, W. A., Ghere, G. S., & Montie, J. (2001). *Reflective practice to improve schools.* Thousand Oaks, CA: Corwin.

CHAPTER 3

Blase, J., & Blase, J. (1999). Effective instructional leadership through the teachers' eyes. *High School Magazine, 7*(1), 16–20.

Blase, J., & Blase, J. (2001). *Empowering teachers: What successful principals do.* Thousand Oaks, CA: Corwin.

Blase, J., & Kirby, P. C. (2000). *Bringing out the best in teachers: What effective principals do.* Thousand Oaks, CA: Corwin.

Chase, B. (2001). To hire and to hold: The quality of teaching must be a school district's top priority. *Education Week, 20*(32), 48.

Cochran-Smith, M., & Lytle, S. (2001). Beyond certainty: Taking an inquiry stance on practice. In A. Lieberman & L. Miller (Eds.), *Teachers caught in the action: Professional development that matters* (pp. 45–58). New York: Teachers College Press.

Drago-Severson, E. (2001, June). *Spencer research grant summary report: Helping teachers learn: Leadership lessons for transformational learning.* Report submitted to The Spencer Foundation, Chicago.

Drago-Severson, E. (2002, April). *School leadership in support of teachers' transformational learning: The dramatic differences resources make.* Paper presented at the annual meeting of the American Educational Research Association, New Orleans, LA.

Drago-Severson, E., & Pinto, K. (2003). *School leadership in support of teachers' transformational learning: Drawing from the well of human resources.* Manuscript submitted for publication.

Greene, M. (2001). Educational purposes and teacher development. In A. Lieberman & L. Miller (Eds.), *Teachers caught in the action: Professional development that matters* (pp. 3–11). New York: Teachers College Press.

Hargreaves, A. (1994). *Changing teachers, changing times: Teachers' work and culture in the postmodern age.* London: Cassell; New York: Teachers College Press.

Killion, J. (2000). Exemplary schools model quality staff development. *Results,* December/January, 3.

Lieberman, A., & Miller, L. (Eds.). (2001). *Teachers caught in the action: Professional development that matters.* New York: Teachers College Press.

Lieberman, A., Saxl, E. R., & Miles, M. B. (2000). Teacher leadership: Ideology and practice. In *The Jossey-Bass reader on educational leadership* (pp. 348–365). San Francisco: Jossey-Bass.

Little, J. W. (1993). Teachers' professional development in a climate of educational reform. *Educational Evaluation and Policy Analysis, 15*(2), 129–151.

Little, J. W. (2000). Assessing prospects for teacher leadership. In *The Jossey-Bass reader on educational leadership* (pp. 390–418). San Francisco: Jossey-Bass.

Osterman, K. F., & Kottkamp, R. B. (1993). *Reflective practice for educators: Improving schooling through professional development.* Thousand Oaks, CA: Corwin.

Sindelar, P. T., Yendal-Silva, D., Dow, J., & Gonzales, L. D. (2002). *School culture: Can it be a predictor of student achievement?* Paper presented at the Annual Meeting of the American Researcher Association, New Orleans, LA.

Sparks, D. (2000). Winning schools demonstrate value of staff development. *Results,* December/January, 2.

Sykes, G. (1999). Teacher and student learning: Strengthening their connection. In L. Darling-Hammond & G. Sykes (Eds.), *Teaching as the learning profession: Handbook of policy and practice* (pp. 151–179). San Francisco: Jossey-Bass.

CHAPTER 4

Blase, J., & Blase, J. (2001). *Empowering teachers: What successful principals do.* Thousand Oaks, CA: Corwin.

Boston Plan for Excellence and the Boston Public Schools. (1999, December). *Professional development spending in the Boston public schools.* Boston: Boston Public Schools.

Chase, B. (2001). To hire and to hold: The quality of teaching must be a school district's top priority. *Education Week, 20*(32), 48.

Darling-Hammond, L., & McLaughlin, M. W. (1999). Investing in teaching as the learning profession: Policy problems and prospects. In L. Darling-Hammond & G. Sykes (Eds.), *Teaching as the learning profession: Handbook of policy and practice* (pp. 376–411). San Francisco: Jossey-Bass.

Drago-Severson, E. (2002, April). *School leadership in support of teachers' transformational learning: The dramatic differences resources make.* Paper presented at the annual meeting of the American Educational Research Association, New Orleans, LA.

Drago-Severson, E., & Pinto, K. (2003). *School leadership in support of teachers' transformational learning: Drawing from the well of human resources.* Manuscript submitted for publication.

Drago-Severson, E., & Pinto, K. (in press). From barriers to breakthroughs: Principals' strategies for overcoming challenges to teachers' transformational learning. *The Journal of School Leadership.*

Elmore, R. F., & Burney, D. (1999). Investing in teacher learning: Staff development and instructional improvement. In L. Darling-Hammond & G. Sykes (Eds.), *Teaching as the learning profession: Handbook of policy and practice* (pp. 263–291). San Francisco: Jossey-Bass.

Johnson, S. M., Birkeland, S., Kardos, S. M., Kauffman, D., Liu, E., & Peske, H. G. (2001). Retaining the next generation of teachers: The importance of school-based support. *Harvard Education Letter, 17*(4), 8, 6.

Killion, J. (2000). Exemplary schools model quality staff development. *Results,* December/January, 3.

Pappano, L. (2001). When two teachers = one job. *Boston Sunday Globe,* May 13, L5–6.

Sparks, D. (2000). Winning schools demonstrate value of staff development. *Results,* December/January, 2.

Virginia Education Association (2000, April). Public and private school differences go deeper than dollars. *Virginia Journal of Education.*

Wyatt, E. (2000). Success of city school pupils isn't simply a money matter. *The New York Times,* June 14, A1, B6.

CHAPTER 5

Athey, I. (1970). *Educational implications of Piaget's theory.* Waltham, MA: Ginn-Blaisell.

Cochran-Smith, M., & Lytle, S. (2001). Beyond certainty: Taking an inquiry stance on practice. In A. Lieberman & L. Miller (Eds.), *Teachers caught in the action: Professional development that matters* (pp. 45–58). New York: Teachers College Press.

Dewey, J. (1944). *Democracy and education.* New York: Free Press. (Original work published 1915)

Dewey, J. (1974). *Experience and education.* New York: Collier. (Original work published 1938)

Dewey, J. (1991). *How we think.* New York: Prometheus Books. (Original work published 1910)

Drago-Severson, E. (1996). *Head-of-school as principal adult developer: An account of one leader's efforts to support transformational learning among the adults in her school.* Unpublished doctoral dissertation, Harvard Graduate School of Education, Cambridge, MA.

Elmore, R. F. (2002). The limits of "change." *Harvard Education Letter, 18*(1), 8, 7.

Friedman, V. J. (1997). Making schools safe for uncertainty: Teams, teaching, and school reform. *Teachers College Record, 99*(2), 335–370.

Fullan, M. (2003). Implementing change at the building level. In W. Owens & L. S. Kaplan (Eds.), *Best practices, best thinking and emerging issues in school leadership* (pp. 31–36). Thousand Oaks, CA: Corwin.

Hannum, W. (2001). Knowledge management in education: Helping teachers to work better. *Educational Technology, 41*(3), 47–49.

Harri-Augstein, S., & Thomas, L. (1991). *Learning conversations.* London: Routledge.

Kegan, R. (1982). *The evolving self: Problems and process in human development.* Cambridge, MA: Harvard University Press.

Kegan, R. (1994). *In over our heads: The mental demands of modern life.* Cambridge, MA: Harvard University Press.

Kolb, D. A. (1984). *Experiential learning: Experience as the source of learning and development.* Englewood Cliffs, NJ: Prentice Hall.

Kruse, S. D. (1997). Reflective activity in practice: Vignettes of teachers' deliberative work. *Journal of Research and Development in Education, 31*(1), 46–60.

Lampert, M., & Ball, D. L. (1999). Aligning teacher education with contemporary K–12 reform visions. In L. Darling-Hammond & G. Sykes (Eds.), *Teaching as the learning profession: Handbook of policy and practice* (pp. 33–53). San Francisco: Jossey-Bass.

Little, J. W. (2000). Assessing prospects for teacher leadership. In *The Jossey-Bass reader on educational leadership* (pp. 390–418). San Francisco: Jossey-Bass.

Little, J. W. (2001). Professional development in pursuit of school reform. In A. Lieberman & L. Miller (Eds.), *Teachers caught in the action: Professional development that matters* (pp. 23–44). New York: Teachers College Press.

Meier, D. (2002). *In schools we trust: Creating communities of learning in an era of testing and standardization.* Boston: Beacon.

Miller, L. (2001). School-university partnership as a venue for professional development. In A. Lieberman & L. Miller (Eds.), *Teachers caught in the action: Professional development that matters* (pp. 102–117). New York: Teachers College Press.

Pappano, L. (2001). When two teachers = one job. *Boston Sunday Globe,* May 13, L5–6.

Rogers, D. L., & Babinski, L. (1999). Breaking through isolation with new teacher groups. *Educational Leadership, 56*(8), 38–40.

Schön, D. A. (1987). *Educating the reflective practitioner.* San Francisco: Jossey-Bass.

Senge, P. M., Kleiner, A., Roberts, C., Ross, R. B., & Smith, B. J. (1994). *The fifth discipline fieldbook: Strategies and tools for building a learning organization.* New York: Doubleday.

Sparks, D. (2000). High-powered professional development for high-poverty schools. *Principal Leadership, 1*(14), 26–29.

Stokes, L. (2001). Lessons from an inquiring school: Forms of inquiry and conditions for teacher learning. In A. Lieberman & L. Miller (Eds.), *Teachers caught in the action: Professional development that matters* (pp. 141–158). New York: Teachers College Press.

Weiss, C. H., & Cambone, J. (2000). Principals, shared decision making, and school reform. In *The Jossey-Bass reader on educational leadership* (pp. 366–389). San Francisco: Jossey-Bass.

York-Barr, J., Sommers, W. A., Ghere, G. S., & Montie, J. (2001). *Reflective practice to improve schools: An action guide for educators.* Thousand Oaks, CA: Corwin.

CHAPTER 6

Blase, J., & Blase, J. (2001). *Empowering teachers: What successful principals do.* Thousand Oaks, CA: Corwin.

Darling-Hammond, L. (1999). Target time towards teachers. *Journal of Staff Development, 20,* 31–36.

Drago-Severson, E. (1996). *Head-of-school as principal adult developer: An account of one leader's efforts to support transformational learning among the adults in her school.* Unpublished doctoral dissertation, Harvard Graduate School of Education, Cambridge, MA.

Kegan, R. (1982). *The evolving self: Problems and process in human development.* Cambridge, MA: Harvard University Press.

Kegan, R. (1994). *In over our heads: The mental demands of modern life.* Cambridge, MA: Harvard University Press.

Leithwood, K., & Jantzi, D. (2002). Thoughts behind "transformational leadership effects on school organization and student engagement with school." In M. Wallace (Ed.), *Learning to read critically in educational management.* Thousand Oaks, CA: Sage.

Leithwood, K., Jantzi, D., Ryan, S., & Steinbach, R. (1997, March). *Distributed leadership in secondary schools.* Paper presented at the annual meeting of the American Educational Research Association, Chicago.

Lieberman, A., & Miller, L. (Eds.). (2001). *Teachers caught in the action: Professional development that matters.* New York: Teachers College Press.

Rallis, S. F., & Goldring, E. B. (2000). *Principals of dynamic schools taking charge of change.* Thousand Oaks, CA: Corwin.

Zehr, M. A. (2001). Teacher leadership should be strengthened, report says. *Education Week, 20*(32), 5.

CHAPTER 7

Ball, D., & Cohen, D. (1999). Developing practice, developing practitioners: Toward a practice-based theory of professional education. In L. Darling-Hammond & G. Sykes (Eds.), *Teaching as the learning profession: Handbook of policy and practice* (pp. 3–32). San Francisco: Jossey Bass.

Becerra-Fernandez, I., & Stevenson, J. M. (2001). Knowledge management systems & solutions for the school principal as chief learning officer. *Education, 121*(3), 508–518.

Blase, J., & Blase, J. (2001). *Empowering teachers: What successful principals do.* Thousand Oaks, CA: Corwin.

Brookfield, S. (1995). *Becoming a critically reflective teacher.* San Francisco: Jossey-Bass.

Cochran-Smith, M., & Lytle, S. (2001). Beyond certainty: Taking an inquiry stance on practice. In A. Lieberman & L. Miller (Eds.), *Teachers caught in the action: Professional development that matters* (pp. 45–58). New York: Teachers College Press.

Darling-Hammond, L. (1998). Teacher learning that supports student learning. *Educational Leadership, 55*(5), 6–11.

Darling-Hammond, L. (2003). Enhancing teaching. In W. Owens & L. S. Kaplan (Eds.), *Best practices, best thinking and emerging issues in school leadership* (pp. 75–87). Thousand Oaks, CA: Corwin.

Drago-Severson, E. (1996). *Head-of-school as principal adult developer: An account of one leader's efforts to support transformational learning among the adults in her school*. Unpublished doctoral dissertation, Harvard Graduate School of Education, Cambridge, MA.

Elmore, R. F., & Burney, D. (1999). Investing in teacher learning: staff development and instructional improvement. In L. Darling-Hammond & G. Sykes (Eds.), *Teaching as the learning profession: Handbook of policy and practice* (pp. 263–291). San Francisco: Jossey-Bass.

Hackney, C. E., & Henderson, J. G. (1999). Educating school leaders for inquiry-based democratic learning communities. *Educational Horizons, 77*(2), 67–73.

Hawley, W. D., & Valli, L. (1999). The essentials of effective professional development: A new consensus. In L. Darling-Hammond & G. Sykes (Eds.), *Teaching as the learning profession: Handbook of policy and practice* (pp. 127–150). San Francisco: Jossey-Bass.

Hole, S., & McEntee, G. H. (1999). Reflection is at the heart of practice. *Educational Leadership, 56*(8), 34–37.

Kegan, R. (1982). *The evolving self: Problems and process in human development.* Cambridge, MA: Harvard University.

Kegan, R. (1994). *In over our heads: The mental demands of modern life.* Cambridge, MA: Harvard University Press.

Kegan, R., & Lahey, L. L. (1984). Adult leadership and adult development: A constructivist view. In B. Kellerman (Ed.), *Leadership* (pp. 199–230). Englewood Cliffs, NJ: Prentice Hall.

Killion, J. (2000). Exemplary schools model quality staff development. *Results,* December/January, p. 3.

McKibben, M., & Joyce, B. (1986). Psychological states and staff development. *Theory Into Practice, 19*(4), 248–255.

McLaughlin, M. W., & Zarrow, J (2001). Teachers engaged in evidence-based reform: Trajectories of teacher inquiry, analysis, and action. In A. Lieberman & L. Miller (Eds.), *Teachers caught in the action: Professional development that matters* (pp. 79–101). New York: Teachers College Press.

Neuman, M., & Simmons, W. (2000). Leadership for student learning. *Phi Delta Kappan, 82*(1), 9–12.

Osterman, K. F., & Kottkamp, R. B. (1993). Change and continuity in supervision and leadership. In G. Cawelti (Ed.), *Challenges and achievements of American education* (pp. 158–186). Alexandria, VA: Association for Supervision and Curriculum Development.

Rasmussen, K. (1999). Reflective teaching: Make it your mission. *Education Update, 41*(5), 3.

Rogoff, B., & Lave, J. (Eds.). (1984). *Everyday cognition: Its development in social context.* Cambridge, MA: Harvard University Press.

Schön, D. A. (1987). *Educating the reflective practitioner.* San Francisco, CA: Jossey-Bass.

Taylor, K., Marienau, C., & Fiddler, M. (2000). *Developing adult learners: Strategies for teachers and trainers.* San Francisco: Jossey-Bass.

CHAPTER 8

Collins, P. (1993). The interpersonal vicissitudes of mentorship: An exploratory study of the field supervisor-student relationship. *The Clinical Supervisor, 11*(1), 121–135.

Compton, R. S. (1979). The mentoring dynamic in therapeutic transformation. *The American Journal of Psychoanalysis, 37*(3), 115–122.

Daloz, L. (1983). Mentors: Teachers who make a difference. *Change, 15*(6), 24–27.

Daloz, L. (1986). *Effective teaching and mentoring: Realizing the transformational power of adult learning experiences.* San Francisco: Jossey-Bass.

Daloz, L. (1999). *Mentor: Guiding the journey of adult learners.* San Francisco: Jossey-Bass.

Daloz, L. A. P. (2000). Transformative learning for the common good. In J. Mezirow and Associates (Eds.), *Learning as transformation: Critical perspectives on a theory in progress* (pp. 103–123). San Francisco: Jossey-Bass/Wiley.

Darwin, A. (2000). Critical reflections on mentoring in work settings. *Adult Education Quarterly, 50*(3), 197–211.

Drago-Severson, E. (2002, April). *School leadership in support of teachers' transformational learning: The dramatic differences resources make.* Paper presented at the annual meeting of the American Educational Research Association, New Orleans, LA.

Fagan, M., & Walter, G. (1982). Mentoring among teachers. *Journal of Educational Research, 76*(2), 113–118.

Galvez-Hjornevik, C. (1986). Mentoring among teachers: A review of the literature. *Journal of Teacher Education, 37*(1), 6–11.

Huling-Austin, L., Barnes, S., & Smith, J. (1985, April). *A research-based development program for beginning teachers.* Paper presented at the annual meeting of the American Educational Research Association, Chicago.

Hunt, D. M., & Michael, C. (1983). Mentorship: A career training and development tool. *Academy of Management Review, 8*(3), 475–485.

Kegan, R. (1982). *The evolving self: Problems and process in human development.* Cambridge, MA: Harvard University.

Kegan, R. (1994). *In over our heads: The mental demands of modern life.* Cambridge, MA: Harvard University Press.

Kegan, R., & Lahey, L. L. (2001). *How the way we talk can change the way we work: Seven languages for transformation.* San Francisco: Jossey-Bass/Wiley.

Killion, J. (2000). Explore research to identify best instructional strategies. *Results,* March, 3.

Kram, K. E. (1983). Phases of the mentor relationship. *Academy of Management Journal, 26*(4), 608–625.

Levinson, D., Darro, C. N., Kline, E. B., Levinson, M. H., & McKee, B. (1978). *The season's of a man's life.* New York: Ballantine Books.

Levinson, D. J., & Levinson, J. D. (1996). *The season's of a woman's life.* New York: Knopf.

Little, J. W. (1990). The mentor phenomenon and the social organization of teaching. *Review of Research in Education, 16,* 297–351.

Merriam, S. (1983). Mentors and protégés: A critical review of the literature. *Adult Education Quarterly, 33*(3), 161–173.

Otto, M. L. (1994). Mentoring: An adult developmental perspective. In M. A. Wunsch (Ed.), *Mentoring revisited: Making an impact on individuals and institutions* (pp. 15–26). San Francisco: Jossey-Bass.

Pappano, L. (2001). When two teachers = one job. *Boston Sunday Globe,* May 13, L5–6.

Saphier, J., Freedman, S., & Aschheim, B. (2001). *Beyond mentoring comprehensive induction programs: How to attract, support, and retain new teachers.* Newton, MA: Teachers21.

Wollman-Bonilla, J. E. (1997). Mentoring as a two-way street. *Journal of Staff Development, 18,* 50–52.

CHAPTER 10

Ackerman, R. H., Donaldson, G. A., & van der Bogert, R. (1996). *Making sense as a school leader: Persisting questions, creative opportunities.* San Francisco: Jossey-Bass.

Ackerman, R. H., & Maslin-Ostrowski, P. (2002). *The wounded leader: How real leadership emerges in times of crisis.* San Francisco: Jossey-Bass.

Barth, R. S. (1990). *Improving schools from within: Teachers, parents, and principals can make the difference.* San Francisco: Jossey-Bass.

Donaldson, G. (2001). *Cultivating leadership in schools: Connecting people, purposes, and practice.* New York: Teachers College Press.

Drago-Severson, E. (1996). *Head-of-school as principal adult developer: An account of one leader's efforts to support transformational learning among the adults in her school.* Unpublished doctoral dissertation, Harvard Graduate School of Education, Cambridge, MA.

Houston, P. D. (1998). The ABCs of Administrative Shortages. *Education Week, 44,* 32.

Kegan, R., & Lahey, L. L. (2001). *How the way we talk can change the way we work: Seven languages for transformation.* San Francisco: Jossey-Bass.

Kelley, C., & Peterson, K. D. (2002). The work of principals and their preparation: Addressing critical needs for the twenty-first century. In M. S. Tucker & J. B. Codding (Eds.), *The principal's challenge: Leading and managing schools in an era of accountability* (pp. 247–312). San Francisco: Jossey-Bass.

Klempen, R. A., & Richetti, C. T. (2001). Greening the next generation of principals. *Education Week, 21*(15), 34, 36.

Sykes, G. (with King, C., & Patrick, J.). (2002). Models of preparation for the professions: Implications for educational leadership. In M. S. Tucker & J. B. Codding (Eds.), *The principal's challenge: Leading and managing schools in an era of accountability* (pp. 143–200). San Francisco: Jossey-Bass.

Tucker, M. S., & Codding, J. B. (Eds.). (2002). *The principal's challenge: Leading and managing schools in an era of accountability.* San Francisco: Jossey-Bass.

Wagner, T. (2001, January). Leadership for learning: An action theory for school change. *Phi Delta Kappan,* pp. 378–383.

CHAPTER 11

Drago-Severson, E. (1996). *Head-of-school as principal adult developer: An account of one leader's efforts to support transformational learning among the adults in her school.* Unpublished doctoral dissertation, Harvard Graduate School of Education, Cambridge, MA.

Drago-Severson, E. (in press). *Becoming adult learners: Effective principles and practices for daevelopment.* New York: Teachers College Press.

Drago-Severson, E., Helsing, D., Kegan, R., Broderick, M, Popp, N., & Portnow, K. (2001). Three developmentally different types of learners. *Focus on Basics,* 5(B), 7–9.

Kegan, R. (1982). *The evolving self: Problems and process in human development.* Cambridge, MA: Harvard University Press.

Kegan, R. (1994). *In over our heads: The mental demands of modern life.* Cambridge, MA: Harvard University Press.

Kegan, R., Broderick, M., Drago-Severson, E., Helsing, D., Popp, N., & Portnow, K. (2001). *Toward a "new pluralism" in the ABE/ESOL classroom: Teaching to multiple "cultures of mind"* (NCSALL Monograph #19). Boston: World Education.

Kegan, R., & Lahey, L. (1984). Adult leadership and adult development. In B. Kellerman (Ed.), *Leadership: multidisciplinary perspectives* (pp. 199–230). New York: Prentice Hall.

Index